THEOLOGY OF MINISTRY

THEOLOGY OF MINISTRY

Thomas Franklin O'Meara, O.P.

PAULIST PRESS
New York/Ramsey

Library of Congress
Catalog Card Number: 82-60588

ISBN: 0-8091-2487-4

Published by Paulist Press
545 Island Road, Ramsey, N.J. 07446

Printed and bound in the
United States of America

CONTENTS

ABBREVIATIONS

As	*L'Assemblée liturgique et les differents rôles dans l'assemblée* (Rome, 1977) (Conferences Saint-Serge, 1976)
C	*Concilium*
CBQ	*Catholic Biblical Quarterly*
Ch	H. Küng, *The Church* (New York, 1967)
DS	Denziger-Schönmetzer, *Enchiridion Symbolorum* (New York, 1967)
EHM	Y. Congar, *L'Ecclésiologie du haut moyen-âge* (Paris, 1968)
Ek	J. Hainz, *Ekklesia. Strukturen paulinischer Gemeinde-Theologie und Gemeinde-Orndung* (Regensburg, 1972)
ESA	Y. Congar, *L'Eglise de S. Augustin à l'époque moderne* (Paris, 1970)
G	D. Power, *Gifts that Differ: Lay Ministries Established and Unestablished* (New York, 1980)
HO	*The Sacrament of Holy Orders* (Collegeville, 1962)
J	*The Jurist*
LMD	*La Maison-Dieu*
LThK	*Lexikon für Theologie und Kirche*[2] (Freiburg, 1957–1968)
MC	Yves Congar, *Ministères et communion ecclésiale* (Paris, 1971)
ME	A. Lemaire, *Les ministères dans l'Eglise* (Paris, 1974)
MM	J. Delorme, *Le ministère et les ministères selon le Nouveau Testament* (Paris, 1974)
MO	A. Lemaire, *Les ministères aux origines de l'église* (Paris, 1971)
MThZ	*Münchener Theologische Zeitschrift*
MWS	B. Cooke, *Ministry in Word and Sacrament* (Grand Rapids, 1976)
MY	E. Schillebeeckx, *Ministry* (New York, 1981)
NRT	*Nouvelle Revue Théologique*
PP	Y. Congar, *Power and Poverty in the Church* (London, 1964)
ST	Thomas Aquinas, *Summa Theologiae*
Syst	P. Tillich, *Systematic Theology* (Chicago, 1951–1963)
TI	Karl Rahner, *Theological Investigations*
TS	*Theological Studies* (Washington)
TWNT	*Theologisches Wörterbuch des Neuen Testament* (*Theological Dictionary of the New Testament*) (Grand Rapids, 1964–1976)
VIIF	A. Flannery, ed., *Documents of Vatican II* (Dublin, 1975)

PREFACE

I have tried in this book to sketch a fundamental theology of ministry: to present a theory which would address the present situation in which ministry is expanding even as the single office of priest or pastor is entering a new position, one amid a gathering of Christians willing to serve the church amid the turmoil of the world.

This book might be called, too, a cultural metaphysics of ministry. It does not give a model diocesan plan, nor, on the other hand, does it claim to resolve the numerous exegetical and historical questions which ministry raises. Written by a theologian, these pages have the task of offering a description of ministry as past Scripture and present movements suggest what the Holy Spirit intends ecclesial service to be today. This turns out to be a theology of grace which views God's presence in the world as the source, milieu and goal of ministry.

These pages are also partly a cultural history of ministry, for I believe that the forms of church life exist on that edge where revelation meets civilization. The constellations of culture are the catalysts of ecclesial forms. From history we gain not a unique model of ministry divinely bestowed; rather, from cultural history we gain an understanding of the adaptability of the church, and we learn why the Christian community assumed Celtic, Syriac, Hellenic forms, and why the church today searches out suitable forms, old and new. A cultural phenomenology of ministry not only looks at the offices, liturgies, architectures and politics of the church in different periods, hoping to glimpse their underlying essence, but because a historically grounded theology is realistic, a theology of ministry refuses to rest until it has found not only words and laws but real life and present grace.

The literature on ministry has grown rapidly. For me, not only study but experience has been a helpful source. To be a minister in the church over the past decades has been to experience one of the deepest upheavals in church structure in Christian history. The following pages try to be faithful to revelation in ministry and also to explain lucidly why ministry is changing—indeed, why under the aegis of the Spirit it must change. My own experience found a positive reception for these ideas when they were presented not only throughout the United States but in Canada, New Zealand and Nigeria.

This book has been written out of a long ecumenical experience. I believe that change and expansion in the ministry are taking place in most Christian churches and in most parts of the world although without strict synchronicity. Both poles of the dialectic—expansion and monoformity—are particularly intense, however, in Roman Catholicism. Problems and examples are normally drawn from my Christian tradition, but the underlying issues and my theological interpretation of ministry are intended to serve a spectrum of Christian churches.

The fundamental theologian lives in the uneasy region on the boundary between revelation and philosophy, Scripture and cultural history. There creativity meets fidelity. I have tried to take seriously the exegetical and historical literature on ministry but I have not felt the need to reproduce their detailed bibliographies which are available to the reader in works I cite.

The following pages are theology, not revelation. They are new and limited and faithful. They ask why in the churches a new vision of ministry has appeared. It seems that societies live by laws and political struggles, but in fact they live by ideas. So, too, with the church; ideas (some of which are charisms) are important and amicable—amicable because they claim no ultimacy but explain something of life today and tomorrow.

How forcefully history influences each of us and how much we are products of an epoch and its culture. The grace of the kingdom of God announced by Jesus has a worldwide destiny unto all the races and civilizations of earth's family. Leo the Great, in his sermon for that great festival of grace and civilization, Epiphany, drew together service, grace and kingdom: "The obedience of the star, which drew the three wise men out of their country and led them to recognize and adore the King of heaven and earth, calls us to imitate its humble service: to be ministers, as best we can, of that grace which invites all men and women to find Christ."*

*Sermon, "In epiphaniae solemnitate III," in *Patrologia . . . Latina* (Migne) 54, p. 244.

CHAPTER ONE
Ministry: Between Culture and Charism

What is a church?

A building for Sunday worship? A community of people?

What if the plan of God for Christians was that few should administer churches but everyone should serve Christ and the world?

What does it mean to be a Christian? To receive or to act?

What if action on behalf of the community were an ordinary part of living in a Christian community? Rather than being the prerogative (or the burden) of a small number of Christians, what if ministry were the commission and the glory of all the baptized?

The following pages have one goal: to present ministry not as a vocation for the few but as a facet of baptized life. Ministry is a horizon in the life of the Christian community. A woman, a man is baptized not into an audience or a club but into a community which accepts a vision which is believed and touched but not seen; into a community which is essentially and unavoidably ministerial. Churches are clusters of people with a world to serve.

Christianity, however, is repeatedly tempted to turn its ministerial faith into passive and liturgical membership, to alter the body of Christ into a caste system, to understand baptism as insurance rather than as commission.

Just as Christian faith is communal, so Christian community is ministerial. Some of the weaknesses of Christianity today flow from the church minimizing, obscuring or withholding ministry.

In the New Testament, Jesus (and his Spirit) does not invite his fol-

3

lowers to passive secular life but to a life which is faith but also service to the kingdom of God. These are not clichés which justify their repetition by claiming that everything done neatly or soberly in the world is a Christian ministry. Not all human activity is ministry, but all baptized men and women are called at times to some precise ministry for the reign of God. That call comes with baptism, but it comes too from the Spirit throughout life.

The world and the church are foci around which the streams of creation, sin and grace swirl. Today both world and church question the old and the new identity of the church. Thinking about ministry is no secondary, merely pragmatic assignment. Nor is the theology of ministry only the latest program for the parish. Ministry has become the normal and forceful way to confront that aspect of Christianity which has absorbed almost all theological attention over the past four centuries: the church itself. Today, new theory and new praxis in ministry challenge the church to appear and to act differently, to become itself.

1. The Explosion of Ministry

A burst of ministry has followed upon the ecclesial event of Vatican II and the social upheavals of the 1960s. It was not dictated by the Council, or even by the churches. It has, however, steadily grown over two decades both as a wave of expansion in ministry and as a question for church structure. All of this is part of a cultural upheaval whose roots lie in a search for freedom, ministerial efficacy, maturity and social equality within the church.[1]

Until recently "ministry" was a Protestant word. Now it describes a new situation in the Roman Catholic Church where more and more people want to be, claim to be ministers and where priesthood and vowed life have developed into a variety of ministries. Other Christian churches are experiencing similar alterations in their pastoral structure as women enter the pastorate and as men and women look for other ministries. Programs for training in varied ministries proliferate as parishes and dioceses expand their staffs. Fifteen years ago there was the Roman Catholic priest, the nun in the parochial school, the Protestant minister. Now it is *de rigueur* for everyone to be in the ministry.

What we call an "explosion" of ministry is pluriform. A worldwide phenomenon, it affects cultures and churches differently. First, the renewal of the local church, priesthood, episcopacy and life in vows initiated by Vatican II led to practical consequences such as the shift of many men and women from one ministry to another. The freedom of self-renewal has initiated a long process of establishing a realistic identity—between the too sacral and the too secular—for members of a technological society whose faith has led them to such a serious commitment as fulltime ministry. The critique of historical church structures by the ecumenical movement and by Vatican II opened the church's life to evaluation and change in areas which had remained unaltered for centuries.

The result of this ecclesial self-criticism, structural renewal and search for identity touched the ministry in three ways. First, many new ministries became important, e.g., in health care, penal institutions, adult religious education, and new paths (other than those of pastor, priest, sister) led to ministry. As a result thousands of Christians in fact entered the ministry—without vows or ordination. Second, an era of numerous candidates for priesthood and vowed life came to an end. This time of great abundance was not as normal or as lengthy as many would think, but nevertheless a decline of numbers indicated a need for new approaches to ministry if the churches were to meet the opportunities of the times. Third, outside of Europe and North America, factors such as emphasis upon the local church, decline of large numbers of expatriate priests and sisters and numerous theological and pastoral openings for baptized men and women in ministry could only shake the entire ecclesiology of missionary countries. Their churches' life had depended on imported celibate ministers. While Latin America, Africa and Asia developed their own theology and liturgy, the old, imported, largely baroque ecclesial structures seemed unresponsive to the needs of a growing Christian population which could no longer depend for word and sacrament upon the infrequent visits of dedicated foreigners. Unofficially, ministers and ministries were begun and expanded.

This brief sketch shows us the complexity of the present "expansion," "alteration," or "explosion" in ministry—a worldwide movement begun by profound changes in theology and praxis. This complexus of shifts both increases and decreases the number of ministers—but is always moving towards expansion and diversity in the ministry.

What caused this explosion of ministry? It was not mandated by universal or local churches, nor by bishops or curia in Geneva or Rome. New theologies of the church and liturgy prepared the way, but new perceptions and forms of ministry quickly passed beyond the ideas of theologians. Church ministry expanding throughout the world suggests that the Holy Spirit is intent upon a wider service, a more diverse ministry for a church life that will be broader in quantity and richer in quality.

We can look at ministry through two different perspectives—society and church—and from each gain understanding as to why in our times both nature and grace have led the ministry to seek out a new activity and therein a new theology.

a. From within Society

The world is growing. The number of people living on this planet expands geometrically. At the same time, people are not content merely to subsist in a changeless life punctuated with rare moments of contentment, but they search for a fuller life summed up in some kind of freedom. Quality in Christian life, as well as increase in population and a search for freedom, are forces which have led Christians to expect wider ministry in their churches.

The church understands that its mission to the world is not the preservation of European culture, nor a heroic if rare contact through missionaries with distant tribes. The church is a collective ministry and it serves the multiform presence of grace in the diverse social consciousness of the world. The church lives out its life amid the religions and political movements of the world, and the message it preaches addresses the cultures and organizations which represent the aspirations of the world.

Each country is a microcosm of our expanding and searching world. By 1970, the Roman Catholic Church in the United States had a large population of Christians interested (if not formally active) in the life of the Church. After being minister to the immigrants and the neighborhoods, the Catholic Church, like other Christian churches in America, was in danger of becoming merely an organization for millions of people swept up in fear over numbers, relevancy and participation. The American church-going public is highly educated; raised in a Christian milieu, it is searching for real community, meaningful liturgy and continuing education in faith and ethics. Could the ministry become less aristocratic, distant and automatic? Could it develop a variety of services to an educated, adult church? A church membership grown in quantity and concerned over the quality of life could only lead to an expansion of the ministry—or to a paranoid withdrawal of the clergy and a slow apostasy of the members.

Other countries—Brazil, Germany, Nigeria, India—are experiencing the same dynamic. The church is caught between a flood of numbers and an individual quest for maturity.

The church, national and local, has been asked to address a variety of personal and social needs of volatile American life. New religious movements, ethical issues, social questions, personal upheavals—before so many requests a single minister could only fail. The church, by definition a community, found itself no longer the center of permanent communities but a fragile point of stability (or of contradiction) in a storm of disintegrating structures and new movements. The monoform ministry of priest and pastor was asked to meet all these needs. Without leaving the traditional roles of liturgical leader, preacher, administrator and teacher, the pastor was to be involved in politics, social issues, community building, family and individual counseling. The legitimate and healthy needs of the community would dismay and destroy any minister who assumed them all.

Churches did not retreat from this new situation but tried to take it seriously at both the parish and diocesan levels. There was a realization that the Gospel now must address many needs, and the time of the pastor could no longer be monopolized by sermon or sacrament. Marriage and family were embattled; people live longer today; the ministry could hardly neglect the large number of Christians who were retired, sick, elderly and dying. The 1960s had spotlighted the poor and disenfranchised—these were not a few needy cases but entire segments of the population of American cities. Family, justice, education—even slight involvement in these would lead to advocacy in the political arena and to a critical look at liturgy and preaching within the local church.

Two areas which occupied local churches more were education and liturgy. Before the 1960s, the church had concentrated upon educating children. Suddenly, something rather obvious was pointed out. People live most of their lives as adults, and Christianity is very much a faith for adults, for it exists within life and death, hope and tragedy, cross and resurrection. The community needed to maintain Christian education for children and develop better programs for adults. At the same time, Vatican II, through a never-ending panoply of liturgical changes, introduced diversity and personal meaning into the liturgy. Elements of creativity should enter the liturgical celebration of baptism, marriage and the eucharist. No longer was liturgy a sacral routine, distant and monolithic. There were eucharistic canons for children, frequent anointings for the sick, charismatic meetings and a variety of ceremonies for marriage and anniversaries.

Who was the pastor? The creator of vibrant liturgies or the teacher applying evangelical ethics to social problems? Or the patient counselor, or the social activist? Before the pressure placed upon the church's single ministry, the minister or priest had only two choices: to retreat, feeling unappreciated, into a hostile cynicism toward the new church and contemporary society; or to accept tremors of Gospel and Spirit and welcome into ministerial partnership men and women desirous of ministry and well-educated for a specific service.

b. From within the Church

Vatican II was a council intent upon pastoral improvement, and it prepared in various ways for a new theology and structure of ministry. First, it returned the basic Christian ecclesial emphasis to the local church; the local church not only had an identity and vigor but, in diocese, region and nation, it should respond to its needs. Second, both the bishop and the laity (but not the priest and the parish) were highlighted. After a long period of overemphasis upon sacrificial eucharist and sacral priesthood, baptism was given a new appreciation. Baptism made the Christian—but baptism raised the issue of a universal ministry incumbent upon all the baptized.

Of particular importance was the church's new look at its traditional ministries. Contrary to the medieval position, the Council affirmed that the ministries of bishop, presbyter and deacon were distinct. They were not simply a step up or a step aside from a priesthood imitating Christ's. They had their own identity, their own ordination. The bishop ceased to be defined as a venerable or glorious version of a priest. Official documents referred to the priest by his more accurate designation as presbyter. Finally, the ministry of diaconate was restored. Deacons were no longer seminarians in their final year of study who functioned at liturgies but were men, frequently married and holding other jobs, who shared in the official ministry of the church. Moreover, these fathers and husbands, plumbers and teachers were ordained, and ordained to a ministry which was not the priesthood. The restoration of the diaconate, the view of priest as presbyter and therefore assistant to the bishop, and the restoration of the bishop not as papal vicar or exalted priest but leader of the local church—all of these were practical statements that the church had more than one ministry, that not all ministry was priesthood, and that ministry was not necessarily joined to celibacy. The ministry of the local church had changed from being a group of priests led by a super-priest to a bishop with assisting, distinct ministers called presbyters and deacons. Could there be other assistants in the ministry? Other ministers and other ordinations?

Today we often hear of a decline in the numbers of diocesan clergy, a decline in the number of priests at work in Europe, in Latin and North America. A diminishing diocesan clergy is not the problem, however, and pessimistic statistics may be camouflage for much larger theological issues, those of an expanding ministry.

Even if the number of priests in large, urban dioceses were to triple, or return to earlier large numbers, before the new demands upon ministry by quantity and quality, this would not give the church enough

So where does that leave us today

?

priests. As we have pointed out, the number of Roman Catholics has grown and the expectation of church life has expanded. The crisis in the number of priests could not be solved by a greater number of clergy; it touches upon a change within the life of the healthy Christian communities. *Lay Involvement*

Moreover, in the past the priest carried out a limited administration and liturgy while sisters attended to schools and hospitals. Now it is not clear that a pastor or presbyter either can or should perform all of the central areas of ministry, reaching from liturgy through religious education to peace and justice.

It is unrealistic to imagine a golden age of many vocations, for that age did not have to minister to the vast churches of today, and many of those large numbers of priests and sisters never remained within the active ministry. In Latin America and Africa, there never was a period when a celibate clergy reached an indigenous and extensive level. Other areas have always been dependent upon Europe and North America for ministers.

The expansion of the ministry is not, then, a random or annoying occurrence but an aspect of a new church which is, for the first time in many centuries, worldwide. Size, expansion and potential point out the limitations of the past and the possibilities for the future.

What a strange coincidence that as the needs of the church and society pointed to a wider ministry, there have emerged so many thousands of people intent upon ministry. Men and women, sisters, brothers, priests, teachers, and activists prepared themselves at professional and graduate schools for a specific ministry. Thousands of religious women, Benedictines, Sisters of Mercy, Dominicans, Franciscans, moved into a variety of new ministries in education, social care, justice and health care. In some communities, over a third of the members moved into new ministries, and it was difficult to convince sisters and brothers that they should not seek out an activity closer to the center of the kingdom of God. The result of all this was that the face of the church changed; the "parish plant" was no longer an accurate architectural symbol for the community—church, school, rectory, convent. The ministerial staff, like the ministry itself, worked beyond the buildings. The priests were joined not only by principals and teachers in schools but by colleagues working in adult education, liturgy, health-care and social action. Behind this reconstruction was a subtle shift of ministerial models: the local church was not a fixed site to which people came during some periods in their life, but became less and more. Churches set up series of concentric circles of ministry which moved from the leaders to all fulltime and professionally trained ministers out through levels of parttime ministers to all of the baptized. In the acceptance of the team or staff model of ministry, an expansion beyond the monoform, monastic and sacerdotal ministry was clearly visible.

During this same period, in the Roman Catholic Church, thousands left the vowed life and male priesthood. Then, too, it was clear that the era of numerous vocations—from 1945 to 1960—was ending. The ministry was both declining and expanding—it all depended upon how you looked at it. There were fewer seminarians but thousands in theological schools; fewer men and women active in parochial schools but many more in social action.

We have a particularly vivid illustration of the new situation in ministry in the changes which have occurred in seminary and theological education. Motivated by an effort toward academic respectability and by the need to offer an education which was theologically deeper and pastorally more responsible American Roman Catholic seminaries in the early 1960s joined their Protestant counterparts and sought accreditation from state and church. Many schools were no longer only seminaries but graduate schools in theology and pastoral ministry. Roman Catholic schools admitted women, married men and Protestants and trained them for various ministries. Fearful of a dilution of priestly identity by such schools, many diocesan seminaries did not follow this course but preserved the ethos of the Tridentine seminary. Even they, however, served at times as centers for non-seminarians in ministerial education. The United States was soon filled with open seminaries, universities, theological schools and summer programs educating thousands for ministry. By the mid-1970s, it was clear that in the United States (Protestant churches were moving more hesitantly) Roman Catholicism was conducting a dual system in theological and pastoral education, and both tracts could not escape the milieu of wider ministry.

This same desire to prepare for a new and diverse ministry is evident at the level of an individual church, a parish, a campus, a diocese. The student of ecclesial structures can find examples of all of these "churches" engaged in running their own schools for ministry. There are dioceses who do not see themselves as running primarily a Tridentine seminary but as developing a program of education for the full ministerial potential of the Christian ministry. A Lutheran parish, dismayed by the absence of an alternative to the single pastorate in the diaconate, started its own school to train Lutheran deacons, a collective ministry which includes men and women in many services. A large, urban state university campus, left bereft of any clergy by a disinterested archdiocese, led a Roman Catholic sister to realize that ministry would exist at the university only if she began a school of ministry for the students. In large archdioceses, schools of ministry for minorities are springing up, with modest goals but with serious theology. Finally, we can view the large theological educational programs of universities and motherhouses as schools for ministry; ultimately the people they educate have come from and will return to direct, explicit Christian ministry.

It may be that theological and ecclesiastical leadership in the church will remain with Europe and North America well into the next century. The structure of the church, however, is another matter; for ultimately the church is not a belief or a law but a social reality. Social realities live out of the dynamic of their people, or they die. By the year 2000 the church in Asia, Africa and Latin America will comprise fifty-eight percent of the world's Christians, but seventy percent of the world's Roman Catholics. By the end of this century, Latin Americans will make up close to sixty percent of the world's Catholics.

The need to expand the ministry exists throughout the world.[2] In the Andes, in West Africa, in the Philippines, the same ecclesial struggle exists, the same resources of willing ministers asking how a mono-form church office expands into ministry. What is clear is that, while the single Christian ministry cannot do all that is demanded of it, there is no lack of Christians driven by some spirit or other toward ministry.

A brief phenomenology of the world and church over the past twenty years helps us understand why the priesthood and ministry could not but change. The experience of the diversification of ministries appears like a life-plan sprung from the subconscious of the church. It is collective charism intent upon realization. The *comunidades de base* of South America recall the ministerial staffs of hospitals and campuses in North America. The charismatic communities in the northern hemisphere, traditional in many ways, spontaneously find their own leaders, healers and prayers as must African Christian villages which are visited rarely by a priest.

It is always dangerous to interpret the mind of the Holy Spirit. Nevertheless, by contemplating social and ecclesial forces recently set in motion, we can see why that Spirit (which is the horizon of developing life within the Body of Christ) cannot but draw its churches throughout the world to a dynamic diversity capable of bearing all that its charisms would bring to the world today. Now we can understand that our time does resemble the first decades of the church; for we too have needs and opportunities worthy of the Spirit's diaconal charisms and we look for a maturity in the Body of Christ.

2. The Challenges to Ministry

Change seems always to be unexpected. This alteration in the churches, however, where ministries such as educator, liturgist, community organizer or minister to the sick and aging (inconceivable fifteen years ago) have become a normal part of many dioceses and parishes, presents challenges for the churches, challenges which will not disappear or be resolved by prayers that both church and society might return to an earlier, simpler time.

The first challenge is to explain and guide positively the expansion of the ministry. We need a theological interpretation of these ministers: some have a full seminary education, some have had a night-course; some are shaping their ministerial field and their ministerial identity while others are reviving traditional church evangelism; some are married, some are not; some serve within liturgy, others on the streets. This diversification of the ministry which invites the theologically educated and the committed parishioner to fulltime and parttime ministry obviously offers a unique opportunity for the church to grow. Without a realistic theology of ministry, however, this opportunity could be lost. The charismatic wells would dry up and be replaced by a pastoral schizophrenia over why formal church ministry has been snatched back by a hierarchy to remain a prize for the few.

The second challenge is to heighten the importance of the traditional ministries of presbyter and bishop even as they are complemented by other fulltime services. A fundamental theology of ministry takes nothing from their identity but locates them realistically within the church, within other diverse and parallel ministries. This wider view of ministry does not remove or dilute the ministries of leadership but rather etches their limits and outlines their more difficult responsibilities. For to be a leader of an adult community at prayer and evangelization is different from being the solitary, sacral mediator of an audience.

Unless these challenges are met, two events will take place. The churches throughout the world will lose the opportunities for growth and service which they now glimpse and the traditional ministries will, in a solipsistic victory, alienate themselves from the rest of the church. Devoid of challenge and isolated from their fellow Christians from whom they have kept the grace of ministry, these ministers will attract mediocre, passive men interested not in service but in performance. If what we might call a charismatic invitation to ministry is allowed to die without response, the church's next age will be one filled with ecclesial illnesses; if the stimulus to ministry is not explained with a mature realism, churches will become confused, empty, and Christians invited by the Spirit but rejected by human authority will drop out in anger.

Because this movement involves the being of a church, the baptized person and the Spirit in history, expansion in ministry is a reconsideration of the Christian church itself. Like icebergs in spring, vast pieces of cultural history, of Christian faith, of beliefs and pieties, of ways of being minister and community today meet, crash, disappear, remain.

Ministry is a hope and an opportunity for the churches. We can see that where the present situation in ministry is both crucial and creative—in the middle class parishes of parts of the United States, in the *barrios* and *comunidades de base* of Latin America, in the numerous but clergyless cities and villages of Nigeria or Zaire—the time and the opportunity must be seized. History gives us examples of the alternative: parts of Europe which never recovered from the clash between a sacral clergy and an Enlightenment society; Japan where in the sixteenth century a Christian church of hundreds of thousands could be successfully terminated in a few years because there was no ministry apart from the foreign missionaries and from a few Japanese educated in a Western, Tridentine seminary. Words such as "charism," "ministry," "inculturation," and "community" describe the very being of the church, and so the theologian's task is to look for wisdom and coherence in history, for principles and direction in revelation.

3. Toward a Fundamental Theology of Ministry

In this book's Preface I described the following pages as "a fundamental theology of ministry," "a cultural metaphysics of ministry," "a theology of grace." It is grace and history which bring limits and unity to the following interpretation of ministry: the principle by which life and service in the Christian community are viewed is the development of charisms of life and ministry in different eras of cultural history.

A look at the fragmentary records of ministry in the first churches leads us to see more intensely the variety in church structure over almost two millennia, and then we grasp the incomplete but expanding ministry today. We have not a historical record but rather an insight into the variety and unity in ministry. History shows the inner nature and the inner creativity of what Jesus and his Spirit gave to the world as service to the kingdom of God. To know history is to be set free. The New Testament's theologies of ministry are richer, more demanding and more varied than we expect, and the history of ministry is not a set of norms of limited successful realizations. The forms of cultural history are principles of church life and self-interpretation.

A fundamental theology of ministry is ultimately a theology of grace. Grace, the presence of the Triune God, is with history the source of our attempt at a coherent theology of ministry. Ministry begins with Spirit's charism; the goal of ministry is to serve the kingdom of God which theologians have called "grace." The promptings which lead the worldwide church toward an expansion of ministry are charisms of the Spirit. So the following fundamental theory of ministry is also a theology of Spirit and grace.

Every theology is existential, transcendental and correlative. This theology of ministry begins with personal calls for wider ministry to sustain the church in this time of opportunity and risk; it is transcendental because it describes the history of the collective consciousness of the church precisely as endowed with charisms and services of nurture, growth and enrichment. It is correlative because its method is to relate the ministerial charisms of the Spirit to cultural history, in the first century, in key subsequent cultural periods, and in our present time.

So, the perspective of grace within culture guides and limits the following pages where the nature, promise and forms of ministry are outlined.

a. Thinking about Ministry

When we think about something, we circle around the subject; we dive into and explore it; we stand back and gaze. Thinking is not memorizing or calculating but calm and happy reflection. Thinking is the reflective side of life.

Theology is the thinking side of belief. Everyone has some kind of faith. Everyone, too, has a theology; for the human being cannot stop thinking (if only in the inner recesses of one's own existence) about the mystery of elusive life and approaching death. Rather than being the special domain of scholars, theology—thinking about belief—is ordinary reflection on the mystery of God's presence in time.

Both thinking and faith stand on the boundary between history and eternity, and that makes both difficult. That vast mystery we call "I" is both self and world. We can know past events and persons; we can search out and express the universe's laws. Life, however, also has its historical and psychic limitations. Through Kant, Marx, Freud, Jung and Einstein we have learned how conditioned our mental life is. Our psychological world is just that, a world, with its own surging seas and high mountains. We are not screens upon which a movie of history is projected, or a black glass wall upon which a series of eternal images are flashed. We fashion our world; partially, we make the world; we exist as history.

The forms which the church and its ministries assume amid cultures and epochs are part of our ancestry. Some human beings live in "an era that works": for instance, Byzantium in the seventh century, Paris in the thirteenth, Holland or Bavaria in the seventeenth. The forms of their liturgy and church (like their art) seemed to them to be something which would always be there: lasting, solid, eternal, beautiful. So there is always the desire to turn thinking into preservation, to keep in the church what was once good and useful as a mode eternal.

Thinking about ministry is theology reflecting upon the church. To think about being-the-church is not easy, however. The ministry like all of the church lives between the power of the Gospel and the poignant needs of this or that person.

What is intriguing about the word "theology" is that its Greek root does not describe well what the word means. Christian theology is not information about God but a revelation from God about ourselves. Christian theology is better described as God's anthropology than as our science of God. Theology is an active, dialectical pondering about self and Presence which moves in one direction through history to the Incarnate Word, Jesus of Nazareth; and, in the other direction, through the diversity of today's world to billions of individual people. Theology is correlation. Not a content of holy ideas but an action, theology always preserves the revelation of God yet breaks out into a permanent dialogue with the world. Theology is the co-relation between two poles: the first pole is the revelation of God; the second is the situation to which the Christian, especially the Christian minister, must speak. This is how Paul Tillich described his method.

> Theology, as a function of the Christian Church, must serve the needs of the Church. A theological system is supposed to satisfy two basic needs: the statement of the truth of the Christian message and the interpretation of this truth for every new generation. Systematic theology uses the method of correlation. It has always done so, sometimes more, sometimes less, consciously, and must do so consciously and outspokenly. . . . The method of correlation explains the contents of the Christian faith through existential questions and theological answers in mutual interdependence. In using the method of correlation, systematic theology proceeds in the following way: it makes an analysis of the human situation out of which the existential questions rise and it demonstrates that the . . . Christian message (is) the answer to these questions. . . . The analysis of the human situation em-

ploys materials made available by man's creative, self-interpretation in all realms of culture. Philosophy contributes, but so do poetry, drama, the novel, therapeutic psychology, and sociology.[3]

Although the passage is Paul Tillich's, the method he described has been that of every important and successful theology. Origen, Augustine, Aquinas, Luther—all have insisted upon the necessity of relating the Christian message to their own society. A theologian was creative precisely because he or she saw a new situation, met culture daringly, drew from the riches of the Christ-event the right word and power in the thought-forms of the time. A theology for one age can never be fashioned in advance for another society. Theology (as distinct from Scripture) implies a particular audience to which it speaks. Revelation is the fullness of Christ as our definitive religious figure and God's word to us.

A theology of ministry is thinking about how the church should live today; it flows from a dialectical format. On the one hand, there is an interest in the forms and models through which the church has developed its ministries and its styles of ministry. Not the canons of a provincial council nor the pages of a famous theologian (there is little discussion of the theory of ministry between the year 100 and the year 1000 A.D.) hold our attention. Rather, it is the form-cluster, the cultural model which tells us about the life of the church. We want to know why the church in this or that era interpreted itself so—why it described itself once as New Israel and later as New Rome. Then we can see the limitations received from the history of forms as well as the lasting essence of the Christian community.

b. The Church in History

The blood of the church is history. Paradoxically, the longing of the human race for the divine and eternal has led theologians and churchmen to describe the church as above or beyond history. The church, however, is not eternal. Its life is not a divine life which watches the passing of centuries. We should not turn the irrevocable presence and mission of the church promised by Jesus and his Spirit into an existence for the church which is apart from history. The church survives but is not always triumphant; the church does not die but it does partake in the uncertainties and tensions of history.

The church, rather than being eternal and perfect, is eminently historical. Just as it is difficult for human beings to affirm that Jesus of Nazareth was true man as well as true God, so it is difficult to affirm the church as word and sacrament of the kingdom of God and at the same time to let the church live not only in but out of history.

When religion is escaping life for the eternity of God, there is a fear of the historical. Time sweeps all before it, not only all men and women but all civilizations. To a neophyte or neurotic in religion, history seems the great enemy, for it challenges the rituals and forms of religion. True, history in its flood leaves nothing unchanged, but it is equally true that the Judaeo-Christian incarnation of humanity and religion embraces history. Incarnation accepts history, looks for salvation in history, views history as moving forward to a fulfillment which will give meaning to all stories and to all of history. We need to look for the other side of history: not violence but creativity.

The situation of the church is history. A theology of ministry is first and foremost a study of history: forms of ministry come from certain periods in history. The incarnation of the Word of God took place in Jesus ben Joseph. This incarnation continues in the church, the Body of Christ.

When a theology is grounded in history, it has some hope of touching reality. The following pages attempt to explain through words but not to explain words. Even holy and ancient words do not ultimately explain anything as active and personal as one human being serving the presence of God in another man or woman. In charting ministry we cannot be content with verbal justifications, whether they are the gift of hierarchies or of theologians; but, like the New Testament with its fresh metaphors and concrete proclamations, we must push our discussion of priesthood and charism until we have reached their reality in psyche and society.

"The situation of the church is history." Must the church like all the institutions of civilization become an antique? Will it end in ruins or self-parody? History shows the wounds and failings of the church but also its survival. Precisely when the church pretends to be eternal it is vulnerable to the ravages of time; for nature and human life are shot through with change. When the church tries to hold back history and neurotically assumes the mask of an age that is dead or dying, history appears harsh. The church wants to stay with this or that civilization and will not admit the evils that history might in its course correct. In short, the church will not live by faith and hope, and its leaders plan not a mission but a museum.

History is trends, changes, wars, migrations, plans, deaths. The products and patterns of ingenious civilizations which fill our galleries instruct us in the life-cycles of history. We see that every period had limitations, that history becomes incarnate in culture, and that history never shows to one epoch all it has to display. History is not only the situation of the church, it is the church's mentor.

Spanish Catholicism and Norwegian Lutheranism show us historical ways of being-the-church. The more we enter into the history of the church, the less we fear history. Social forms, liturgical signs, a language and a style of preaching and praying, charisms before government—these are the flesh and blood of the church's life. Through them grace acts upon us; or fails to act.

The church will not end, but churches do end. For over six hundred years there was no more dominant force in Christianity than the Syrian church. Theologians, preachers and poets were numerous; centers formed monastic schools and sent missions into China or to Ethiopia. Antioch, Nisibis, Damascus—the bishops of these great centers could hardly have imagined that their power and glory would end, but today Syrian Christianity, though alive, is hardly of any importance. Few even know how great was its history. When we gaze upon the carved crosses of Celtic Christianity at Kells, we have the opportunity to enter for a moment into yet a different church. With its dual, episcopal-monastic organization, its pleasure in missionary travelogue and its druidic interest in all types of spirits and creatures, Celtic Christianity peacefully wove a rich cultural tapestry, Latin and Gaelic. Now it barely remains. The lesson, however, from these two examples is not hopelessness before the onslaught of time, but the variety and greatness of the union of Spirit and culture in the churches.

The famous philosopher of our century Martin Heidegger came to the conclusion that the deepest meaning of reality itself was the history of culture. Temporality and historicity penetrated into the marrow of every person and every object.[4] Metaphysical meditations led Heidegger to conclude that history was not an evolution; history does not have as its primary purpose forward improvement. Later times are not always better than earlier times; Gothic art is not inevitably an improvement over Greek or even Mycenaean art. Civilizations are unique products of an epoch, and one age of history is not better than another but different. Time, Heidegger decided, is like a planetary lighting-process and culture is the collection of forms, symbols, institutions and thought-forms which one period brings to our attention. But—and this is important—when one set of lights goes on, another goes off. No time is perfect, no age is the standard, no culture was sublimely integral or especially theonomous. There never was a golden age.

Every church looks back to its golden age. The church of Byzantium looked back to the time of the great theologians and fathers of the church; the churches of the Reformation imagine that the sixteenth century was a time of singular evangelical freedom; how much effort Roman Catholicism spent in the past hundred years trying not only in theology but in art and educational theory to reproduce the thirteenth century. If there was an *âge d'or* for the church, then faith in community life would not be a life of the spirit but a life of a scholar or an aesthete. A single golden period would accomplish the impossible; it would contain the entirety of the Kingdom of God, and it would have harnessed all the powers of the Holy Spirit and the collective Body of Christ. The idea of a single normative, historical time for the church is dangerous and close to idolatry, for it locates the Spirit of God within very finite limitations. Moreover, it strikes at the mission of the church (and how often evangelism has been crippled because the fullness of the Gospel was hidden in the propagated civilization of its preachers) as it communicates that the church is not capable of nourishing the mustard tree of Christ living in all times or spreading to the ends of the earth.

Christianity is a sacramental and international faith, and so it could not be content with an empty temple, a gray room. Not only language and symbol but theology and social structure come as gifts from history's cultures. The metaphors of Judaism, the hierarchy of Neoplatonism and the lapidary orders of Rome not only preach but form the Gospel. In the New Testament, the early churches have many metaphors, several theologies, no canons. In the fourth century, Ephrem, the Syrian, described the church in flowery poems, while in the West Ambrose hammered out a logical and legal relationship between two corporations, church and state. History is the means by which the church is continually incarnate in culture. Through the churches, the lighting-process of history shows the kingdom of God in one set of ideas and symbols; but that time too must come to an end so that another constellation, another luminous display can engage men and women with new insights into the richness of Christ.

In an ecclesiology similar to Heidegger's philosophy of the selective lighting process of cultural history, Hans Küng points out the difficulty in finding the essence, the nature of the primal reality of the church. There is such an essence, and the origins of the church hold and pass on a normative reality for the Christian community. And yet, nowhere and at no time do we find the essence of the church perfectly isolated.

> Every age has its own image of the Church, arising out of a particular historical situation; in every age a particular view of the Church is

expressed by the Church in practice, and given conceptual form by
the theologians of the age. . . . There are fundamental elements and
perspectives in the Church which are not derived from the Church
itself; there is an "essence" which is drawn from the permanently de-
cisive origins of the Church.

In short, the "essence" of the Church is not a matter of metaphysical
stasis, but exists only in constantly changing forms. If we want to discover this original and permanent "essence," given that it is something dynamic rather than something static and rigid, we must look
at the constantly changing historical "forms" of the church.[5]

We need historical liberation in our theology because Christian
ministry has been particularly susceptive to what we might call a process of eternalization. The priesthood changed little after the year 1000;
its piety identified closely with the priesthood of Jesus. The ministry
which we have today is meager; ministerial forms are bare. We need to
uncover the rich origins of ministry, to learn how history and culture
have highlighted and limited ministry through two millennia.

History is not only the church's life and situation, it is the church's
cross. Time brings pain and the church feels the pain of change. The
mission of the church, "to the ends of the earth," knows the archetype
of life and death; not that the church is caught up in a pagan cycle of
demise and rebirth but, like its Lord, it exists in the spring of life out of
death. To be faithful to the commission to preach to all nations, the
church at times must die to itself. The church experiences the death of
its labors in this period, the migration of its members from this or that
region, the end of what had once been the right theology and liturgy.
All of this is a crucifixion. Yet, the faithful church can experience this
not as death but as Christian mystery; from the death of the church's
glory (even of grace) springs forth new life. "Unless a wheat grain falls
on the ground and dies, it remains only a single grain; but if it dies, it
yields a rich harvest" (Jn 12:24). Life out of death is the ontology of the
church as it is for all of human life in this world.

c. The Church in Culture

If the blood of the church is history, the flesh of the community of
Christ is culture.

The forms through which the church acts on behalf of the Kingdom of God come from the culture of a time and a place. The Word of
God assumed the culture of a particular tradition. He selected a lan-

guage and its way of expressing reality, a landscape and a poetry with its limitations. The Church lives within cultures. Human beings are effectively addressed and personally touched within their psychic and cultural worlds. All that we said above of history—its service to the Gospel, its glory and its limitations—is true of culture as it touches the church. The verbal system of a language expresses something new about the past and future of Christ; one mythology prepares for the crucifixion and resurrection differently than does another. The sacred space and holy symbols of this architecture will invite, even enclose, the Spirit in their own way. Ultimately, no culture can express the reality of the Gospel of Christ fully; after a hundred cultures have fashioned liturgies, mysticisms, ecclesiologies, the Gospel remains waiting even deeper explorations.

It is not enough to admit in theory the illuminating role of culture for the preaching of the Gospel. More and more churches are accepting the fact that while they must critique their cultural narrowness, they must simultaneously accept life from culture's form. The ramifications of a cultural ecclesiology for Africa and Asia or for Los Angeles and Amsterdam are only beginning to be accepted.

Ministry is a fullness, a pleroma, a mine awaiting new excavations. Just as there is an essence of the church in history, however, so too there is a fullness of ministry in and through cultures. But we human beings—limited in time and church—never meet all the ways and depths of ministry. We fall again and again into the ethereal theory that our ministry alone is God's. What we call a perfect priesthood, above history and time may be, of course, only an imperfect mixture of elements from Rome in the fifth century or from France in the Baroque.

Looking at the sociological images, the cultural realizations in classes and clothes and ecclesiastical powers, Hans Küng describes a pageant of length and variety.

> Pastoral ministries have undergone several changes as we can see if we think of the varied forms they have assumed in the course of the centuries . . . the Corinthian pastors . . . the ascetics and monks and the basilical clergy and court bishops . . . medieval simple priests, canonists, court chaplains, spiritual princes, curial officials and warring popes to the clergy and missionaries and the worker priests of modern times.

> A long and highly varied procession comes to our eyes as we look back down the centuries; it reminds us not only of the relativity of clothes and social symbols but also of the external and internal forms

of the ministry as such. The different forms it took were not dictated by the special commission given to the clergy, nor by the original Christian message, but by all kinds of cultural, social, political and psychological factors.[6]

Culture is the great life-source for all that continues in history. The ecclesiologist and minister must be not only theologian but cultural observer. World-fashioning and world-maintaining, meaning is produced by the variety of cultural ideas, symbols, structures and buildings. Philosophies and theologies create the "world" and maintain this particular form of world which lives, and then struggles and fades.

That venerable and often controversial aspect of the Christian church, tradition, can be described as the history of Christian community manifest in cultural forms and articulated in theology, liturgy and prayer. The distinction between the primal but lasting nature of the church and its forms is at the basis of tradition: the church is committed to the past even as it searches for ministry today.[7] There was an extraordinary variety in the first decades among the Christian churches when Easter and Pentecost were new. Every subsequent generation looks to that experience: not as to a confining law but as to a revelatory experience rich with more and more possibilities for ministry. Modern theology interprets tradition not as written norms but as the living consciousness of the Christian community reflecting upon itself (its world and its ministries) and its past.

Tradition includes not only wisdom from past epochs but failures. Upon closer inspection we see that the history of ministry is often a "negative tradition." The church has long periods of *not* having this or that ministry; earlier ministerial forms or faithful interpretations of ministry were not retained. A devolution implies a negative tradition, i.e., the historical record is often not one of hammering out ministerial forms but of letting ministries and structures of community life fade away. Centuries passed during which there was no discussion of ministry outside of that concerning the spirituality of the celibate male priest. Negative tradition does not transmit fully Gospel and Spirit in tradition.

We should hesitate to glorify our own age or the first century. Nevertheless, there seems to be an affinity between our times and the first decades of Christianity from the point of view of ministry. The theology of the sacraments of initiation, the inculturation of local churches, the rediscovery of important church ministries and the revitalization of venerable ones—these are the sources of the present ambiguous growth-decline of ministry. Added to this is a healthy rediscovery of the charismatic balancing the clerical. Ministry, like a volcano overflowing, seeks in a world grown smaller a wider horizon.

All of this has its affinity with the world and faith of the first generations of Christians. René Laurentin observes:

> In the New Testament period as in our own, a vast pagan world offered unprecedented opportunities of communication, an extraordinary mixing of cultures, intense and sometimes anxious inquiry about the meaning of human life, vigorous religious movement and the need for a genuine experience of life in the community. In the New Testament period as today, crisis and change provoked creativity. The New Testament is an example of the predominance of movement over system which is a widely proclaimed goal today.

> The period of the New Testament had also undergone the most radical experience of declericalization ever seen; this was characteristic of the transition from the Old Testament and pointed the way to a purification and a transcendence which would not be a negation of the sacred but a sacralization of life itself within the living body of Christ.

> The first and most important lesson is that the ministries of the New Testament are functional; their goals are determined by the service of the community and not by the bureaucratic apparatus. . . . Another important aspect found in the New Testament is that ministries are fundamentally missionary.[8]

Perhaps the similarity between the first century and our own times comes from the awareness that Christ sent his followers to be ministers of the good news to all the earth. After Pentecost, the church came to the startling conclusion that it was destined not for Jews alone, nor for just Antiochenes or Corinthians, but for all the world. There have been centuries when that insight was paramount in the church's consciousness and centuries when it was forgotten. Karl Rahner has written that the decades after Vatican II have in the midst of rapid change brought back the same insight, the same shock, the same truth.

> Theologically speaking, there are three great epochs in church history, of which the third has only just begun and made itself observable at Vatican II. First the short period of Jewish Christianity. Second, the period of the Church in a distinct cultural region, namely that of Hellenism and of European culture and civilization. Third,

the period in which the sphere of the church's life is in fact the entire world. These three periods signify three essential and different basic situations for Christianity and its preaching.

This means that in the history of Christianity the transition of Christianity from one historical and theological situation to an essentially new one did happen *once,* and now in the transition of the Christianity of Europe (with its American annexes) to a fully world religion it is starting to happen for a second time.[9]

This book is not a defense of novelty in ministry, nor a liberal program for the future. It is an explanation of what in fact is happening. The expansion of the ministry, the entrance into ministries by Christian men and women, variants in seminary and theological education, the manifest confusion about who realistically is or is not in the ministry— none of this was programmed by theologians or by bishops. It happened.

Ministry at any time lives within four worlds: (1) the world of the thought-forms of the time expressed abstractly in philosophy; (2) the teaching of the church at this time (theology); (3) the services provided in ordinary church life; (4) the social context in which people live. Sometimes these come together, sometimes one or more of the four worlds are apart from each other and society tears into its own flesh or the church fails to develop a healthy life.

The following chapters are held together by an analysis of grace within historical culture. The major issues in ministry are looked at from a biblical (chapters Two to Four) and then from a theological point of view (chapters Six and Seven); the bridge between these two sets of chapters is formed by a look at the major incarnations of ministry in history (chapter Five).

NOTES

1. On the extensive changes in Roman Catholicism after 1962 cf. P. Hebblethwaite, *The Runaway Church* (London, 1975); G. Noel *The Anatomy of the Catholic Church. Roman Catholicism in an Age of Revolution* (New York, 1980); W. McSweeney, *Roman Catholicism. The Search for Relevance* (New York, 1980); L. Gilkey, *Catholicism Confronts Modernity* (New York, 1975).

2. On the explosion of ministry throughout the world, cf. in *Pro Mundi Vita: New Forms of Ministries in Christian Communities* 50 (1974); *Basic Communities in the Church* 81 (1980); *The Institutional Church in the Future* 82 (1980); *Parishes without Priests* 80 (1979); *New Forms of Lay Ministry in Western Europe* 82 (1980); D. S. Amalorpavadass, *Ministries in the Church in India*

(New Delhi, 1976); W. Buhlmann, *The Coming of the Third Church* (Mary-knoll, 1979); *Asian Colloquium on Ministries in the Church* (Manila, 1977). H. M. Legrand, "Bulletin d'ecclésiologie," *Revue des sciences philosophiques et théologiques* 59 (1978) 645ff. M. Singleton, "New Forms of Ministry in Africa," *Pro Mundi Vita* 50 (1974). W. Burrows, *New Ministries: The Global Context* (Maryknoll, 1980); F. Klostermann, *Gemeinde—Kirche der Zunkunft (Thesen, Dienste, Modelle)* (Freiburg, 1974) 1. Writings on this topic have been com-posed by the Latin American bishops at Puebla (1979), the German bishops (1977), the French bishops (1973), and the Asian bishops (1977). On the history of the theology of ministry in the past decades cf. the *Bulletins* written by Yves Congar since the 1930s, and the historical survey of Bernard Cooke in *MWS*, pp. 1–32.

3. *Syst* 1, pp. 31, 60. For an application of Tillich's correlation to the vari-ous levels of ministry cf. E. and J. Whitehead, *Method in Ministry* (New York, 1980), pp. 3ff.

4. M. Heidegger, *Identity und Difference: Vom Wesen der Wahrheit;* the section *"Zeitlichkeit und Geschichtlichkeit"* in *Sein und Zeit.*

5. *Ch,* p. 4.

6. *Ch,* p. 437. "We can and should recognize the seriousness and depth of a spiritual change in a culture; for the consequences of such a shift in the limits and range of experience and understanding for the life of (Christian) faith call for a state of preparedness and give a mandate for a new interpretation of it. . . . When our ways of understanding reality, our models, our whole intellectual and spiritual equipment begin to shift and alter, the way we think about the faith as a whole will be different too." E. Schillebeeckx, *Jesus* (New York, 1979), pp. 579f. On models, see A. Dulles, *Models in the Church* (New York, 1974); P. Granfield, *Ecclesial Cybernetics* (New York, 1973); T. O'Meara, "Philosophical Models in Ecclesiology," *TS* 39 (1978) 3ff.; J. Theisen, "Models of Papal Minis-try and Reliability," *American Benedictine Review* 27 (1976) 270ff.; P. Chirico, "Dynamics of Change in the Church's Self-Understanding," *TS* 39 (1978) 55ff. M. Fahey, "Continuity in the Church Amid Structural Change," *TS* 35 (1974) 415ff.

7. W. de Vries describes his history of the structural ecclesiology of the first seven ecumenical councils (a particularly challenging area for this ap-proach) as a study of the structure of the church unfolding itself under the di-rectorship of the Holy Spirit in different historical forms; cf. *Orient et Occident* (Paris, 1974), p. 7.

8. R. Laurentin, "The New Testament and the Present Crisis in Ministry," *C* 7(1971), 7, 14. "On the basis of theological criteria I think that preference must be given to the first Christian millennium as a model for a future shaping of the church's ministry—albeit in a very different, modern historical context—and in particular to the New Testament and the pre-Nicene period." *My,* p. 67.

9. K. Rahner, "Towards a Fundamental Interpretation of Vatican II," *TS* 40 (1979) 721f.

CHAPTER TWO
The Kingdom of God and Its Ministry

Because we are interested in sketching a fundamental theology of ministry, we will begin not with issues such as sacramental character or episcopal office but with the forces in history which gave rise to church and ministry. God comes to us as kingdom, as Spirit, as grace, and out of this horizon of the divine within cultural structures and individual personalities come Christian community and its ministries.

1. Jesus and the Kingdom of God

Jesus Christ preached not a religion nor an institution, not even himself. He preached the kingdom of God.

Contemporary Christianity is rediscovering that Jesus, God's Word in human person, during his ministry on our planet was a prophet of what he called the kingdom or reign of God. This powerful but unseen reality of God's presence to humanity is the central message of Jesus of Nazareth: all else flows from this burning core. The kingdom of God is a zone which exists between the ineffability of God and the liminality of all that is human; "kingdom" is a word for the loving, active plan of God in history and for our fragmentary and distorting appropriation of God's presence in our lives.

Jesus did not preach primarily the formation and triumph of an institution we call "church." As an itinerant, sometimes apocalyptic herald, he proclaimed the advent of God, describing this "kingdom" in metaphors and parables. He warned of its challenge to the rich and the

26

priests; he pointed out its presence in honest soldiers, sorrowing prostitutes and repentant exploiters of the poor. The realm of God was not only a hope but a power overcoming the tragedy of history. Jesus joined it to faith in God, or to love for another suffering human being, or to conversion from sin, dishonesty and egoism. "Jesus came into Galilee, preaching the gospel of God, and saying, 'The time is fulfilled, and the kingdom of God is at hand; repent, and believe in the gospel' " (Mk 1:14f.).

Ernst Troeltsch's succinct observation may be one of the great insights modern theology has given us: "Jesus did not bring the kingdom of God; the kingdom of God brought Jesus." We see Jesus as the result and center not only of Israel's history but of all religious history. Jesus is not a demi-god in a strange land, but the prophet and priest of horizons of God's power. The location of Jesus within the kingdom of God need not reduce Jesus to an ethical teacher; for he presents himself as the incarnation of a presence of God evolving beyond a past religion— he is the explosion of God's Spirit now and in the future.

What is the kingdom of God which Jesus announces and whose coming in history has brought not only the Christ but his Pentecostal Spirit? We ponder the metaphors for God's presence, and suddenly we find that the church has stepped in front of the kingdom. Frequently there have been periods, colorful if exaggerated, when political kingship claimed priesthood and ministry. At his coronation, the son of Charlemagne was clothed not only as emperor but as deacon. Some officeholders of the church lived out their ministry not as itinerant evangelists but as battle lords.[1] The kingdom of God is not the power of this world, although the history of the church is a record of that temptation—and of the church's acquiescence. Nor is the church a sacral city substituting on earth for the kingdom. The church is human (even if Spirit-filled), but the kingdom is God's presence. The way we view the reign of God present in and after Jesus will determine the vitality and accuracy of our vision of Jesus' call to ministry. Since all ministry ultimately serves the kingdom of God and since the church itself—as ancient mosaics portray—is a *deacon* of the Trinity, we must begin a theology of ministry with a contemplation of God's presence in history.

The kingdom of God is the central symbol of the message of Jesus.[2] It is easy to say what the kingdom of God is not: the kingdom is not any one civilization or culture, not any particular nation or empire; not this philosophy or world-view nor this political or economic movement. God's plan and direction is greater than any individual or collective cultural enterprise; more than history, more than the history of the world's religions, more than art and more than economic equality.

From the preaching of Jesus, we learn through similes that there is a dynamic influence of God in our midst, a presence perceivable only through belief. Its standards and its work, its very style of working, are not those of the world's ambition and sensuality but are love, service, a dying to self and a rising. The kingdom of God is not a condition after biological death but is the inner core of life and history, a dynamic intensifying and expanding after the coming of Jesus of Nazareth.

Ephesians translates these images of God's reign into a theological ontology and a cosmic plan:

> For he has made known to us in all wisdom and insight the mystery of his will, according to his purpose which he set forth in Christ as a plan for the fulness of time, to unite all things in him, things in heaven and things on earth.

> In him, according to the purpose of him who accomplishes all things according to the counsel of his will, we who first hoped in Christ have been destined and appointed to live for the praise of his glory (Eph 1:9).

Before creation, before the tragic turn of our fallen race, this planet emerges from God marked by a plan. The plan includes me, born of love and destined for eternal life. This plan is mysterious not in the sense of hidden information or divine trick, but mysterious in its concreteness and in its paradox. The plan of God moves from cosmic peace and power through sin (exemplified and climaxed in Jesus at Golgotha) and through our own suffering and sin to life triumphant.

> The hour has come for the Son of man to be glorified. Truly, truly, I say to you, unless a grain of wheat falls into the earth and dies, it remains alone; but if it dies, it bears much fruit . . Father, glorify thy name (Jn 12:23, 28).

What is the plan, the "reign of God," if it is not a religious empire or a set of saving ideas? We—unacquainted with kings and kingdoms— might name it an atmosphere, a horizon.[3] The contemporary world lives within certain horizons; they are the way a society works, the way people think. Horizons are the world-views and the cultural perspectives of a time. A horizon, whether one of technology or art, can at first seem to be far less concrete than a machine gun or a computer, but ultimately the horizon has produced the pieces of machinery. A horizon is the most important thing in the world, for it determines the cultural life of people. A horizon can produce the architecture of a Bernini or the death-camps of a Himmler. A horizon pervades our conscious and un-conscious life, suggesting forms and directions. It may emphasize the present or throw the entire populace into a sacrificial struggle to master the future.

The kingdom of God is not simply the mind of God or a future heaven. God's vision-plan for the future and for a beloved humanity does not remain an idea or a possibility but surrounds every person. Not only "kingdom" and "reign" but words like "salvation," "redemption," "grace" designate this horizon of God's presence. God's being—al-though it is as intimate to us as we are to ourselves—is not our product, for even our response to it is a gift of the horizon. The atmosphere of God's plan is expansive, future-directed, within but not of the world; perceived not by statistics but by the eye of faith. Although appearing to be of religion, God's gracious plan transforms and challenges all it touches . . . even religion. Pro-human, it veers away from superstitious bondage to a deity, and turns toward the service of what ultimately is best in us.

Eventually there will be a clash of horizons, for the kingdom of God purifies all lesser realms and judges politics and civilizations. Jesus would not isolate into soul or temple the new presence of God he saw breaking in.

> I saw Satan fall like lightning from heaven. Behold, I have given you authority to tread upon serpents and scorpions . . . and nothing shall hurt you. Nevertheless do not rejoice in this, that the spirits are sub-ject to you; but rejoice that your names are written in heaven (Lk 10:18).

The kingdom of God is the horizon of ministry.

The kingdom of God is the source, the milieu, the goal of ministry. The presence of God in our complex world enables ministry, gives min-istry its life and its freedom. The church, rather than being the dispens-er of ministry, stands with ministry within the kingdom as something derivative, fragile, secondary, temporary. At the end of time, ministry and church will have been absorbed into our life in God.

The loving plan of God is the ultimate revelation and grace made personal in Jesus' life; and his Spirit's activity becomes concrete in his-tory through the church. *Pneuma, charisma,* and then *diakonia* are re-alizations of the wider, intimate horizon Scripture calls "the kingdom of

God." A theology of ministry is basically a meditation on the kingdom, a theology of the Holy Spirit, a contemplative analysis of grace.

2. The Church and the Kingdom of God

In the advent of the kingdom Jesus effected a revolutionary metamorphosis from religion to something new—charism, church. In short, out of Jewish covenant and the structure of the synagogue, alongside the disparate mystery religions there emerged a group of spirit-filled evangelists who called themselves "people," "the saints," "brothers and sisters." In Greek, the elect community was called *"ekklesia,"*—and this word has come down to us as the church.

Among the Gospels, "church" is mentioned only in the *Gospel of Matthew,* and then only three times, in two verses. The kingdom of God is mentioned over a hundred times in the New Testament in a variety of images and stories. The reign of God opens the ministry of Jesus, and in Jesus men and women meet the new advent of God's reign.

Jesus invited followers to join his ministry of evangelization and the first Christians experienced his Spirit calling to discipleship. After Jesus' resurrection, Christian communities pondered the unique, theandric existence of Jesus. They grasped that no Christian ministry can be greater than the ministry of the lord of ministers. Precisely as the incarnate word of God, Jesus is not just an example of divinity but is paradigmatically—in his birth, ministry, crucifixion and resurrection— God's plan in a human being. So Jesus is minister to God: in a special way, Jesus Christ is the work and ikon of the plan. Nevertheless, we may not simply substitute Jesus for the kingdom. ". . . The kingdom of God brought Jesus."

The church, infinitely less, cannot be a ministry to itself. The church is a community of ministers to the kingdom, a limited but sacramental anticipation of God's presence; the ministry is the charismatic power and personal force expanding the kingdom in the world. So the *raison d'être* of ministry cannot be church membership or church obedience or even conceptual orthodoxy, although these may be healthy, intermediate goals. The goal of ministry, like that of the church, is serving the kingdom of God. The church is, individually and collectively, deacon to the Spirit of Jesus.

3. Ministering to the Kingdom

Jesus was in various ways a minister to God's reign. First, while not a cultic priest, he was a *prophet* of the new advent to all who could perceive it (Mk 1:4). Second he described himself as a minister (in Greek, *"diakonos"*) saying that he had come to serve others, not himself, and that loving service transmitted the values of the kingdom of God (Jn 12:26). He was in a striking way an apostle, for his sending had been from God as the inner spirit of God's presence (Jn 8:42).

Ministry lives out of the theology of its community. A church can interpret its relationship to God's reign in different ways—some are correct, and some are perverse. The ministry will follow one of those theologies and will enact it in daily life. A theology of the ministry begins not with church structures but with deeper questions which rise up out of the faith-reflection of the community. Why does the church exist? Why and how has the church survived? What is honestly claimed by the churches and what is their purpose?

If the church identifies itself with the kingdom, the ministers may become domineering ascetics or powerful pontiffs who always claim to be the voice of the will of God. If the church fears that it has almost no contact, in an ontic way, with the horizon of God, the ministers lose themselves in doubt and secularity. They preach timorously but do not enact the kingdom. They substitute personal renewal for divine plan. Roman senators, Germanic princes, English lords, modern businessmen—the ministers of Christ have ended up in all these masques. It is not merely personal ambition which led them into these personae but a false theology of the proximity or distance between the kingdom of God and its community and ministry.

The scandals and missionary failures which come from identifying the church with the kingdom are visible in the ministry just as they are detected in every other aspect of the churches' life. The typical danger for the Roman Catholic and Eastern churches, large and ancient, is to be fixated by the global church. Under the self-satisfied presumption that "the Church" is the divine organism, the universal church would direct all of its ministry into a campaign for itself. Ministry, then, points back to the church, demands only obedience and offers only worship. God's grace is not permitted much freedom; there are no contingency plans for history. This ecclesiology of glory can move to a spirituality of contempt for the world: people are not trusted; whatever is new is sinful. The exact opposite of Pentecost holds sway: because the Spirit is locked up within church structures or returned to heaven unwanted, the missionary is static, formal, content.

Sectarian movements, on the other hand, separate themselves in outrage against this identification of the church with the kingdom of God (but eventually they will fall into the same identification). The older and large church is clearly corrupt, the new movement alone with its apocalyptic coloring is the place of salvation; outside of its purity of Gospel and enthusiastic membership are only theological error and sin. What is originally a burst of healthy New Testament interest in ministries of all sorts born of a humble attention to charisms becomes as anti-world and triumphalistic as the larger church might appear. While the ministry may continue to grow, the sectarian church leadership often turns this success to its own profit.

Before and within the reign of God, ministry has three healthy stances towards the milieu which is both its source and goal.

(a) *as servant.* Ministry approaches the reign of God not as its high priest or banker but as its servant. When the church is tempted to replace the kingdom of God, to adorn itself with divine prerogatives (which are not the same as sacraments and charisms) in neurotic disfigurations of grace and community, the church gives up its basic modality, being a servant of grace, and it strives to be a master. But that is impossible; for, as master, it would replace God. The example Jesus gave to his followers, becoming "deacons," i.e. servants, is no mere piety but (faith and psychology agree) the only non-neurotic stance toward life amid the kingdom. Face to face with the dynamic presence of the ineffable God, one's only sane stance is that of servant. The church's ministry is healthy the more the church models its life upon the life of its founder where apparent humiliation and eternal success, Calvary and Easter, mix. Neither church nor ministry is called to be lord of the reign of God.

(b) *as universal servant.* The church is finite. It is publicly identifiable in place and time, for its members and its structures are known. Theological adjectives such as "invisible," "latent," and "anonymous" should not distract us from recognizing the public nature of the church: a community of baptized men and women voluntarily present and active in Christian community. The church is the center and sacrament of the kingdom but it is not co-extensive with God's presence. The kingdom of God in various degrees flows through the entire human race. All are called to be saved (1 Tim 2:4), and the blood of the cross objectively redeemed not only the baptized but the entire race. The horizon in human consciousness that we call grace is present in some modality or another, as offered, received, rejected, to everyone who is born. So, the ministry exists not to organize outsiders or to polish the baptized but to serve the kingdom of God wherever it may be. Awed by the holiness and mercy of God, ministers serve the mysterious point of intersection between a single personality and the unknown God. The goal of ministry is not ultimately membership or orthodoxy (although these are important, often crucial) but individual relationship with God, the process of becoming that which God's creative love intends in my birth, that is, radical salvation.

Real ministry demands sensitivity, a contemplative attitude for analyzing the way the dialectic of sin and grace has touched this individual. The minister must be a student of grace, a discerner of God's presence. Rather than being frightened by what lies outside the church or discouraged by the church's less than universal membership, the minister through a theology of the transcendence and immanence of God's reign is enabled to be a prophet and an apostle rather than a successful or failed entrepreneur.

(c) *as sacramental servant.* The church and the ministry, however, are more than a pointer to the reign of God. They are more than a preacher of its advent, more than a supportive community of those who believe in a special presence of God in history. If the church and its activities were not more, we would still be waiting—waiting not for the word but for the Word made flesh. In an incarnational faith, ministry exists at the intersection of the human and the divine. The invisible horizon of grace is made concrete in word, celebration and person. We are used to pondering the mystery of ongoing incarnation in the sacraments but we are critical of easy claims that the Spirit arrives in every episcopal utterance. Yet, the ministry not only in its preaching and liturgy but in its myriad of services cannot escape being both flesh and blood and temple of the Spirit.

The church is not a library of religious information, nor an assembly of the saved. The church should be reality and power. The Spirit finds in the interplay of discussion, mutual service, celebration and activity its strongest (if far from perfect) realization on earth. Businesses, universities, factories and the federal government do not intend to concretize the life or values which Jesus declared to be his Father's interpretation of human life.

The church ministers to the kingdom by preaching Jesus in the real situation of the world. The church also ministers to the kingdom by making grace—more abundant and accessible after Good Friday and Pentecost—concrete in word, sign and personal meeting.

The great tradition of the churches, East and West, has never accepted the idea, developed in the past few centuries among some Protestant churches, that the church is only a voice, only a servant waiting upon its Lord. The church is servant and voice, but the church is also reality, a sacrament of the kingdom of God. By sacrament we do not mean a liturgical service such as the sacrament of baptism. The sacramental is the interplay and mix of human and divine horizons. There is an incarnational nature to the church and ministry because ultimate reality is a dual presence of the human and the divine. Hans Küng is right to argue against hypostatizing the church but he errs in seeing little possibility for the church to be a real anticipation of the kingdom.[4] The transcendental nature of God and the eschatological nature of the kingdom are balanced by another dynamic: the incarnation.

The theandric nature of the Word of God illustrates physically God's plan for our race. The definitive religious reality which is the underlying structure of all reality is incarnational, that is, it is an interplay of the human and the divine. The church is not divine; it does, however, partake of the intersection of sin, creation and grace.

We need to find the true meaning of incarnation. Neither Christianity nor local church should aim at reproducing the divine *logos* or Jesus Christ. After the events occurring at the end of his ministry, Jesus lives on in history in a pneumatic way. But, too, the church does not exist as an extension of an utterly distinct Holy Spirit. Cardinal Ratzinger writes: "Christ lives now through the Holy Spirit with its openness and breadth and freedom; this does not exclude an institutional form but does limit its claim, not permitting a simple identification with institutions."[5] Leonardo Boff explains that the sacramental or incarnational nature of the church and its ministry is also of the Spirit. "The church has to be interpreted and presented from the Christ living now as the Risen One; its form of being is something given by the Spirit. The church is the sign, organ and sacrament not of Jesus in the flesh, but of Christ in the Spirit."[6]

The church's ministry really does express, extend and incarnate the reign of God. The minister through word and silence, through service and worship, is not only an occasion of God's presence but an intersection of the human and the divine; both of these dimensions are rooted in Christ who is the incarnate Word in our past history and who exists now in the intense modalities of Risen Lord and Spirit. At the same time, all that is accomplished for the reign of God is totally a result of God's grace active in the community, and the church and ministry are subject to the limitations and paradoxes of nature, sin and grace in every man and woman.

The church is Jesus' Spirit in people.

While servanthood is the style of ministry, the pulse of ministry is the power of the Spirit. It occurs to the theologian that what *Matthew* and *Mark* call the kingdom of God and what *John* and Paul call the Spirit are the same. Both express the great theme of Scripture—of all revelation and religion—namely that God is intimately present in people's lives drawing them forward to an unseen destiny.

4. The Fulfillment of Religion

Our fundamental theology of ministry is searching for what is the primal force behind ministry: the new advent of God. This horizon will burst into faith and redemption, but it will, as grace, also confront history and society. So there will be an unavoidable clash of horizons between revelation—and religion.

Ministry seems closely allied to religion. "Organized religion" has its "ministers" and "priests." The burst of grace into the individual Christians and their communities meets religion. Precisely because the kingdom ushers in new and last times, God's revealing presence in Jesus cannot simply build upon or modify religion. Religion in a fallen race will contain stolid error and idolatry; the Spirit must meet each religion and must face the totality of religion. The New Testament records this impact between the highest terrestrial stage in grace and the general religious struggle of the human race as Jesus encounters positively and negatively his own religion, and then as he enacts in a strange way the sacrifice of religion unto God.

A theology of ministry (especially one which has seen ministry reduced to liturgical priesthood) is grounded upon the conviction that before and after Pentecost the men and women who followed Jesus experienced in a different way that which we call casually "religion." Christ really did fulfill and end something. Ministry is not solely a bloody or bloodless liturgy, the Christian church is not a marble temple of a new covenant, the ministers of Christianity are not brighter and more powerful forms of levitical priesthood; at best these views are partial, close to metaphor. Seeing themselves and God in the light of the coming of the Spirit, the Christians replaced much of religion with community, charism and service. These communities were not a new religion nor a new version of Jewish religion; they were the fulfillment of all religion. Only in that context can we understand how charismatic ministry replaced pagan, cultic and Jewish priesthood.

We pause to consider the fulfillment of religion in the church not to urge a new puritanism but precisely to free sacrament and service from a narrow constraint for wider incarnations in people and actions.

Religion is attraction to the transcendent and holy. But religion has a second, narrower meaning as the localization of the divine in objects and people encircled by mediations and castes, cults and idols. Re-

ligion in this second meaning—not merely in its abuses but in its very
nature—shakes before the new mercy and the new freedom of the kingdom of God. Paul Tillich expressed it in this way.

> There is nò religion as a special function in the Spiritual Community.
> Of the two concepts of religion, the narrower and the broader, the
> narrower does not apply to the Spiritual Community, for all acts of
> man's spiritual life are grasped by the Spiritual Presence. In biblical
> terms: There is no temple in the fulfilled Kingdom of God, for "now
> at last God has his dwelling among men! He will dwell among them
> and they will be his people, and God himself will be with them." The
> Spiritual Presence which creates the Spiritual Community does not
> create a separate entity in terms of which it must be received and ex-
> pressed; rather, it grasps all reality, every function, every situation. It
> is the depth of all cultural creations.[7]

Although we may disagree with Tillich about where the sacramentality
of the depth and ground of the Spiritual Presence have risen up among
us, he helps us to see that the kingdom of God is different from religion,
and that the Christian Gospel and its community should not be one.

The preaching and promise of Jesus is not a new religion nor only
the next stage of one previous religion, that of Israel. To be called Son
of God means to exist as definitive religious prophet. Jesus is addressing
all religion, for he knows that God's kingdom now fulfills, judges, illumines and critiques the religions of the world.

The chronology of evolution has expanded our comprehension of
the length of social life. Anthropology has unearthed a vast spectrum of
religions. The psychological and social structure of religion and their
myriad cultural fulfillments are earlier phases of the kingdom which
God's final reign must lovingly overcome. God's plan for the salvation
of the human race has in Jesus brought history into "the last times."
This apocalyptic eschatology means that religion too has met crisis and
change.

Christians since the ahistorical reappropriation of the Jewish scriptures in the late second century have often believed that the new covenant was merely a clear and fulfilled version of the religion of the old.
In fact, the Old Testament was religion, the New is grace. There is a
considerable difference between the two, and it is grace (as we have
seen) which determines the Christian ministry. Religion demands a
caste of cultic priests while grace encourages a diversity of ministries.

The kingdom of God is not a new privileged set of sacred rituals.
The passion of Jesus was not merely the price of each human's soul but

an objective crisis for the world: the earth trembled, the sky darkened, the Temple's veil split. The world could never be the same, and history after Golgotha was different. Judgment not only came to individuals with an invitation to conversion in grace but judgment came upon cosmic powers, nations and religions.

> And you, who were dead in trespasses and the uncircumcision of your flesh, God made alive together with him, having forgiven us all our trespasses, having canceled the bond which stood against us with its legal demands; this he set aside, nailing it to the cross. He disarmed the principalities and powers and made a public example of them, triumphing over them in him (Col 2:13f).

The cross was a scandalous event of social and religious history. Preaching the cross and resurrection of Jesus of Nazareth, the Twelve found that often their hearers did not comprehend the connection between the coming of the Spirit (the Twelve themselves did not easily grasp it) and the freedom from religion. By baptism, believers accepted the grace rampant in the last times. People and cities long accustomed to the cultic manipulation of the divine and to the purchasing power of ritual were startled by God's wisdom: for through a condemned criminal in a public sacrifice—a grotesque liturgy—God's plan entered its final era.

There are many ways of defining and dividing "religion." Neither philosophers nor cultural anthropologists agree on a single meaning. Religion can mean things: not only vessels and idols, buildings and people, but clothes, rituals, doctrines and writings—all of which pertain to knowing about and influencing the Absolute. Or religion can mean the less defined psychological drive, the mental and emotional urges which are the ground of the concrete realizations mentioned above. There is in every woman and man feelings of dependence (finitude), of incompleteness (mortality), of quest (meaning), and these give rise to religion, to total and personal quest, to a more or less implicit hope and faith.

Religion is one form of culture among others—and yet it is unique; for it is not just one facet of life but is capable of being the matrix of other cultural forms, of being a conscious or unconscious ground for life. Worldview and meaning never escape religion. Modern philosophers and psychologists have concentrated upon this second, broader meaning. Philosophers such as Rudolf Otto and Martin Heidegger and painters like Kandinsky and Klee spoke of the holy disclosed in the spiritual essence of things and situations. Tillich described religion as the substance of culture—the ground of being and the ultimate concern break forth into the concrete forms of architecture, theater, and economics. This understanding of religion is not the enemy of but the prelude to the great modern Christian theological systems. In this understanding of religion, religion is a dimension which both psychology and ontology disclose, and not a province of less sophisticated anthropologies.[8]

When we say that the advent of the kingdom of God in Jesus and his Spirit clashes with religion, even spells the purification of religion, we do not mean this second understanding of religion. Its forms lie deep within our personality. If charism and ministry in a sacramental mode are to be successful, realizations of revelation and faith (and revelation must become concrete to make an impact upon our sensitivity), they must not only address our transcendental religious drives but they must use symbols and events, actions and people to make grace concrete. Since the Enlightenment, scholars and theologians have been announcing the arrival of a secular, religion-less world. Schools and churches were convinced that they should abandon faith in a distinct revelation of God in Jesus Christ in order to be ready and relevant for a society without religion. Of course, such a time never arrived. Today many areas of the human race, even of technological societies, seem even excessively religious. When we argue that the early Christians had a revolutionary grasp of religion, we do not mean they foresaw pure secularity—*ekklesia* metamorphosed into secular city—but that they understood that external, cultic, tribal religion was impotent, and ended by the events of Golgotha.

The reign of God brought judgment to sacral religion with its externalization of human religious drives in buildings, objects, rituals and classes. We can contrast the *transcendental, ecstatic* and *sacramental* religious dimension (in the self-transcendence of ordinary life a person experiences an invitation to "the more," "the holy") with sacral religion. "Sacral" means all manner of things which not only symbolize or present (as the Christian sacrament does) but which may summon or manipulate the divine. In cult, the divine is often controlled; in idols, the transcendent materialized; in priesthood, the holy is mediated. Superstition, magic and idolatry are the accompanying spirits of sacral religion. Such religion brings the perennial temptation to encapsulize the divine. Sacral religion is a phenomenon of extremes: it parades exaggerated claims and it achieves ultimately nothing. Not the dimension of human self-transcendence toward the holy, but the concreteness of sacral religion was what Jesus challenged.

Karl Barth treated religion in his *Romans* and *Church Dogmatics.* He recognized the omnipresence and strength of religion only to deny any positive relationship of religion to revelation. For Barthian theology, religion is simply one aspect of the broken dialectic between God and the human person, nature and grace. "Religion," Barth wrote, "is the one great concern of godless men."[9] The Gospel can throw light on religion only to judge it. For in religion the human person is blind, closed, and so not a believer. It is not so much primal religions on the Amazon or Niger which aroused the Barthian critique but the seeds of idolatry in European religion. Barth argued against the transformation of Christ after 1700 into a founder of an enlightened moral religion. Every social or civic creed must be rejected by the church as darkness.

The modality of Barth's theological enterprise is one of contrast, anti-development, non-analogy. There is grace only in the Word, and there are no areas of implicit faith and grace mediating between Christianity and the religions of the world. Barth's insights into the fallenness of religion are valuable; the question is how widely to apply them. He highlighted the real antipathy between the Gospel and some aspects of religion: the kingdom of God does judge and reject, fulfill and terminate much of what people call religion. But Barth, ambiguous toward culture and too severe in his analysis of the fall, applied his radical critique not just to sacral religion but to human religious drives, to every aspect of the transcendent in culture. So he turned Christianity into an excessively supranatural phenomenon and rendered difficult an appreciation of the long and varied history of religion.

Roman Catholic theology also sees Christ as the special light of the world but as the light of a historical world where there are rings of less faint light before, outside and after the sun who is Christ. The kingdom of God is broader than the church, broader than the explicit, human acceptance of Christ. There is no neutral world. So the world of grace, sin and religion can include precursors of greater grace in Christ. Karl Rahner offers a less neat but more accurate interpretation of sin and grace mixing in religion. Religion is neither demonic nor divine.

> In every religion the attempt is made (at least from the human side) to reflect upon and to set forth the original, unreflected and unobjectified revelation, and in all religions we find moments, made possible by God's grace, of such reflection and realization which have succeeded. But just as God has permitted the guilt of humanity in general, so this works itself into all individual and social dimensions of humanity in a darkening and ruinous way, and this affects the history of the attempts to objectify gracious revelation by human being.

It is only partially successful and is mixed with error and guilty obscurity.[10]

Thus Rahner reaches the conclusion that God gives his presence (which we call grace or kingdom) a special impetus in history, and out of this growing horizon of God comes the Christ.

Rahner agrees that Christianity is not a religion but religion's future. He distinguishes between a subjective aspect (openness to the transcendent and the holy) and religion's objectification in cult and objects. Christianity was not destined to be a religion. "Essentially Christianity is the redemption of religion because the *basileia* which has begun to penetrate can no longer be identified with any single historical world and those identifications which are attempted in the course of history are broken through by the Christian faith."[11] Christianity in a particular form cannot easily be viewed as the resolution of Buddhism. Nevertheless, for the believer, Christianity in its fullest nature renders "all religion and not just the highest form" useless.

The Christ-event brought and brings a challenge and a transformation to religion. The "end of religion" does not argue that our times are happily secular or that the early Christian communities lived without any religious forms whatsoever. Forms from Judaism and from other more or less intense contemporary religious worlds were taken into the life of the *ekklesia*. Nonetheless, we cannot overlook the conscious replacement of much that was essential in Jewish and Hellenic religion by the early churches. In community life, the Christians were not for long a Jewish sect nor did they become a mystery religion.

The reign of God summons every religion to self-purification and draws each religious tradition to a deeper expression because religion has perdured not only as a twisted (even diabolic) distortion of God's Spirit in the world but as a pedagogue and precursor. The school of theology at Alexandria dwelt upon how the Hellenic world (and we can apply this to every great religio-philosophical tradition) was the lamp which brought light through the night until that dawn when the "Sun of justice" appeared. It is the very cosmic and ontological awesomeness of the Christ-event which suggests a revolutionary evaluation of religion—religion not as the inner openness toward God nor as the aesthetics of the holy, but as a drive which too easily is plugged into neurosis and so must be judged. Religiosity, superstition, magic, religiously founded war and racism, numerous forms of ritual mutilation of body and spirit, idolatry dogmatizing despair—into these the kingdom of God comes like a tidal wave crashing into weak dikes protecting swamps.

Because ministry is servant, sacrament and word of the kingdom's grace and God's presence, the stormy backdrop to the realization of Christian ministry is the clash between kingdom and religion.

5. Jesus and Religion

In Jesus' attitude toward religion we have a foundation for the charismatic and communal life of his followers; the development from religion to charism has its roots in the preaching and life of Jesus, and in the interpretation of the Christ by his followers and evangelists.

The relationship of Jesus to human religion and then to his communal Body touches upon two issues which have some importance for a theology of ministry. While an incarnational revelation and an ecclesial people are critical of sacral religion, the incarnation bespeaks sacramentality, the union of the human and the divine, of personality and grace. Jesus and the early church by their use of the material and the human turn away from a faith and life which avoid ikon, sacrament and movement.

Nevertheless, this very sacramentality—its union of spirit and matter—can introduce into the churches idolatry and superstition, sacral class and autocratic power. Secondly, Christian ministry has developed into a single office which has long been called or depicted solely as a "priesthood." A sacerdotal monopoly of ministry urges us to ponder how and why Jesus and his followers understood their assumption into the final times to be a liberation from much that religion purveys.

Both Jesus' preaching and his person addressed religion.

In the New Testament writings we see no single approach to the encounter with religion but at least the beginning of a new attitude. In Jesus God's reign breaks in, finding a climax at Golgotha and the empty tomb; the implications of all this are elaborated by the early communities. A few of these motifs are important for the location of Christian ministry beyond the characteristics of easy power and rigid authoritarianism and exclusivism bestowed by sacral religion.

Jesus of Nazareth was born into a religion where priests and temple cult were of high import. The society which witnessed Jesus' ministry was a priestly society. Jesus was not a priest and, contrary to what one might expect, did not come from a priestly family. He stood throughout his public ministry in the prophetic line of Israel. Jesus belonged to the Davidic (royal) but not to the Aaronic (priestly) line. He did not move from a sacerdotal family to service in the Temple as a cultic intermediary between God and nation. As with the prophets, Jesus faced opposition from the priestly superstructure of his people; for Jesus broke through sacral caste to welcome all as he questioned religious rules as divinely guaranteed absolutes and flared up in anger more at religious hypocrisy than at ethical sin.

Jesus did not reform or renew one sacerdotal religion because this would have fallen short of the revolution which the reign of God was introducing. Priestly areas, however, are present in Jesus' life: the identification of the temple with himself, his sacrificial death in blood, the service and liturgy which he accomplished not in a shrine but in the world, not through sacrifices but through preaching, healing and teaching (Mt 5:21). Jesus' preaching often confronts religion in the form of the Jewish law, and in varying degrees in different Gospels Jesus critiques not so much the impotency as the hypocrisy and tyranny which can flow out of religion. All this culminates in the revolutionary axiom: "The sabbath was made for man, not man for the sabbath; so the Son of man is lord even of the sabbath" (Mk 2:27f.). Jesus' preaching is the authoritative critique and interpretation of God's meaning and purpose in the law, that is, in religion.

By incarnation Jesus is priest. Medieval theology explained Jesus' priesthood through the ontological anointing by the Logos of Jesus Ben-Joseph, the Christ.[12] In the Word made flesh we have the union and interplay but not the confusion of the human and the divine. The divine is present in the human but acts along with ordinary life. In short, the divine is not an arbitrary, theocratic will nor magic power. It is, rather, the invisible presence of God permeating and inviting. There is a certain secularity in Jesus' personal priesthood: not that the presence of God is ignored but that sacrifice and teaching are removed from temple ritual and exist in the open air as part of life. As victim Jesus is not ritually executed by priests at a sacred place among Aztecs or Scythians. Jesus dies as a civil criminal and religious rebel.

In presenting Jesus as a priest, the *Letter to the Hebrews* is an innovation.[13] We must remember that *Hebrews* is not saying that Jesus was in a fact a priest of the Jewish religion, nor the first priest of a new (Christian) religion. Rather the letter proclaims, over against the impotent symbolism of all priesthoods, a reality and action which can be named, analogously, sacerdotal. Jesus, through what appeared to be political evil and personal brutality, changed the structure of the world and so of religion. Rather than arranging symbols which hint at eschatological reality Jesus' person and death explain symbols. They bring the world of religious cult to a fulfillment which would have always infinitely escaped it.

Hebrews' central section explains the superiority of the "religion" or, better, of the "reality-history" of God's new covenant.

Though not a priest among the religions of earth (8:4), Jesus the Christ is a priest of the reign of God and of the human race.

> Since then we have a great high priest who has passed through the heavens, Jesus, the Son of God. . . . For we have not a high priest who is unable to sympathize with our weakness . . . (4:14f).

Mature reflection upon the infinite reality of who Jesus was, and upon what happened in him, leads the author of *Hebrews* to meditate upon the meaning of Calvary. Golgotha was an event in cosmic and religious history. What Israel's covenant and subsequent history teaches is precisely that religion's weakness: a new priesthood had to arise, with a new law (7:11). To describe the role of the earlier law, the writer uses several words which illustrate how it anticipated Christ—as a "pattern," "shadow," "ikon" (8:5; 10:1). Ultimately the law was removed, nullified, replaced by something better. What we have in "law," "priesthood," "commandment" is, of course, the Jewish religion, but the facet stands for the whole. For *Hebrews*, Israel's religion, even granting some superiority, remains a shadowy forecast, similar to every religion, of a fulfilling reality. It is not only Israel's priestly rituals that were impotent before God's being, but in them one senses the feebleness of all cults.

Hebrews' theology draws its readers to the theme of reality: the real effect of Jesus, the unreality of human sin and cult. At times, all is viewed negatively as shadow, or seen positively as pattern, and eventually there is no hesitation in saying: "In speaking of a new covenant, he treats the first as obsolete. And what is becoming obsolete and growing old is ready to vanish away" (8:13).

The daring writer drives home his critique of the unreality of Jewish religion, indeed of all religion outside of Jesus, the God-Man. Repeating rituals is a sign of their impotency, and both priest and devotee when freed from the cultic emotions of fear and gain must glimpse that their entire sacral structure is arbitrary, one without any real connection to God's mercy. This insight into the arbitrariness of religious ritual, however, is hard to gain. Human drives and needs want finite objects and things to be divine and omnipotent. *Hebrews* challenges the objectification of religion and breaks out of the entrapment of humanity by sin and finitude.

> But as it is, Christ has obtained a ministry which is as much more excellent than the old as the covenant he mediates is better.

According to this arrangement, gifts and sacrifices are offered which
cannot perfect the conscience of the worshiper, but deal only with
food and drink and various ablutions, regulations for the body imposed until the time of the reformation.

But when Christ appeared as a high priest of the good things that
have come . . . how much more shall the blood of Christ, who
through the eternal Spirit offered himself without blemish to God,
purify your conscience from dead works to serve the living God (8:6;
9:9ff, 11ff).

Hebrews' powerful Christological paean is constructed out of an
anticipation/fulfillment motif. Its daring vision of the collapse of external Jewish religion is aimed at religion as a cultic arrangement of things
and people to control the deity.

The church is on real, historical pilgrimage wending its way toward that realm into which Christ has entered, ahead of us, through his
Calvary priesthood. The community can and will follow him into redemption through belief in the event of Christ (3:14).

Therefore, brethren, since we have confidence to enter the sanctuary
by the blood of Jesus, by the new and living way which he opened for
us through the curtain, that is, through his flesh, and since we have a
great priest over the house of God . . . (10:19f).

In this coda, we pass from desultory and misty religion to the brightness
of the church. Ultimately the theme of *Hebrews* is the final priest and
his free and redeemed people. Christ's priesthood is unique, for there
remains nothing more, objectively, to be enacted. All who follow Christ
are redeemed and sanctified. What remains is the expansion of the pil-
grim people by preaching the word about Christ's real liturgy to others.

*   *   *

A fundamental theology of ministry circles around that which
Scripture calls "the reign of God." Since ministry is a service to God's
grace, the more ministry comprehends its roots in that horizon of grace,
the more freedom it will have to serve. A description of the encounter
between grace and religion shows that Christian ministry, whether we
call it priesthood or pastorate or diaconate, is destined to be a role and
an act which is separate from self-serving religion's control and imper-
sonation.

This experience of grace as the critique of religion gives us a picture which is only preliminary and which is partially negative. The next chapter will describe the positive unfolding of the grace of the Spirit in freedom and charism—and then in ministry.

NOTES

1. C. A. Bouman, *Sacring and Crowning* (Groningen, 1957); E. Kantorowicz, *Laudes Regiae* (Berkeley, 1946).

2. Cf. N. Perrin, *Jesus and the Language of the Kingdom* (Philadelphia, 1976); J. Bright, *The Kingdom of God* (New York, 1953); R. Schnackenburg, *God's Rule and Kingdom* (New York, 1967).

3. For this theology of kingdom/grace see K. Rahner, *Foundations of Christian Faith* (New York, 1978); L. O'Donovan, *A World of Grace* (New York, 1979); R. Haight, *The Experience and Language of Grace* (New York, 1979); Paul Tillich, *Systematic Theology 3* (Chicago, 1963).

4. *Ch,* pp. 92, 129.

5. J. Ratzinger, *Introduction to Christianity* (New York, 1970), p. 277.

6. L. Boff, *Die Kirche als Sakrament im Horizont der Welterfahrung* (Paderborn, 1972), p. 37; cf. J. Theissen, *The Church and the Promise of Salvation* (Collegeville, 1976). Thomas Aquinas observes that we do not believe in the church as something supernatural but in the Spirit vivifying the church (*ST,* II–II q. 1, a. 9, ad. 5).

7. *Syst* 3, p. 156; on the meanings attached to religion see the writings of R. Otto, N. Smart, J. Wach, T. O'Dea, W. C. Smith.

8. *The Interpretation of History* (New York, 1936), p. 50; on the interplay between culture, history and religion in expressing the Spirit (and the demonic) cf. *Syst* 3, pp. 246f.

9. K. Barth, *Church Dogmatics* (Edinburgh, 1956), 1:2, pp. 299f. The commentary on *Romans* also touches this theme.

10. K. Rahner, "Offenbarung," *Kleines theologisches Wörterbuch* (Freiburg, 1961), p. 267.

11. "Religion," *ibid.,* p. 314. E. Schillebeeckx argues for viewing Christianity as a religion. He locates the early churches within Judaism, and so they absorb naturally a religious structure; Schillebeeckx, however, is arguing against those who would depict a golden age of charismatics free of all religion or forms of Christianity, which era then devolved into "early Catholicism" with its unfortunate religious structures. Religion and its forms have several meanings, and distinguishing them gives us something of the ordinariness and the revolution of the *ekklesia. Christ* (New York, 1980), p. 552.

12. *ST* III, q. 22, a. 1; q. 8, aa. 2, 5, 7; q. 2, a. 10, 2; q. 7, a. 9.

13. Cf. E. Schillebeeckx, *Christ* (New York, 1980), pp. 237ff.; C. Spicq, *L'Epître aux Hébreux* (Paris, 1952); A. Vanhoye, *Situation de Christ* (Paris, 1969). On the Gospel according to John and cultic religion, cf. R. Schnackenburg, "Worship in Spirit and in Truth," *Christian Existence in the New Testa-*

ment (Notre Dame, 1969), 2, pp. 85ff.; F. M. Braun, "In spiritu et veritate," *Revue Thomiste* 52 (1952) 245ff, 285ff.; cf. G. Sloyan, *Is Christ the End of the Law?* (Philadelphia, 1978); W. Trilling, "Amtsverständnis bei Matthäus," *Mélanges ... B. Rigaux* (Gembloux, 1970), pp. 39ff.; H. Kee, *Community of the New Age. Studies in Mark's Gospel* (Philadelphia, 1977).

CHAPTER THREE
Beyond Religion: Spirit, Freedom, Charism and Ministry

1. *The Spirit of Jesus*—"Pneuma"
2. *The New Freedom*
3. *Freedom, Religion and Community*
4. *The Spirit's Gifts*
5. *Diaconal Charisms*

Jesus was the definitive Word of God to us. As the public preacher of God's revealed plan he made inevitable a fulfillment of religion. The backdrop for a theology of Christian ministry is the meeting between the kingdom of God and religion; there the Spirit's charisms and ministries in the people of the church emerge.

What is at stake is an understanding of who God is for men and women, and who men and women are in God's plan. Jesus called followers and disciples. Jesus' ministry to people became striking in his inclusion of the poor, the marginal, the oppressed. He called people to a discipleship that was more than temple priesthood, more than rabbinic internship. What that "more" meant became clear only after Jesus' Resurrection and his Spirit's Pentecost. Slowly it dawned on Jesus' believers that following Jesus and his Spirit meant universal service: service for all, and by all.

By calling a variety of men and women and by a forceful (but not always successful) explanation of the reign of God (Mt 13:11), Jesus showed that others are to carry on his ministry. The kingdom is neither an inner piety nor a cataloguing of anonymous people passively redeemed. History needs shepherds; the harvest looks to workers; the future demands interpreting prophets. After Jesus, his disciples are to go to all of Israel, even to all nations (Mt 28:19).

1. The Spirit of Jesus—"Pneuma"

At Pentecost with the coming of the Holy Spirit, the kingdom of God entered a new, more intense phase. Personalized and universalized in the *Pneuma,* the reign of God gained a communal place and a personal activity in all who believed in and followed Jesus.

The Spirit whose consoling presence is forecast in the *Gospel of John* is the Spirit of Jesus. For the great Pauline letters, the Spirit and the Risen Jesus are expressions of the same power. *1 Corinthians* explains that Jesus became "a life-giving spirit" (15:45). The mode in which the risen Christ lives and works is in the Holy Spirit. The Lord, *Kyrios,* is now Spirit, *Pneuma.* It is important for us to rediscover this proximity of Jesus to his Spirit, for ministry is grounded not so much in the imitation of the historical Jesus as in the personal response to the charismatic call of his Spirit. "Now this Lord is the Spirit, and where the Spirit of the Lord is, there is freedom" (2 Cor 3:17). What Paul is struggling to express is not a full absorption of Jesus into spirit, nor an identity of two persons in God but rather how the eschatological event of the Resurrection altered history and space, and so altered the way in which Jesus is present to us today. Now the Word of God Triune exists not only as the historical Jesus who is *Kyrios* but as the Lord who is at present Spirit, *Pneuma.*

> Through the dynamic structure of the *Pneuma,* the *Kyrios* is not merely someone coming again but is conceived as the Coming One present. . . . The Apostle's eschatology, his ecclesiology, his understanding of Christian life cannot be understood without the identity of *Kyrios* and *Pneuma* as expressed in *2 Corinthians.* . . . Christian existence is given the task through its reception of the activity of the *Pneuma* "in our hearts" (Rom 5:5) to gain a share in Christ, to be a member among the members of the Body being built up by the Spirit (1 Cor 12: Rom 8:9).[1]

At first, comprehension of the accessibility and power of the Spirit eluded even the Twelve. How was their movement distinct from Israel? How was the kingdom not a sect nor a religion? The action of the Spirit not only shook culture but drew the disciples away from traditions and institutions which could not incarnate the omnipresent *Pneuma.*

The horizon which is the Spirit is always a challenge, for there is comfort in religion. An unconditional offer of freedom and personal development is difficult to accept. People fear freedom, mistrust love. The first Christians were slow to comprehend existentially the universality of their mission and why the Spirit went ahead of them into Samaria, Antioch and the Graeco-Roman world (Acts 9:31; 10:44). It might have been preferable and more intelligible to believe that Jesus' kingdom became another religion. The advent of the Spirit was not the coming of a mentor or a judge, a new prophet or a new religion—even the best religion. Rather earth's salvation has revealed itself in a remarkable combination of universality and individuality whose poles are freedom and power. Religion can survive only as fulfilled in the Spirit.

If the sacral structure of telluric religion is fulfilled by the death of Jesus, human religious drives are fulfilled by his Spirit. Like the physical structures of the cosmos existing prior to individual men and women, so the horizon of the Spirit is a sovereign, surrounding presence. At the center of the horizon is freedom. "Where the Spirit of the Lord is, there is freedom" (2 Cor 3:17). How revolutionary it was to introduce freedom into the world of religion; temples and rituals are the opposite of freedom, both for the devotees and for the deities. Yet personal freedom does accompany God's word and life. Arriving in the avant-garde of the kingdom, it is the precursor of an adult life in faith, hope and love. It is the milieu of personal identity; it grounds charism and ministry.

2. The New Freedom

The letters of Paul never stop praising freedom. They are rejoicing, however, not in the end of the social institution of slavery nor in the ability of the baptized to make this or that choice but in a general freedom which is broader and deeper. "For freedom Christ has set us free" (Gal 5:1). For Paul (once in bondage to Pharisaism), and for his hearers (anxious over the uncertainty of their relationship to God and gods), a gospel of freedom came as a liberation from personal burdens. A Pauline letter always breathes a thankful spirit of freedom from the forms and phantoms of impotent religion. "The kingdom of God is not food or drink, but righteousness and peace and joy in the Holy Spirit" (Rom 14:17).

What is this freedom which is the atmosphere of the entire life of the baptized believer in Christ? It is not a slogan, nor is it an interior piety free in prayer but captive in religiosity. It is not a freedom from the antiquated laws of *Leviticus* alone, nor is it a freedom (which in fact appears to be oppression by divine authorities) to purchase a future life. The freedom of the Spirit cannot be an empty trick, like the sign over the entrance to the concentration camp which read: "Work Makes One

Free." To spring this freedom free from abstract sermons and double-talk demands some reflection. Because ministry is not merely external ecclesiastical office but a public way of acting out Christian life, a discovery of freedom is fundamental to any theology of ministry.

We do not have freedom, freedom has us. "So if the Son makes you free, you will be free indeed" (Jn 8:36). Freedom is a word of the Son, a gift of the Spirit. Freedom is not self-liberation from any constraint but a responsible, demanding way of being human. By our response to God's sovereign presence, we become in our belief and our will free: free to enjoy, inherit and spread the kingdom of God. The first Christian men and women, as they emerged out of the baptismal waters, were free as they had never been before.

> Do you know that all of us who have been baptized into Christ Jesus were baptized into his death? We were buried therefore with him by baptism into death, so that as Christ was raised from the dead by the glory of the Father we too might walk in newness of life. . . . So you also must consider yourselves dead to sin and alive to God in Christ Jesus (Rom 6:4, 11).

Christians were free from the uncertainty of their past religious lives because Jesus the Christ was for each individual existential truth and future consolation.

> All who are led by the Spirit are sons of God. The spirit you received is not the spirit of slaves bringing fear into your lives again; it is the spirit of sonship, and it makes us cry out, "Abba, Father!" It is the Spirit himself bearing witness with our spirit that we are children of God. And if children, we are heirs as well: heirs of God and coheirs with Christ, sharing his sufferings so as to share his glory (Rom 8: 14ff).

Even more, their freedom was only a beginning; they were free to continue to live, to live as a new kind of person, to be a "household of God" (Eph 2:19), a "new creation" (2 Cor 5:17).

Free of laws, the baptized were free to exist in the real world of the Spirit which was neither the cosmos of past religions nor the city of ambition, anger and money. Their relationship to Christ was not one of religious obedience but of spontaneous similarity. "But thanks be to God, that you who were once slaves of sin have become obedient from the heart to the standard of teaching to which you were committed, and, having been set free from sin, have become slaves of righteousness. . . . Now that you have been set free from sin and have become slaves of

God, the return you get is sanctification and its end, eternal life" (Rom 6:17ff., 22).

First and foremost, freedom gave accessibility to God through Jesus and his Spirit. "This is why we are bold enough to approach God in full confidence through our faith in him" (Eph 3:12f). Not only had walls broken down between human beings, but veils between God and men and women were rent. Where formerly God was a judge or an idol, now he was a Father; the Lord's prayer invited not superstitious bargaining with a deity but a communing with the divine will in the milieu of his new reign.

> Of this gospel I was made a minister according to the gift of God's grace which was given me by the working of his power. To me, though I am the very least of all the saints, this grace was given, to preach to the Gentiles the unsearchable riches of Christ, and to make all men see what is the plan of the mystery hidden for ages in God who created all things: that through the church the manifold wisdom of God might now be made known (Eph 3:7–10).

Evidently there was a new experience of a new freedom—but freedom from what? Paul gives many answers to this question: law, sin, disharmony, death, evil, hostility towards self and others, endless lust, abuse of God.

The new freedom of the Spirit is very much a freedom from fear: from the fear of not living, of drifting without meaning, of feeling guilty and condemned. It is not the prisoner who utterly lacks freedom, for even within the shacks of the Gulag a person may be eminently free. Jailers have observed Christ and his martyrs giving the impression of being free in a lordly way. We misunderstand life-giving freedom when we name its opposite the limitation of options. The opposite of freedom is fear, and the fundamental fears in human life are the fear that we will cease to exist, the fear that our life, our very self, has no meaning and is foolish and formless, and the fear that we have no value, that we are worthy of hate because we have failed. All of these are in tension with grace, for faith, hope and love reject their venom and vacuousness.[2]

What Paul called "law" is a horizon of human life and not simply the legal books of the Jewish religion. Paul perceived that the law could not solve the problems of death, meaninglessness and guilt. Law like fear, its product, is an opposite of freedom. Law tried to point to salvation but it only intensified personal pain. Where there was law, there was neurotic guilt, vacillation, and despair. The Spirit with the new freedom brought an alternative. "There is therefore now no condemna-

tion for those who are in Christ Jesus. For the law of the Spirit of life in
Christ Jesus has set me free from the law of sin and death" (Rom 8:1,
2). Paul contrasts the pneumatic ("spiritual realities") with its opposite—all that is opposed to the Spirit.

> But you are not in the flesh, you are in the Spirit, if in fact the Spirit
> of God dwells in you. Any one who does not have the Spirit of Christ
> does not belong to him. But if Christ is in you, although your bodies
> are dead because of sin, your spirits are alive because of righteous-
> ness. If the Spirit of him who raised Jesus from the dead dwells in
> you, he who raised Christ Jesus from the dead will give life to your
> mortal bodies also through his Spirit which dwells in you (Rom 8.9–
> 12).

The Spirit had accomplished what religious form could not. Access to
God brought trust in being a loved creation of God, and a grasp of the
paradox of God's plan (life through death). Freedom from the guilt,
pain and hopelessness of attempting to manipulate the divine led to a
positive freedom for life. This freedom in Christian life is not only that
which preachers proclaim but the ground of ministry.

There were still threats to Christian freedom, but they came from
the attraction of the anti-spiritual elements in society; from religious de-
mons not yet fully vanquished; from religious neuroses; from controversy, ambition, self-aggrandizement, pneumatic manipulation.

What is the Spirit's freedom? Life in the Spirit is just that, a life. And
life under grace includes a freedom for giving of self. Now the mode of
that giving is service. "Service" extends the spirit and new law of the
kingdom further into the needy, turbulent world. Service brings about
the new religious law, love. "Now we are discharged from the law, dead
to that which held us captive, so that we serve not under the old written
code but in the new life of the Spirit" (Rom 7:6).

New life in the spirit brings ministry.

Not only life but ministry results from the Spirit and its freedom
gained in baptismal initiation. Not only freedom but action! Paul saw
that the freedom of the Spirit is not a preparation for magic but a contact which flows into activity. The mission of the Spirit bears in it a
drive toward activity, and this service—a being-sent to serve—flows out
of the freedom and community of the Christians.

Nothing is more basic to a theology of ministry than to see how
Christian service is grounded in the Spirit. Shortly we will turn to the
bridge between freedom and ministry—charism. First, however, assisted by our grasp of the revolution which Jesus' coming accomplished in

religion and freedom, we must further examine how the Spirit's liberating presence transformed religion into community and ministry.

3. Freedom, Religion and Community

The first Christians comprehended Jesus' critique and fulfillment of religion and they experienced the new freedom with which the Spirit replaced cult. Christian communities must have sensed themselves to be pioneers in a process of freedom and desacralization. Temple, priesthood, sacrifice, liturgy and laws have been moved from the sphere of the uncertain and manipulative to that of the sacramental and the ministerial.[3] The following chart illustrates that metamorphosis.

RELIGION	CHRISTIAN REINTERPRETATION
one people, tribe or nation	all people, particularly the lowly and socially marginated
temple	the community
priesthood	all the baptized with diverse charisms and ministries
high priest	Jesus the Christ, executed and risen
sacrifice	the political and religious execution of Jesus; secondarily the sufferings, lives and services of the baptized
worship	preaching, daily life
laws	a mature response with freedom and without fear to the preaching and life of Jesus enabled by the Spirit

| magic | the world is loved by God and has been redeemed; it is the place of the Spirit. Baptism, meals, Eucharist, anointing, embraces and layings on of hands nourish the community |
| superstition | faith in the Father and communion with his will as manifest in the kingdom, globally and individually |

The community de-sacralized and personalized the incarnation of Christ. The charismatic indwelling of the Spirit permeated the life of the community. Let us look closely at four characteristics of the *ekklesia's* fulfillment of religion.

(a) *The People.* Religion was intrinsically connected to exclusivity. The tribe or nation had its religion; normally a man or woman could no more move from religion to religion than he or she could exchange racial color or ethnic background. Tribal exclusivity fielded a claim of superiority through and under the gods—an exclusivity which has survived after the collapse of tribalism in nationalism and racism.

Slowly the first Christians realized that not only was the limiting structure of Judaism (priest versus poor, female apart from male) ended, but the Gospel made faith and baptism open to, indeed destined for, all peoples, all races, all social classes, all religions. As if to emphasize this universality, the example and teaching of Jesus would lead one to conclude that if there was a preference, it was for the poor, for those groups living on the margin of respectable society, the casualties of history.

(b) *The Temple.* The temple had several meanings in the self-description of the early Christians but none of these meanings was a sacral building.[4] The human body of Jesus was the place where a unique manifestation of God took place, and so it was on the cross (as the Jewish temple's veil split) and then in the faith of his followers where one found the center of true worship. Since the Christian communities built up the Body of their Risen Lord, they were known as the temple. The new people of the kingdom of God replaced the holy spaces of physical temples. In a communal faith where a public execution had altered ritual sacrifice and where the very *Pneuma* of God had immediately come upon each member, sacral buildings had no meaning. Sacred space is where the divine spirit dwells—but that was in the community of the Lord. "Didn't you realize that you were God's temple and that the Spirit of God was living among you? If anybody should destroy the temple of God, God will destroy him, because the temple of God is sacred, and you are that temple" (1 Cor 3:16f).

In the Spirit, God himself and his *Kyrios,* Jesus, are effectively present in the community despite fragility and weakness among the baptized. This presence, however, is not one of emotional or gnostic enjoyment. Indwelling is mission. The immediacy of the Spirit had rendered the stone buildings of Graeco-Roman paganism and of the newer Eastern cults superfluous; but, too, the locality of the temple, a magical place, is shattered by the evangelical mission of the community. The church receives the Spirit and this builds up the Spirit's living locus. The foundation of this temple is important ministries grounded in Christ: its "stones" are the members of the churches.

> So then you are no longer strangers and sojourners, but you are fellow citizens with the saints and members of the household of God, built upon the foundation of the apostles and prophets, Christ Jesus himself being the cornerstone, in whom the whole structure is joined together and grows into a holy temple in the Lord; in whom you also are built into it for a dwelling place of God in the Spirit (Eph 2:19–22).

The temple, the Body of Christ, is always being built up—there is no community without growth. The metaphor of the temple, in fact, weakens as Paul struggles to give it the quality of expansion. The visible element of the community comes not through its temple and rituals but through its people. In their distinction from the world's ruling powers, active lives of service (where humility and love toward others distinguish them) are more visible than columns and thuribles. The counterbalance to human attempts to domesticate the Spirit is personal and communal ministry.

(c) *Priesthood.* The first Christians were close to the world of ritual sacrifice and temple priesthoods even if the Mediterranean world was losing confidence in their efficacy. They were struck by the insight that Jesus was the last priest. For God, the Suffering Servant's sacrifice needed no further complement. The result of Calvary, an infinite event in space and society and time, was redemption.

The first Christians set up no priestly group to reproduce Jesus or

Golgotha through ritual. The New Testament is very reticent toward priestly language. The Gospels do not refer to Jesus as a priest nor does Paul use the word *hiereus* of Christ, and of course the New Testament writers never describe the ministers of the church as priests.

If no priestly caste is set up among the Christians, Jesus appears in later theology as the high priest par excellence who has come to that position not through birth or special training but through execution, partially at the hands of one religion's temple servants. Because Jesus is both God and human person, he represents both sides of the dialogue between God and us. He is, not cultically but really, mediator. Jesus bridges the gulf of sin which holds back human transcendence from God. He escapes the shadowy unreality of religious rites and dominates on Golgotha the history of the human race.

The later *First Letter of Peter* in a rare employment of priestly language speaks of the Christian community as a "royal priesthood" (2:9).[5] These two metaphors are rooted in the Old Testament, in *Exodus* and *Leviticus,* where the people of God's covenant are promised that they will "be to me a kingdom of priests and a holy nation" (Ex 19:5f). Regardless of how this royal and priestly people is joined to entrance into covenant (baptism), what is clear is the universality of the hieratic among the baptized. In both the passage from *Exodus* and *1 Peter* the priestly nature of the people is not a status but a mission. All of the priestly people are commissioned to declare "the wonderful deeds of him who called you out of darkness into his own marvelous light" (2:9). Pneumatic sacrifices (2:5), actions in charism are the ministry of life and preaching in the Christian. The purpose for being a body of priests is not that Christians might be consoled in a new holy state, nor that they might be in a sacerdotal college imitative of and led by Jesus. When priestly language is used in the New Testament, it is used metaphorically, and the metaphor points to a reality—God's act, evangelism. *1 Peter* does not mention the nature of the Christian community's meeting, nor the role the Eucharist meal played nor what levels of seriousness the instructors held. It does not say that the individual Christian is a priest. Rather it eschews caste by proclaiming a universal priestly people and by transforming the priestly into the ministerial.

We can find four priesthoods in the New Testament. The *first* is that of the agents of religious cult, of those pageants of sin and grace in the world religions. The priesthood in general, of every religion before the coming of the Spirit, is not continued or personified in Christ, although it does find a completion in him. Jesus' own priesthood, the *second* priesthood, is not that of being a high priest within Jewish or pagan religion, even to an extraordinary degree. The priesthood of Jesus both effects and sacramentalizes that which other priesthoods could not accomplish. In goal and power, the priesthood of Jesus turns cult into reality and then brings that human and divine reality in word and life to the human race.

The *third* priesthood is the priesthood of all who in explicit faith and public baptism follow the teaching and life of Jesus. This is a priesthood of men and women conscious that they have been redeemed and given a new existence. It is not a passive, cultic priesthood which happens also to preach or to judge orthodoxy and morality. Rather, the very life of the baptized is actively ministerial to church and kingdom. The liturgist of the Gospel is more accurately described as evangelist or social deacon or prophet than as priest, although "priesthood" nourishes external ministry through sacrament and word in a new style. Not only cult, but preaching, life and love serve the community.

The *fourth* priesthood is that of leaders of communities. There is no reference in the New Testament to the Christian ministry of leadership as a priesthood. Nevertheless, it was inescapable that in a world much concerned with the control of the divine the leaders of increasingly larger and more visible Christian churches should appear not only as charismatic leaders but as hieratic figures of large assemblies. But this history of the resacerdotalization of the ministry of leadership belongs to a later period and need not detain us here. For we want to understand the depth and universality of the primal Christian revolution in ministry—a death and transfiguration of religion through freedom into grace and service.

Paul in *Romans* did employ priestly terms in an intentional but metaphorical way. First, they expressed the ordinary life of the Christian: "Present your bodies as a living sacrifice, holy and acceptable to God, which is your spiritual worship. Do not be conformed to this world but be transformed by the renewal of your mind that you may prove what is the will of God, what is good and acceptable and perfect" (Rom 12:1, 3). The words "sacrifice" and "worship" recalled the temples and their smouldering offerings, but this world has been transformed into a life which is both free of arbitrary rituals and committed to the active will of God in public life.

Paul's second meaning of cult altered to ministry was preaching: "the grace given me by God to be a minister of Christ Jesus to the Gentiles in the priestly service of the gospel of God, so that the offerings of the Gentiles may be acceptable, sanctified by the Holy Spirit" (Rom 15:16). Paul's ministry of evangelization was his liturgy; in this passage he took facets of priesthood out of the temples and used them as metaphors to present the real liturgy of worldwide public preaching. In *Phi-*

lippians, the daily life of the Christian in its distinctive morality and hopeful faith in the future was a worship of God, a sacrifice not to be consumed in the present but enhanced and fulfilled in the future (2:17).

The liturgist in the Hellenic world was someone whose acts of sacrifice and benediction represented the world of the sacral publicly to the people. Paul transposed terms from political liturgies or Judaism as he proclaimed that his mission was to all the nations and was public through the cosmic, universal and eschatological event of God acting in Jesus Christ. "Paul's sacrificial ministry is not a personal, charismatic undertaking but an authorized and delegated mandate which is accomplished through charism and existence. Paul conducts in his liturgy a ministry and office for the totality of the world, describing (it) not only as *diakonia* . . . but as *oikonomia.*"[6] This is not only a spiritualization of cult but a change from the uncertain, idolatrous realm of the sacral to the real: real in the sense of going beyond the impotent symbols of cult to the life and death of Christ; real in the sense of being mandated by that grace (the reality of God) which is moving to the universality of the eschaton.

Worship, or what we call the liturgy, in the early communities was no arbitrary work in rubrics and rituals. Preaching, evangelization and Christian life were sacrifice, liturgy and priestly office. The Eucharistic meal possessed a central role in the life of the Christian community. Nevertheless, that manner in which Jesus, crucified and coming, was made manifest happened through a meal, through bread and wine: basic, ordinary, celebratory foods of humanity.

(d) *Magic and Superstition.* Part of the long history of human religion is superstition and magic. Twin activities of religion, they often are not eradicated but only suppressed in higher faiths. They appeal to the human desire to know and to control. Magic is a way of controlling the deity; superstition is a way of knowing what only the god can know. Magic claims to transform the created into a sign of power of the creator; superstition claims to draw from the finite knowledge of the infinite or the future. The preaching of Jesus ended these drives to manipulate the divine, for it rendered them unnecessary. The world is loved by God, so loved that he sent his Son. If the world is redeemed and if the human person is surrounded by the Spirit of God, the old dichotomy between finite and infinite, matter and spirit, is ended. The early Christians claimed to be "the way," "the saints," "the community," "the people." With the gifts of the Spirit which the individual receives no one needs to control magically the world of matter. When the creator is love, there is no need to dominate creation through bribing powers. After Jesus, there are no performing intermediary magicians because a Christian has direct access to the Father through the Son and the Spirit.

The opposite of superstition is the triad of faith, hope and love, all grounded not in the arbitrary will of God but in his loving plan. Superstition wants control and knowledge to escape threats to human existence, and magic wards off the dangers of a diabolic or unknown cosmos. Jesus and his spirit, however, bring a presence and plan which need not be feared, even before death. Jesus' prayer is an illustration of the termination of superstition, for it is not a prayer that our will for the future be given to us, but that we learn to commune with God's will. The *Our Father* reaffirms our entrance into God's kingdom, communes with God's will for us, petitions for little more than existence and benediction. Prayer for the Christian is not only not superstition; it is hardly even petition since the *Our Father* asks God simply to place us in his plan, his will, his kingdom.

All the words we might use to describe this metamorphosis within the early Christian *ekklesia* from sacral worship to communal charismatic life are deficient. It is a "desacralization" but it is not a "secularization," for the dimension of the sacramental, the interplay of the human and the divine, are more present than ever. The goal of this process is not a worldly absence of religion but the incarnation of the divine in the human and historical.

> Some "desacralization" of the Christian ministries can only be a purification. The temple of God is wherever two or three are gathered in the name of Christ, who is then in the midst of them. But the group must meet or be summoned in the name of Christ, and it is from this that the ministry which summons, assembles and completes the believers in the name of Christ receives its meaning as a sign. The minister is a sign that the gathering is not a merely human gathering but a summons by God's grace to believe in his love, the love of which he gave a pledge in the wonderful deeds he performed in Jesus Christ, and of which the ministers are no more than official heralds through preaching and liturgy.[7]

The early Christians understood themselves as a chosen people for all and they omitted necessarily caste-theologies which derive from mediating priesthood. But every age must learn anew this profound shift: the church as the Body of the risen Christ passes repeatedly through what occurred historically in Jesus Christ—the surpassing of religion.

4. The Spirit's Gifts

The certitude that each believer and each church lived in times characterized by the reception of the Spirit gave the Christians a new dynamism. "Charism," "gift," "pneumatic (event, reality, power)," and "service" are words for the silent action of the Spirit in a Christian personality and community. The Spirit's intense coming is a sign that Jesus truly introduced, in the fullness of time, the reign of God.

The presence of the Spirit of Christ in an individual is called by Paul "charism." Etymologically charism has tones of graciousness, joyful liberality. The gift is the love, mercy and future life which God makes available and real in Jesus. Paul did not create the word, *charisma,* but he gave it a new, theological nuance and richness. He sometimes turned "spiritual" into a noun, speaking of powers given by the Spirit as *pneumatika,* but Christians have preferred the other term, charism. The interplay of the two words explains not a bizarre enthusiasm but the source of charism in the Spirit.[8] "Charism" is found many times in Paul and rarely outside his writings. We do not have to conclude, however, that Paul's ecclesiology built upon charism is a narrow projection of his ideas or of the experiences of the Corinthians. Some exegetical and theological evaluations of charism have for over a century represented a form of what we might call the spark or photon theory. Among ordinary people in early Christian communities, the theory explains, there appeared sparks of supernatural activity, powers full of seizures and miracles. A passage from *Romans,* however, suggests that we see charism as a richer word, expressing several meanings of the Spirits's contact. "The charism of God is eternal life in Jesus Christ, our Lord" (6:23). Here we meet a primal charism, the background to the more specific activities of the Spirit—new life. Charism joined God and Jesus Christ to Christian existence and so was the very way of living in the kingdom of God, in the Spirit of Jesus risen. There are pneumatic gifts of many kinds only because there is this charismatic ground from which all flow.

Charis, gift and life, does not reward activity but causes action. Paul calls charisms "energies" (1 Cor 12:6, 11). This third member of a hermeneutical triad of the Spirit (*charisma, pneumatikon, energēma*) also leads to ministry.

> Now concerning spiritual gifts (*pneumatikon*), brethren, I do not want you to be uninformed . . . Now there are varieties of gifts (*charismaton*) but the same Spirit; and there are varieties of service (*diakonion*) but the same Lord; and there are varieties of working

(*energēmaton*) but it is the same God who inspires them all in every one. To each is given the manifestation of the Spirit for the common good (1 Cor 12: 1, 4–7).

Perhaps these different Greek words represented nuances, theologies, movements whose precise identities are lost to us, but the nature of the Spirit's activity in variety is clear. We should not conclude that each word defines a different ecclesiology or pneumatology but rather that the reality described is power from the Spirit. The community's life, freed from religion, is embraced by the horizon of the Spirit. The Holy Spirit works charismatically in the psyche of each Christian. The horizon of the Spirit in baptized men and women is a life which is charismatic in terms of its source, but diaconal in terms of its goal. Spirit leads to ministry.

Romans offers a theology of the Spirit as life and power. Here the *charismata* of the Christians are different in different people but all result from union with God in Christ. Examples are teaching, prophecy, preachers, ministers of mercy and aid, and a general *diakonia.*

> For as in one body we have many members, and all the members do not have the same function, so we, though many, are one body in Christ, and individually members one of another. Having gifts that differ according to the grace given to us, let us use them: if prophecy, in proportion to our faith; if service, in our serving; he who teaches, in his teaching; he who exhorts, in his exhortation; he who contributes, in liberality; he who gives aid, with zeal; he who does acts of mercy, with cheerfulness (Rom 12:4–8).

None of these charisms is essentially miraculous or ecstatic but all are necessary aspects of church life. Then Paul illustrates communal diversity-in-harmony by the theological analogy of the Body.

In *1 Corinthians,* the Apostle mentions first spiritual gifts, and then charisms, ministries, powers; an exemplifying list of what is given to the baptized follows: preaching, healing, prophecy, instruction. The Body is offered to unify a second list of gifts: apostles, teachers, leaders, workers of power. Christian freedom, ministry and diversity are referred back to the Spirit.

> Now there are varieties of gifts, but the same Spirit, and there are varieties of service, but the same Lord; and there are varieties of working, but it is the same God who inspires them all in every one. To each is given the manifestation of the Spirit for the common good. To one is given through the Spirit the utterance of wisdom, and to

another the utterance of knowledge according to the same Spirit, to another faith by the same Spirit, to another gifts of healing by the one Spirit, to another the working of miracles, to another prophecy, to another the ability to distinguish between spirits, to another various kinds of tongues, to another the interpretation of tongues. All these are inspired by one and the same Spirit, who apportions to each one individually as he wills (1 Cor 12:4–11).

The effect and gifts of new life in the Spirit are closely related to ministries. The Spirit does not effect an interior, mystical, homeostatic life in the community, and the community is not one of adorers or attendants waiting for an absent God. Although there are a few indications that charisms are occasionally related to Christian life itself, for the Romans and Corinthians Paul links charism to ministry; on the other hand, there are no lists of ministries in the early community which are not related to the Spirit's diverse energy.

Frequently Christian groups have thought of charism as a spectacular personal gift or a miraculous phenomenon. Although Paul has heard of effects of the Spirit which seem to have been extraordinary, he always leads *pneumatika* and *charismata* back to ministry for the community on behalf of expanding the good news of and in Jesus; back to ordinary, daily life and to love. Inward maturity, holiness, and outward growth are the goals of the church, not flamboyant miracles. Charism in the Pauline ecclesiology is not the alternative or rival to daily ministry but the source of ministry.

Modern exegesis and theology have been characterized in the field of charism/ministry by a drive to separate the two, to pit pneumatic power against community. Overly intent on finding at the origin of Christianity (and of every belief) a tension between liberty and order, between humanity and grace, Protestant scholars overlooked the context of charism—Body of Christ—and charism's fulfillment—minister. Adolf Harnack rejected connections between charisms and the lasting, central, traditional ecclesiastical offices, while E. Schweizer has followed him in seeing a dual structure in the early churches: one part was exclusively charismatic, more or less unrelated to ministry. R. Sohm concluded that the tension between office and charism illustrated a primal opposition between structure and spirit.[9] H. F. von Campenhausen described insightfully the depth of the charismatic empowering of the Pauline churches but then concluded that there could be in these communities no "legal system," or "formal authority"; that "free fellowship developing through the interplay of spiritual gifts and ministries" fully excluded "office," "authority," and "elders."[10] These theologians' language portrayed the Spirit as soaring freedom snatching the baptized from lurking Jewish or Gentile structures which could contain only the arrogance of human authority.

Turning to exegetes, we find the same modern German theory. Rudolf Bultmann interpreted "the prophets" as ecstatic, independent preachers whose teaching about Jesus, the later church decided, was not dependable.[11] E. Käsemann tempered this approach first by pointing out that one cannot read later theology and church polity into the New Testament, and second by emphasizing the ordinariness of early church life and the universality and diversity of charisms. There is no divine gift which does not bring with it a task, no grace which does not move to action.

> Our definition of charism is the concrete form and individuation of the grace of the Spirit, because every Christian is a partaker of grace and of the Spirit; it is implicit also in our account of the body of Christ which we described as being composed purely of charismata and of those endowed with them. There is no passive membership in the body of Christ. Every Christian stands equipped and ready for service. . . . "Everyone has his charisma from God" (I Cor 7:7). Ecclesiastical egalitarianism is thus ruled out of court. God does not repeat himself when he acts, and there can be no mass production of grace. There is differentiation in the divine generosity, whether in the order of creation or of redemption. Equality is not for Paul a principle of Church order.[12]

The Body of Christ motif as well as the breakthrough of Spirit guide Käsemann's theology of charism and ministry as he argues for an ordinary diversity in the community.

> When he talks about the body of Christ, Paul is dealing with problems presented by largely enthusiastic congregations. Unlike today, the point is not to arouse "the laity" to activity. Rather, the multiplicity of gifts, possibilities and demonstrations is threatening to break up the unity of the church. The task of the paraenesis is to give the theological reason for the unity in the midst of multiplicity, to put that unity into practical effect and then to preserve it. The watchword is solidarity, not uniformity. Paul finds it important for the church to remain polyform. Only in this way can it pervade the world, since the world's reality everyday is not to be conformistic. Uniformity is petrified solidarity. People who are the same have nothing to say to one another and cannot help one another. They remain introverts and cannot do justice to the constantly differing situations of life. Consequently the ecclesiology which is stamped by the

motif of the body of Christ must radically maintain and effect the priesthood of all believers. The fact that for a long time people were only capable of deducing purely hierarchical structure from this ecclesiology is grotesque.[13]

Yet Käsemann feels pressed to argue that the first Christians knew no ecclesial order and that charism is present in an existential act of ministry. The confusion of charismatic display with ministerial identity has been set aside but the identification of order and permanency with oppression seems to remain. The Tübingen exegete contrasts the enthusiastic ministry of the Christians under the leadership of the prophets whose theology is apocalyptic with a later anti-gnostic ministry of the first century; he sees in *Matthew* protests not against the Judaism of Jesus' time but against later attempts at church ordering (7:22; 23:8); and in *Acts* he sees a theology of the cross becoming through tradition and structure a theology of glory.[14]

In all of this we find a negative dialectic between law and Gospel, a hostility between individual and social nature (both sinful) and grace. Structure is mistaken for authoritarianism. This takes attention away from the real counterpart of charism: not the threat of authority but the fulfillment of ministry.[15]

The Roman Catholic mind tends on the other hand to see harmony between grace and creation, spirit and structure. But Catholicism later gave its own coloring to the relationship between charism and ministry in Paul. Strangely enough, a harmony between the charismatic and the ecclesial had for a long time been set aside by medieval and baroque theologies. The emphasis upon hierarchical ministry constituted by legal code was so strong that the charismatic had to flee to the edge of church life, to the monastery and spiritual life where from an esoteric world women and lay persons were permitted occasionally to utter a prophetic word. The history of ecclesiology and mysticism shows how comfortable it is to draw a sharp line between the charismatic/ministerial and the priestly. As early as the third century, the great church was frightened by the Montanist ecstatics, who no doubt retained true facets of charism in ministry. Control through priestly rather than charismatic office came to the bishops, but the charismatic dimension reappeared in Egyptian monasticism and in groups of educated women in fifth century Rome and Jerusalem. It entered anew through the founders of religious orders and, though often informally, through mystics who were theologians and teachers. The frequent explication of *charismata* as extra-ordinary and transient graces comes not from Pauline theology but from later centuries, each with its own reason for separating spiritual excess from legal church office and for offering some place of activity in the church for women and laity. Charism is defined over against the ordinariness, the stable sacramental power of office. Freedom and spirit are in the charism; obedience and church are in the priesthood. The church may need the charismatic for inspiration, but the charismatic ultimately must yield to the authority of the church. Teresa of Avila is the charismatic—Bañez, her confessor, is the Dominican priest. Francis of Assisi is the charismatic—Innocent III is the ecclesial center. Thomas Aquinas summed up this split by a distinction between charism (*gratia gratis data*) and public ministry (*officium*). While offices lead people to justification and sanctification, because of their particular intensity and because of their inspiration of people in the world, these "freely given graces" are transitory and clearly distinct from the official ministries of the church.[16]

The medieval distinction between transient charism and permanent office neither accurately depicts the early church's theology of charism nor helps us to understand the expansion of ministry today. Roman Catholic ecclesiology (and spirituality) has now moved away from the past marginalization of charism just as it has moved away from the identification of ministry with one office. Hans Küng explains how charisms are universal and primal, but not miraculous.

> We have seen that charisms are everyday rather than fundamentally exceptional phenomena, that they are various rather than uniform in kind, and that they are found throughout the church rather than being restricted to a particular group of people. . . . Hence one can speak of a charismatic structure of the church which includes but goes far beyond the hierarchical structure of the church . . . it (charism) signifies *the call* of God, addressed to an individual, to a particular ministry in the community, which brings with it the ability to fulfill that ministry.[17]

But Küng too shows an affinity with the German tradition of tension between charism and office. He seems to fear admitting any permanence or ordinary structure in the Pauline, charismatic ministry. He contrasts it with a Jerusalemic ministry of special appointment. He has let imagined conflict between Semitic and Hellenic churches, between structured diversity and free charism, disrupt his correct instinct that charism grounds ministry. Words like "presbyter" and "bishop" distract Küng, for where those words are present he sees a non-charismatic system in which authority and appointment existed.[18] This he contrasts with the vitality of the Pauline communities. In fact, mature scholarship is wary of interpreting the Greek words for early ministries by their later meanings. Küng is reading back into *episkopos* and *presbyteros* the post-medieval ecclesiology which he fears. There is no reason to suppose that the Spirit of Jesus was shy in the Semitic churches. Antioch and Jerusalem seem also to be filled with invocations of the Spirit upon people destined to ministry (Acts 2:17). The absence of the word "charism" does not mean that the theology of Spirit fashioning ministry through charism was unknown. The elements of this ecclesiology are present in *Acts,* and in *Ephesians.*

Bernard Cooke, on the other hand, accepts the fundamental charismatic structure of the church's ministry but distinguishes between temporary and permanent charisms. He accepts the line which moves from Spirit through charism to ministry.

> Ministerial role is the expression of charism. Not only such manifestly "charismatic" activities as prophecy are rooted in this empowering by the Spirit, but also regularized teaching and structured governing. This means that one cannot simply contrast "charism" and "institution" in the life of the church. Institutions themselves are meant to be the organs through which the Spirit-animated community expresses its life.[19]

Office (or a commissioning thereto) does not alone create ministry and charism but rather is a formulation of the ministry into a public legal status. Ordination is the public designation of the Christian to office, and it both approves and vitalizes the charismatic in public ministry. We will return to this later when we look at the sources of ministry.

Cooke's encyclopedia of information on ministry develops an exegetical analysis of the interplay between charism and ministry, avoids inserting the later Roman *ordo* or *officium* into the discussion, and ignores the Germanic bent for finding tension between *charisma* and *diakonia.*[20] He finds a harmony between Spirit and human spirit which seems to agree with Paul's recurring *telos* for charism: the building up of the church in the world. The Body of the Lord Jesus who was crucified and is now risen expands to become the ecclesial Body of Christ through the intermediary action of the Spirit by whom the Lord (the "head") builds up his church (the "body") in a total unity. While the different linguistic presentations of the action of the Spirit in Greek may reflect nuances and groupings, they do not clearly lead to a radical divorce between Spirit and ministerial structure.[21]

Charism is a dialogue. To be a son or daughter of God excludes being a plaything of either divine or diabolical powers. The merely sensational is not the charismatic. Paul rejects the idea that the Spirit acts in bizarre or arbitrary ways. Signs and wonders also occur in the pagan religions and cults (1 Cor 12:2) but in the Holy Spirit there is not just power but also order, utility, consolation and success. The Spirit holds within its being infinite possibilities and so the individual members of the community have their own pneumatic identities. They are not the playthings of the *Pneuma* but free, adult partners. Each Christian receives from and responds to the Spirit out of his or her own clear, limited identity. Since the Spirit and the Lord Jesus are one with the Father-Creator, there can be no conflict between my God-given biological identity, and the personal gift of the Spirit, my membership in the kingdom of faith. My charismatic identity is not utterly different from my psychological personality. My charisms will find in myself potentialities they can draw forth, for the Spirit will not ask me to be what I am not in the mind and plan of God. Charism will not lead me in a way which is destructive of my given personality, nor will spiritual gifts utterly transform my one identity. *Gratia perficit naturam*—"Grace brings nature to completion." The Pauline metaphor of the body suggests that Thomas Aquinas' theological axiom of extraordinary ordinariness throws light upon the theology of charism. We will return to this in a later chapter.

What are the characteristics of charism which declare its relationship to ministry? First, charism's action is not a pure theophany; in Jesus we see that God's grace is incarnational and evangelistic; so too in the life of the Christian. Second, charism is not the creation or possession of the individual Christian. Charism is God's gift, the active presence of the kingdom of God permeating an individual. The Spirit is free, and charisms respect the sovereignty of God and the individuality of the person. Similarly, although the charismatic activity of God is for the good of the church, it is never radically created or fully controlled by the church (although the community's charisms are asked to discern the charismatic life of individuals and full-time ministries). Ministry is not an institutional product of the church but a realization of the pneumatic life of the community present in structure, diversity and unity. The church is the place, but not the solitary creator of ministry.

Drawing upon an interpretation of Pauline theology, we have been arguing that professional, central ministry in the church—teaching, preaching, leadership—does not form a second, ordinary and official structure over against the charismatic. Rather, charism is diaconal. Charism is the source and foundation of every ministry whether this be temporary or lifetime. There should be no successful ministry to grace which is purely institutional or where a Christian without vocation or gift has been officially but not spiritually established as public minister. Every vital ecclesiology draws its inspiration from the Spirit working in the world. Structure is the bridge from divine charism to real service. "Our competence is from God, who has made us competent to be ministers of the new covenant" (2 Cor 3:5, 6).

5. Diaconal Charisms

Sometimes both visionary and hierarchy picture the Christian community in a schizophrenic way: for the former, charism displays supernatural powers and proclaims a God-appointed alternative to the offices of a too powerful church; for the latter ministry is conceived as office and ends up as an ossified institution because it has separated itself from the Spirit. Without a close and direct relationship of charism to ministry the source of ministry is diluted and its responsibility to the Spirit's plan (realized in both tradition and creativity) is lost.

Paul welcomed all spiritual gifts, refusing to be embarrassed by or hostile to whatever was spiritually healthy. Nevertheless, he minimalized the sensational gifts and accented those which were public services to the Gospel. In *1 Corinthians* he may be contrasting flamboyant *pneumatika* found in sectaries with diaconal, ordinary charisms. Inevitably he led charisms to the life of the church and emphasized their nature by giving examples of ministries which would build up the community. Charism exists "for the common good" (1 Cor 12:7). The key to the interplay of charism and ministry is found in Paul's repeated statement of their common goal: growth of the field's fruits (1 Cor 3:7), building the temple of the Spirit (1 Cor 3:16); the growth of the body (Rom 12:4). Harmony is brought to a diversity of important ministries and to innumerable communal services by the goal, "a unity in the work of service (*diakonia*), building up the body of Christ" (Eph 4:13). The kingdom has yet to be fully realized, the churches are to spread.

Far from charism being opposed to ministry, ministry is mediated from the Spirit to personality by charism: diaconal charisms.[22] A fundamental theology of grace in ministry and a historical-cultural sociology of church structure point to a theology of charism leading at times during a Christian's life to service. There is a corporate thrust to the gifts of the Spirit—the early church's life is played out as a mission to the world. While it is true to say that office and ministry must be understood in the broad horizon of *charis* and *charismata,* it is also true to point out the permanent but not frantic goal of the pneumatic and charismatic in explicit service to the Gospel.

Paul's difficulty was the opposite of the one faced by the medieval or baroque church; he was faced with an explosion of charisms and he hoped for a panoply of ministries. Early Christian communities would not have understood a limiting of charism or ministry to an elite.

Paul used the metaphor of organism to illustrate diversity, unity, power and lack of rivalry. Clearly, the lists of diaconal charisms in *Romans, Corinthians* and *Ephesians* are not intended to exhaust or control charisms or ministries. The lists do show that the manifestations of the Spirit are not to be rudely curtailed. A sign of living as a Christian is to have at times in one's life charisms which are ministry. We have had a paucity of realized charisms in the church and only one full-time ministry. Now more and more Christians do ministry. We have an expansion of the priesthood into several full-time ministries; we have hundreds of parishioners who wish to work not simply in church social life but in ministry.

Charism is the contact between the horizon of the life of the Spirit and a personality. There can be many charisms ranging from momentary inspirations to life-long decisions fraught with risk. God's inspirations are often concerned with the depths of my personal faith or with my relationship to others. Not all charisms are diaconal, but at times in a Christian's life, we suspect, invitations will be given to serve the church. Secondly, not all charisms are church ministry, but all church ministry is grounded in charism. The Christian lives within a life of the Spirit, and some facets of life are ministerial; the church lives within an atmosphere of ministry, and this ministry should come not from purely legal constitution but from the charism of its people.

An individual's life has its continents and its oceans; life follows cycles when one interest pattern dominates over others. The ages of a man's or a woman's life are the terrain to which the Spirit sends its calls. There is an ebb and flow to baptismal ministry which follows the life of the individual Christian. Invitations to full-time ministry come according to the patterns of a recipient's life. We will return to this topic later when we consider the source of ministry and ordination.

The charisms which come to each baptized man and woman receive their diversity through their goal: healing, consoling, service to the socially impoverished, preaching, teaching, public evangelism, leadership of liturgy and community. Pauline theology rejects the ecclesiology which holds that the ideal situation in the church is one charism and one ministry, leadership. The ministry of leadership is mentioned by several names in the New Testament, but this ministry is not always clearly first. Leadership at times seems to flow out of another defined, external ministry, e.g., prophet, and to exist to serve ministry, not to bestow it (1 Cor 16:15). Ministry is not solely leadership, nor is it a vague charity to others or a community style where every service can be done by everyone. The history of ministry shows a tendency to reduce ministry to priest, bishop or administrator with a subsequent reaction to replace office with universal and free charism. The theological harmony between charism and ministry should exclude monoformity as well as competition. The analogy of the body challenges the idea that some charisms and ministries are essentially superior to others in the eyes of the Spirit and the church. In the diversity of ministry we find each particular ministry's identity and, too, its power, humility and holiness.

The word *diakonia*, ministry, in the New Testament sometimes means a particular kind of church action (Rom 12:7), and sometimes it means the general term which includes all the serving and evangelistic roles in the community (Eph 4:12). A service of services, it flows forth from Christian life and community and then is channeled into various Christian presentations of the word and power of God's new covenant. *2 Corinthians* contrasts the past religious "ministry of death" with the new "ministry of the Spirit" (3:7, 9).

This ordinary Greek word for serving and attending upon someone has not fared well in translation. The abstract Latin, *ministerium,* can easily become an office, even a rather servile one, and was in fact replaced in Western Christianity by *officium.* The Reformation wanted to rediscover the style in the word "minister" but centuries of too close contact with state churches or middle class ethos have obscured the active and servant nature of the word; Roman Catholics until recently saw "minister" as Protestant. But the English words "serve" and "service" have their own difficulties. In a society increasingly devoid of a servant class, a description of church offices and roles as services and of their holders as servants borders on piety or poetry. The contemporary rediscovery of the word "ministry" with its sharp etymological challenge in service as well as its dynamics of a diversified ministry looks towards a theological reappreciation of every church office as activity serving grace, and of the style of that activity as inescapably one of service—service of people, service of the Spirit in people.

In Jesus, the source of community and discipleship, we have the origin of the word and its accompanying style. Jesus' activity on behalf of the kingdom in which he invites others to share is marked out not by the style of an apocalyptic seer or a royal administrator but by the style of the diaconal, of the active and faithful servant.

> You know that among the pagans the rulers lord it over them, and their great men exercise authority over them. It shall not be so

among you; but whoever would be great among you must be your servant—even as the Son of man came not to be served but to serve, and to give his life as a ransom for many (Mt 20:25–28).

In this passage the verb form of *diakonia* stands in marked contrast to "lord over"; perhaps this saying of Jesus is the foundation for Pauline theology naming church and charismatic activity in a global sense as service. Words and actions from the Last Supper as recorded by *John* and *Luke*—the union of foot-washing with the acceptance of the Passion, the commissioning to intimate ministry and the promise of the Spirit—complement the injunctions of the Synoptics about the style of preaching. The New Testament describes an existential and divine authority in Jesus and a real authority in the subsequent churches, but neither authority escapes the paradoxical and difficult modality of service.[23] In *Romans,* Jesus is described in his historical life as a servant (15:8), a deacon of God's truth and of the Father's promise, and the entire fundamental theology of ministry is summed up: ministry to the active plan of God. The very real abasement of the waiter (an office for a slave in many civilizations) passes through the abasement of the founding moment of the church, Calvary, and then finds a new style in Jesus and his Spirit for serving the historical mystery of God's plan.

*   *   *

We must leave to exegetes the relationships and nuances in the words "charism" and "service" in the writing of the New Testament and be content with establishing both as normal aspects of community life and with bringing both back together as a couplet. Every ministry is grounded in charism; some charisms in each Christian lead to ministry. Diaconal charisms come to baptized men and women in various modalities during their lives. Now we can turn to further characteristics of the fundamental ecclesial structure of the early churches and ask about the diversity and arrangement of ministers, men and women, whose work is so wondrous that they are called co-workers with God (Col 4:11).

NOTES

1. I. Hermann, *Kyrios und Pneuma* (Munich, 1961), p. 145.
2. P. Tillich, "Being, Non-Being and Anxiety," in *The Courage To Be* (New Haven, 1952).

3. "Its (*Hebrews'*) starting point is the insight that all human sacrifices, all ritual and cultic attempts to reconcile oneself to God, have remained helpless and futile works of man. . . . The hour of the cross was the cosmic day of reconciliation. There is no cult other than this one and also no priest other than the one who fulfilled this liturgy, Jesus Christ. . . . Whoever reads the New Testament attentively will see that it is—despite the differences that it otherwise exhibits—at all points characterized by a deep knowledge of the radical termination of the foregoing history of religion signified and effected in the Christ-event. What was said about Jesus, who was, juridically speaking, a layman, and about the profane character of his death appears here once again: that day (the day of his death) manifested the holiness of the apparently profane and the non-holiness of the previously religious. . . . From a historical point of view, Christ's death was not a cultic activity or event but an occurrence belonging very much to the realm of the profane." J. Ratzinger, "Priestly Ministry: A Search for Its Meaning," *Emmanuel* 86 (1980) 250ff. On the fulfillment of sacral religion, cf. J. Blenkinsopp, *Celibacy, Ministry and the Church* (New York, 1968); G. Schrenk, "Iereus in the NT," *TWNT* 3, p. 263; H. Wenschkewitz, *Die Spiritualisierung der Kultusbegriffe. Tempel, Priester und Opfer im Neuen Testament* (Leipzig, 1932); G. Klinzing, *Die Umdeutung des Kultus in der Qumrangemeinde und im Neuen Testament* (Göttingen, 1971); J. M. R. Tillard, "La qualité sacerdotale du ministère chrétien," *NRT 95* (1973), 481ff.; *MM*, pp. 408ff. Treating the new self-interpretation of the early Christians over against that of pagan and Jewish priests are S. von Dunin-Borkowski, "Die Kirche als Stiftung Jesu," *Religion, Christentum, Kirche* (Kempten, 1913), 3, pp. 55ff.; J. Jungmann, *The Place of Christ in Liturgical Prayer* (New York, 1965), pp. 146ff.

4. On the temple, cf. Y. Congar, *The Mystery of the Temple* (Westminster, 1962); R. Brown, *The Gospel According to John,* 1 (New York, 1966), pp. 121ff; J. D. Davies, *The Gospel and the Land* (Berkeley, 1974).

5. J. H. Elliott, *The Elect and the Holy* (Leiden, 1966): "This activity (a holy life of obedience and well-doing) is basically a witness oriented towards the world and complements a second aspect of the community's responsibility, the proclamation of the word of salvation and mercy . . . The same community called a *ierateuma* ("priesthood") was charged with a charismatic ministry and ordered according to a certain sense of office." *Ibid.,* p. 224.

6. H. Schlier, "Die 'Liturgie' des apostolischen Evangeliums," *Martyria, Leitourgia, Diakonia* (Mainz, 1968), p. 251. Cf. P. Seidensticker, *Lebendiges Opfer* (Münster, 1954); P. van Bergen, "La vie quotidienne vécue comme culte," *Sainteté et vie dans le siècle* 2 (Rome, 1965), pp. 81ff. E. Hajemann, "Worship in the World," *Commentary on Romans* (Grand Rapids, 1980), pp. 326ff; C. Wiener, "Hierourgein (Rom 15, 16)," *Studiorum Paulinorum Congressus* (Rome, 1963) 2, pp. 399ff.

7. J. Colson, "Ecclesial Ministries and the Sacral," *C* #80 (1972), p. 74; cf. *Ministère de Jésus-Christ et le sacerdoce de l'évangile* (Paris, 1966); J. P. Audet, *Structures of the Christian Priesthood* (New York, 1968); H. Schlier,

"Grundelemente des priesterlichen Amtes im NT," *Theologie und Philosophie* 44 (1969) 168ff; A. Vanhoye, "Sacerdoce commun et sacerdoce ministeriel," *NRT* 97 (1975) 191ff. Y. Congar, "Le sacerdoce du NT," *Les Prêtres* (Paris, 1968); "Situation du sacré en régime chrétien," *La liturgie après Vatican II* (Paris, 1967) pp. 385ff; "Le sacerdoce de l'évangile, le sacerdoce aaronique et les sacerdoces paiens," *Sacerdoce et laicat*.(Paris, 1962), pp. 91ff; D. Donovan, *The Levitical Priesthood and the Ministry of the New Testament* (Münster, 1970); W. Pesch, "Priestertum und das Neue Testament," *Trierer Theologische Zeitschrift* 79 (1970) 65ff. On the permanence of the sacred in Christian life, H. Mühlen, *Entsakralisierung* (Paderborn, 1970); M. Simon et al., *Le Retour du sacré* (Paris, 1977); E. Syndicus, "Entsakralisierung: Ein Literaturbericht," *Theologie und Philosophie* 42 (1967) 577ff.

8. *Ek,* pp. 334, 338ff. On the accepted theory that charism must be separated from office, cf. pp. 362ff. "Charisms . . . do not establish a constitutive difference in the depth of the church but they act solely on the level of action." U. Betti, *Au service de la Parole de Dieu* (Gembloux, 1969), p. 252; MC, p. 46; cf. G. Hasenhüttl, *Charisma, Ordnungsprinzip der Kirche* (Freiburg, 1969). For a survey of the word, B. N. Wambacq, "Le mot 'charisme,' " *NRT* 97 (1971) 345ff. *Charis* is "the grace which encounters a person as the person is called to the Christian condition, claiming, commissioning, enabling for service. The grace-character of the Christian condition is perceived in the enabling and preparing or serving. It is striking that Christ is the initiator, the giver." J. Gnilka, *Der Epheserbrief* (Freiburg, 1971), p. 206. Schillebeeckx' *Christ* (New York, 1980) is largely a theology of grace drawn from the ontic presence of the *Pneuma* of Jesus Risen but it does not pursue the extension of *charis* into ministry.

9. A. Harnack, *The Constitution and Law of the Church* (New York, 1910), p. 236; E. Schweizer, *Church Order in the New Testament* (London, 1961), p. 183; R. Sohm, *Kirchenrecht 1* (Berlin, 1892); cf. Y. Congar, "Rudolf Sohm nous interroge encore," *Revue des sciences philosophiques et théologiques* 57 (1973) 263ff.

10. H. F. von Campenhausen, *Ecclesiastical Authority and Spiritual Power in the Church of the First Three Centuries* (Stanford, 1969), p. 71.

11. *Geschichte der synoptischen Tradition* (Göttingen, 1964), p. 135.

12. "Ministry and Community in the New Testament," *Essays on New Testament Themes* (Naperville, 1964), pp. 73, 76.

13. "The Theological Problem Presented by the 'Motif of the Body of Christ,' " *Perspectives on Paul* (London, 1971), p. 119.

14. "The Beginnings of Christian Theology," *New Testament Questions Today* (London, 1969), pp. 83ff; "Ministry and Community in the New Testament," p. 92.

15. "There is only one principle and it is theological, a theology of the cross where the crucified Jesus is always first in theology and in the church's consciousness; it searches out every aspect of a *theologia gloriae* which in the church might lead to "ecclesiological metaphysics." ". . . Motif of the Body of Christ," p. 117.

16. *ST* II—II q. 171, intro.; I—II, q. 111, aa. 1,4,5.

17. *Ch,* p. 188.

18. *Ibid.,* p. 420. Hasenhüttl distinguishes between charismatic ministries and other services for the general good of the community which are "purely human and sociological callings that one that is conscious of being temporary" (*Charisma,* p. 354). Such a distinction ignores the charismatic nature of all ministry against the backdrop of sin and grace. C. Journet gives an original if bizarre form to the scholastic distinction between charism and office by describing the ordained hierarchy as those who generated the church formally through teaching and administering the sacraments; other Christians in the apostolate serve or transmit supernatural truth and grace through influence and example. Cf. *The Apostolic Hierarchy* (New York, 1954), pp. 9f.

19. *MWS,* p. 198.

20. *Ibid.,* pp. 43–55; 197–212. H. Mühlen looks at the structures of the early church from the dialectic of desacralization—pneumaticization, and calls attention to the replacement of honor by personal identity. *Entsakralisierung,* pp. 259ff.

21. Cf. K. Kertelge, "Einleitung," *Das kirchliche Amt im Neuen Testament* (Darmstadt, 1977) pp. 1ff.; E. Ellis sees pneumatics including various modes of speaking, teaching, preaching (prophecy) and observes that the stable sages in Qumran resemble the Christian charismatics. " 'Spiritual Gifts' in the Pauline Community," in *Prophecy and Hermeneutic in Early Christianity* (Grand Rapids, 1978) pp. 26ff. Similarly Gerd Theissen, *Sociology of Early Palestinian Christianity* (Philadelphia, 1977) sees the Twelve to be "homeless, wandering charismatics" founding activist groups all of whom are involved with a call and life "over which they have no control" (pp. 8f.). Such an anomalous view of charismatic resembles the medieval Catholic, static isolation of the charism apart from office.

22. "For Paul, ministries are charisms, gifts of God for the good of all; the ministries of apostles, prophets and teachers come at the head of the charisms given to the church . . . , essentially ministries of the Word. These ministries do not, however, exhaust the gifts made by God to his church. There is still place for a multitude of other gifts and functions for which language and vocabulary remain quite flexible." *MM,* p. 62. Supporting the linear linking of charisma and diakonia are Hainz, Hasenhüttl, Cooke and Lemaire. For Käsemann, in *1 Corinthians,* "*diakoniai* are interchangeable with the *charismata.*" "Ministry and Community in the New Testament," p. 65. Expressing reservations about the flow from charism to ministry is U. Brockhaus, *Charisma und Amt, Die paulinische Charismenlehre auf Hintergrund der frühchristlichen Gemeindefunktionen* (Wuppertal, 1972), 237ff.

In the context of the new discussion of office, ministry and charism, the exegete F. Hahn observes the intention of Paul to join "spiritual gifts" and "activities" with *diakonia.* "He (Paul) spotlights the spiritual gifts not because of their particular mode of appearance but because they are to be, at the same time, *diakoniai;* for this reason he lists gifts and tasks as charisms which until

now were not viewed as the activities of the Spirit (Rom 12:8; 1 Cor 12:28)."
"Charisma und Amt," *Zeitschrift für Theologie und Kirche* 76 (1979), 424.
Hans Küng's emphasis is placed upon the charismatic aspect rather than on its
union with the diaconal structure and ordinariness in ecclesial and evangelical
service.

    23. *PP,* pp. 38ff.

CHAPTER FOUR
Primal Ministry

The New Testament describes charism and ministry mainly in specific ministries whose names are taken from the act of ministry, e.g. preaching, teaching, evangelizing, healing. These names and actions differ according to place, culture and time. Because diversity of ministry is such a crucial part of the contemporary expansion in ministry, and because over the centuries there has been a canonization of a few ministries during which ordinary Greek words became sacral Roman and European offices, we must look at the structure of ministry among the first Christian churches. This requires a theology of ministry to remain with the Scriptural records a while longer before moving to the transit of ministry through the centuries, and then to the exigencies of ministry today.

1. Primal Experience

The New Testament does not describe a pageant to be worshiped or imitated; rather, the diverse books—letters, narratives, gospels—give an interpretation of life. In contrast to our monoform, perduring model of priesthood, the record of early Christian communities presents a panoply of ideas and forms. The ecclesiologist wants to avoid solving complex problems of exegesis without appearing naive or satisfied with a fundamentalist literalism. The theologian looks for basic insights from the depth of the New Testament which are the stimuli for an interpretation of a particular facet of Christian faith.

The richness of the New Testament world, at least in the area of ministry, has been obscured. We experience less of the being of the church than the first churches did. So we develop a fundamental theology of ministry in the light of the experience of the first Christians and we turn to early church life not because it is old but because it is primal. Primal means near to the source: in this case, near a source which faith holds to be quasi-infinite. The first communities were not only chronologically close to Pentecost but their freedom in religion and their creativity in community show that this proximity was one of being profoundly formed by the Spirit. The first churches are not only first but primal: in them the new and lasting rebirth of human life in the Spirit appears not fully but radically and strikingly. Our interest is not in antiquity but in proximity; first churches reflect the primal event of the birth of Christian faith and community. We are interested in the self-consciousness of the early church not to revivify exactly this or that form but to see through these forms what the churches view in culturally diverse ways as essential and charismatic.

Christian faith has always held that not only was Jesus' preaching and life normative but that the first generation of his disciples—called the apostolic generation—was privileged in what they saw and perceived. Their witness because of its immediacy was special. They remain primal; but early churches are not simply the first Christians receiving their marching orders from Jesus, Peter or Paul. If that were so, these churches would have presented one set of lasting forms. The church today would not reflect the church in 1200 A.D. or 1600 A.D. but only in 50 A.D. The first witnesses and the first generations of believing disciples are primal because they are immediate; they have a lasting significance because they are also creative.

We find less ecclesiology in the New Testament than we would like. What we know of Paul's ecclesiology is highly conditioned by circumstances at Corinth (a milieu which we do not completely understand), and we know little of the inner way of life of the Jewish churches in Antioch or Caesarea, and only something of early Rome and, later, of Ephesus. What is striking for the theologian of ministry is that in this area the New Testament is richer than are the subsequent centuries of Christian reflection and practice. The later history of ministry strikes one as a diminution. Ministry shrinks, ministry is institutionalized, ministry becomes priesthood and is grafted on to canonical posts from charismatic roots. Not every area of the Christian faith undergoes this diminution; for instance, the dialogue between grace and the human personality is more extensively developed as the centuries pass. In ministry, however, reflection on faith undergoes some impoverishment after A.D. 90. Yet, history of ministerial diversity and expansion retains seeds and patterns of an earlier variety, and while diversity still struggles to be present in the fourth century, by the Middle Ages earlier paradigms are present not in ministries but in monks and nuns. Our attraction to this primal time is, then, a legitimate one.

Ecclesiology, like Christology and the theology of grace and free will, displays a diversity in the New Testament. The difference in social and cultural backgrounds of the men and women who entered Christian communities rendered the churches diverse. The religious and political structures in which they had been raised were not destroyed by baptism and the Spirit but often contributed to the manner of living in community. Different regions of the Roman Empire held different views of the world and its future, and from this array of social, ethnic and religious structures the first churches could not help but draw institutional forms.

The New Testament's books are not systems of polity but often writings of circumstance. They are incomplete, their situation is not fully known, and their styles are diverse. We learn about ministry in a collection of writings of different literary genres drawn from several linguistic and religious worlds. There is a view of ministry in letters to communities in Corinth (in turmoil) and in Rome (not yet seen); there is *Acts* which presents the first decades of the church but not always without the interpretation of later decades. *1 Peter, Hebrews,* and *Revelation* come from quite different areas and eras. Through all of this, the difficult task of exegesis is to penetrate behind the letter of the text to authors and communities capable of influencing the structures described as well as the written text.

Raymond Brown has attempted to draw out of particular New Testament writings some characteristics of an early community, the Johannine *ekklesia.*[1] Before 120 A.D., he detects three distinct periods in this particular community: (1) within the mid-century Judaism during the composition of the Fourth Gospel (up to 90 A.D.), a time of evangelism, climax and confidence; (2) a time of inner controversy indicated by the three Johannine letters; (3) a time of decline moving into the expanded institutionalization beyond Ignatius of Antioch and up into Tertullian's pneumatic Montanism. We mention Brown's analysis not for its particular insights into ministry—the Johannine literature has other interests—but to illustrate the evolution, complexity and the lacunae which each distinct type of Christian community—Johannine, Corinthian, Roman, Antiochene—presents to the theoretician of ministry studying the early church. Hence the theologian (now beyond comparing titles in the New Testament) looks to exegetes not only for an analysis of a particular ministry—prophet, presbyter—but for a sociological picture of communities with defined theology and ethos determining a particular ecclesial structure.

All the writings of the New Testament bear witness to the existence of ministry—actions and people nourishing the churches. That these functions and people appear in various forms does not mean that the form of ministry was of no interest to Christians, or that ministry in the church can be allowed to be today a secular, bureaucratic activity which in its ordinariness shies away from the Spirit. Just the opposite is true; New Testament ministry is not simply organization and work but the very activity of the Spirit in co-workers. The typology of ministers is important. Between charismatic anarchy and secular passivity there were, in the first churches, groups able without the burden of tradition to develop in different ways. L. Goppelt writes:

> From the very beginning, we can observe in the organization of the church, as in the service of worship, the same characteristic tension between historical forms and pneumatic freedom. The church conducted herself as a living organism in keeping with the consultational forms which she had taken over in an attitude of uninhibited independence from the Jewish tradition, yet she never made these forms into a constitution.[2]

The contours of what we can learn from the New Testament of the first churches and their ministries (even when we must study them carefully and indirectly through later churches) help us to appreciate a diversity of pattern, suggest a possible chronology of development, and sum up characteristics owned by churches of Jews and Hellenes, Romans and Syrians.

2. A Realm of Ministries

Three New Testament writings—*Romans, 1 Corinthians,* and *Ephesians*—give lists of ministries. Each expresses a community living in different geographical and social environments and in more than one decade of the first century.

Now there are varieties of gifts, but the same Spirit; and there are varieties of service, but the same Lord; and there are varieties of working, but it is the same God who inspires them all in every one. To each is given the manifestation of the spirit for the common good. To one is given through the Spirit the utterance of wisdom and to another the utterance of knowledge according to the same Spirit, to another faith by the same Spirit, to another gifts of healing by the one Spirit, to another the working of miracles, to another prophecy, to another the ability to distinguish between spirits, to another the interpretation of tongues. All these are inspired by one and the same Spirit who apportions to each one individually as he wills.

For just as the body is one and has many members, and all the members of the body, though many, are one body, so it is with Christ (1 Cor 12:4–12).

For as in one body we have many members, and all the members do not have the same function, so we, though many, are one body in Christ, and individually members one of another. Having gifts that differ according to the grace given to us, let us use them: if prophecy, in proportion to our faith; if service, in our serving; he who teaches, in his teaching; he who exhorts, in his exhortation; he who contributes, in liberality; he who gives aid, with zeal; he who does acts of mercy, with cheerfulness (Rom 12:4–8).

And his gifts were that some should be apostles, some prophets, some evangelists, some pastors and teachers, to equip the saints for the work of ministry, for building up the body of Christ, until we all attain to the unity of the faith and of the knowledge of the Son of God, to mature manhood, to the measure of the stature of the fullness of Christ (Eph 4:11–14).

Two of these lists are certainly by Paul and were written not long after the midpoint of the first century; the third is perhaps by a group of Paul's disciples who were writing a few decades later.

These appear to be illustrative not exhaustive. Exegesis and ecclesiology, after the medieval period, tried to harmonize these lists or reduce them to a single set of ministries, those of the medieval Roman Church. Actually, the lists tell us more about the theology of ministry than they do about its precise structure. It is easier to conclude that ministry was active, diverse and flexible than to derive a job description of the ministries listed.

None of these lists includes *episcopos* from which our term, bishop, comes; "*diakonia*" in *Romans* means a specific role resembling perhaps that established in *Acts* while in *Ephesians* the term is a generic one of all ministries. There is, of course, no mention of a priest (*iereus*) nor even of the kind of advisory elder (*presbyteros*) from which etymologically our English word "priest" is derived. Nevertheless, there are ministries of leadership called shepherd, helmsman, foreman or president (Eph 4:11; 1 Thess 5:12) but these seem flexible terms for a necessary ministry of leadership, and not titles for an all-encompassing director.

Our English words may confuse rather than assist an understanding of what a particular ministry did. The "apostles" mentioned above were not the twelve apostles but members of the community evangelizing new mission fields outside the community; the "prophets" were not seers into the future but gifted public preachers of God's revelation to the community; "deacons" may be a generic term for ministry to which all the baptized are called.

The period in which kingdom, charism and ministry burst upon the scene evolved several styles and forms some of which disappeared into history. Exegetes now struggle to arrange the temporal and cultural lines in the ministries mentioned in the New Testament. Let us pause to give some chronological order to this dynamic of ministry.

First, there was the ministry of Jesus (c. 27 to 30 A.D.); second, the first communities were in Jerusalem, Antioch and Damascus where Jewish forms, presbyterial and prophetic, would be prominent (30–45); third, the wider foundations of Gentile churches by the Twelve and by other apostles gave an internal prominence to teacher, prophet and apostle (45 to 70); fourth, bishop, presbyter and deacon (as a specific ministry of care assisting leadership) more and more arranged, and in some ways replaced, the earlier stages (70 to 110). This gives us two triads in the first century; the first is apostle-prophet-teacher; the second is bishop-presbyter-deacon. How the Christian churches throughout the Roman Empire moved from the first triad to the second is unclear; how they co-existed is uncertain. But these two patterns, not just the second, are key stages in the development of ministry in the seventy years after Pentecost.

André Lemaire offers the following typology, arranging the varied New Testament ministries and detecting layers and movements of ministries. Lemaire draws from the fragmentary network of people and roles mentioned in different writings of the first century three separate types of ministry: (1) listed services in a community; (2) Paul's co-workers and their goals; (3) leadership in the community.[3] None of the three categories fully excludes the others. The shepherds and helmsmen in the first group are also in the third. Lemaire's approach, not based upon one New Testament writing nor upon a group of unclear activities which appear in several writings, gives us a view of the situation in the middle of the first century and allows us to see what forces lay beneath developing church titles.

a. Activities in the Community

Paul's enumeration of ministries does not have as its purpose the presentation of an ecclesiology but the affirmation that ministry in the church is diverse. He lists not so much offices as people; and gifts which stand out in the community's life as significant ministries. Today church offices appear to Christians as distant, liturgical but supranatural; originally, however, they were activities derived from life: an "apostle" was someone sent on a mission; a "prophet" spoke publicly; a "deacon" was a servant.

Exegetes point out how *1 Thessalonians* mentions ministers in a general way by using the terminology of work: laborers and foremen. Perhaps this describes a first level of ministry when zeal and the service were paramount, when specificity and title were not as important as the expansion of the *ekklesia* and charismatic harmony.

Apostle, prophet and teacher have a prominence in *1 Corinthians* and *Romans,* and then in *Ephesians.* Overtones of this triad survive into later documents. The ministry of the *apostle* was not that of the Twelve Apostles but of missionaries officially sent by their church some distance to preach the Gospel or as travelling representatives of a community (Gal 4:14). "The first place given to the 'apostles' in this triad marks clearly the missionary orientation of the church, particularly the church of the Antiochene tradition at this early period."⁴ *Evangelist* means a public preacher who aimed at converting his hearers; exegetes are uncertain as to whether this minister worked more at the local level than on distant journeys. The *prophets* enjoyed a central place because they were the ordinary preachers within the community. Their exhortation and encouragement was homiletic (1 Cor 14:3). *Acts* spoke of this ministry as one of leadership in Antioch and Jerusalem (4:36; 13:1), while the *Didache* suggested that their preaching led to leadership at Eucharist and in the church.⁵ It is not surprising that Paul and the Twelve would conceive of leadership and evangelization as going together (while they would hardly be singling out the marginal activity of forecasting the future): "Search the gifts of the Spirit, above all, that of prophecy" (1 Cor 14:1). While research is needed to uncover the meaning of apostles and prophets, the *teachers* are less opaque. Associated with the prophet-preachers they may have been Christians occupied with the serious teaching and instruction of the revelation of God in Christ. Some experts suggest they reflect a rabbinical form. We know that the mystery religions, too, had not only ritual and fellowship but serious instruction both before and after initiation.

These three activities—external evangelization, preaching and assembly leadership, teaching—formed the core of the community. New Testament lists, however, show other ministries and they should not be neglected or shunted aside. These are ministries of healing, of consoling, of serving those in need. Perhaps Paul implied that these are arranged around the core ministries, but they are no less charisms, pneumatic gifts and ministries. All of these charisms/ministries are *diakonia*, and *diakonia* implies the building up of the community.

Now we can better understand the list of *Romans* 12; as with *1 Corinthians* 12:28 there is a break in the enumeration after the gift of "exhortation" (*paraklesis*)—the construction changes and introduces charisms drawn from personal attitudes: simplicity, zeal, etc. Prophecy, ministry, teaching and exhortation proceed from a group which is like the triad, apostle, prophet, teacher. In *Romans* Paul is thinking of the life of apostleship, and prophets and teachers are clearly expressed by prophecy, teaching and exhortation. This triad of ministries might be viewed as a bridge between the early communities' charismatic universality in ministry and the later emergence of an increasingly centralized episcopacy.

b. The Co-Workers of Paul

The *Acts of the Apostles* as well as the Pauline letters record many proper names of people who are introduced as co-workers (*sunergos;* Phil 2:25) in the ministry. No doubt other Apostles drew Christians into their ministry, but few names of these early Christians have been preserved, while with Paul we have close to one hundred and fifty co-ministers. Some of these ministers were men, some were women. Some traveled with Paul, some were only known to him; some were evangelists on the road, and some were residents of a house where a Christian *ekklesia* gathered. These people cannot be fitted into one type of church office. Clearly, all are not presented as bishops or presbyters. When they are called *diakonoi*, not all are what later centuries will mean by deacon and deaconness. In *Colossians*, Tychikos is described as a faithful deacon and co-servant of the Lord (4:7); in *Philippians*, Epaphroditus is called a "comrade in arms" and "brother" (2:25), an "apostle" and a "co-worker" and finally a "liturgist" to Paul's needs. *Romans* ends with a long list of personal greetings: first to Phoebe, Paul's "sister" and the "deacon" of the church in Cenchreae (16:1); then to important "co-workers in Christ Jesus," Prisca and Aquila (16:4) and to outstanding apostles Andronicus and Junia (more than likely a woman) (16:7). E. Ellis has highlighted the importance of this wide and varied group who are called not disciples (*mathētai*) but co-workers (*sunergoi*).

The large number, cutting across traditional religious lines of Jew and Gentile, slave and free, male and female, and the absence of official titles are striking. Among these ministers, fidelity to the message of Jesus and zeal for its spread are most important; nourishing all of this are personal and financial support and the deepest support of prayer. Support, activity, harmony in church life and belief are summed up in the ultimate title of brother and sister, and Ellis wonders whether this is not in fact an important designation of those who work with Paul in the ministry of preaching.[6]

This variety of co-workers in the ministry and this primal level of personally intense but officially vague designations of them by Paul is important. Its imprecision and potential creativity will annoy us if we expect to find a single schema of church office. We may miss the theological significance of the first believers raised to the level of co-worker. The insight given into the life of the churches will, however, encourage us if we are looking for characteristics of universality and spontaneity among the first Christians.

We find women in the ministry not first in a movement after 1970 but in names recorded in the New Testament. Full membership in the Christian community for women was a revolution for the first century. The rivals of Christianity—Jewish, neo-platonic, Mithraic—did not admit women to full initiation. As an ecclesiological principle we must ponder the excited proclamation of Paul in *Galatians:* "There is neither Jew nor Greek, there is neither slave nor free, there is no male and female" in Christ (3:28). Women were among the followers of Jesus from the beginning. They were faithful to the end, and the Gospels enhanced their role on Good Friday and Easter. Since ministry at the level of belief and theology derives not from human social arrangement (although this influences the realization of ministry in a culture), after the coming of the Spirit to all, we would expect ministry in the Christian churches to be open to all the baptized. One of the many recent books and scholarly studies on this topic concludes:

Women were admitted to baptism and membership in the Church without qualification, from the outset (unlike the Gentiles). Women were members of the earliest community which formed the nucleus of the Church (Acts 1:14f) and were among those who received the Spirit at Pentecost (Acts 2:1ff). Ministry, which derives from the gifts of the Spirit communicated by baptism, was open to women.

There is evidence that many of the functions which later were associated with the priestly ministry were in fact exercised by women, and no evidence that women were excluded from any of them. There were women instrumental in the founding of churches (Acts 18:2, 18f., 1 Cor 16:19, Rom 16:3f.); women with functions in public worship (1 Cor 11:5); women engaged in teaching converts (Acts 18:26). Women prophets are attested (1 Cor 11:5, Acts 21:9). In Paul's greeting at the conclusion of *Romans,* a woman minister (*diakonos*) of the church at Cenchreae is named, and very likely a women apostle (Junia—Rom 16:7). Thus, while male leaders may have been more prominent and numerous in the early Church and while women's activities may have been somewhat limited by what was culturally permissible, many roles which ultimately were associated with the priestly ministry were evidently never restricted to men.

The limitations presently placed on women's role in the Church and the arguments advanced in support of those restrictions must be evaluated in light of the evidence for ministerial co-responsibility and for the presence of women in ministries in the Church of the New Testament period.[7]

It falls outside of a fundamental theology of ministry to decide the details of the presence of women in ministry past and present. The interplay of Jesus' kingdom in community does offer principles whose roots in baptism and charism can be limited to a natural group—one race, one sex—only with difficulty. Later we will look at the historical context for the reduction of ministry.

c. Ministry of Leadership

If the words for ministries in the first communities are words of action and service, this implies a perennial critique of any church office whose reality lies mainly in honor and title. In the first century, ministry came not only from the Spirit and the Twelve but from the community itself. The ministry of coordination and leadership was not the whole ministry but one important ministry among others, with responsibilities and limits.

At the opening of *Philippians,* Paul greets the community with its overseers and ministers (*episkopois kai diakonois*). In *Acts* the title of "elder" is prominent (it is absent from the major Pauline letters) and addresses those responsible for the churches at Jerusalem, Antioch, even at Ephesus. These three terms, of course, are, in history and etymology if not in description of office, the source for the three ministries given special emphasis by Christianity: bishop, priest, deacon. They seem to represent different cultural systems of the ministry of leadership in the community. We do not know what their relationship is to

Pauline terms for leadership: foreman, helmsman, shepherd. Nevertheless, we have no evidence for a Christian church which did not contain a ministry of leadership (although we cannot give that ministry one title), just as we have no example of an ekklesia which had only a ministry of leadership. The pluralism in name and description is a further illustration of cultural and ecclesial diversity in the first century.

Exegetes have thought that one title, *presbyteros,* indicated the Semitic background of elder while episkopos came from the Gentile churches. R. Brown suggests that "a more plausible theory is that we have here a reflection of two strains of Judaism which came into Christianity. The synagogues of Pharisaic Judaism had a group of *zegenim,* 'elders.'. . . In addition to such *zegenim* the Dead Sea Scrolls community of the New Covenant had officials who bore the title *mebagger. . . ,* supervisor, overseer."[8] Brown concludes his recent study of "bishop" in the different communities of the New Testament by pointing out a difference in manner and exercise of supervision in different places and different periods as well as in official terminology. The American exegete views the vacuum left by the death of the great leaders of the first decades after Jesus as exerting pressure for a more uniform structure of the church. "By the 80's–90's the presbyter-bishop model was becoming widespread, and with the adjustment supplied by the emergence of the single bishop that model was to dominate the second century until it became exclusive in the ancient churches."[9]

Some exegetes offer a particularly fruitful opinion that the "deacons and bishops" in *Philippians* do not represent two distinct offices but stand for all of those in ministry and leadership in the community. It may well be that at the time of Peter and Paul these were not specific ministries like teaching and healing but were global names for all or some ministries and for those who held directional ministries. The core of fulltime ministers would be addressed as "ministers and overseers." Paul attached little importance to titles and he was not preoccupied with consistency in titles. The New Testament writings sometimes speak of "ministers" (or "ministry") not as denoting the deacon of the third century church but as describing every Christian active on behalf of the church. The more important ministries would be ones of leadership and direction in a community of ministry. This would help explain why in the later letter to the *Ephesians* the diversity of ministries stands out but no mention is made of bishops, presbyters and deacons (4:4), while *Acts* speaks of presbyters in Ephesus (20:17). J. Gnilka writes:

> Individual holders of ministry and administration do not stand out in
> a special way in Paul's letters. From this we conclude that the com-

munities first bear responsibility for themselves, that each person living in the community was considered to share in the responsibility of
the community . . . that the various "community-offices" are effects
of the Spirit, and that both ministers and leadership roles are within
these effects of the Spirit.[10]

This view of ministers and overseers as a generic term serves as a
bridge between primal variety and the later reduction to three offices; it
frees us from a too limited early definition of deacon and bishop, for we
see them not as a single empowered office but as a generic occupation of
service. Later generations could look not only at ministry but at leadership as potentialities from which more than one precise diaconal form
might be drawn forth. In fact, through the centuries, as title perdured
and office changed, really different ministries were in fact to be drawn
out of "deacon" and "priest."

Two aspects of this survey of the levels of ministry may surprise us.
First, varied work and a widespread invitation to ministry joined with
the harmony of the community. Everything was subjected to the service
of that which is most important, the kingdom of God. Second, the roles
of authority and leadership emerge from the community and exist in
tension with many ministries. But by the end of the first century, the
fulltime ministry of leadership has achieved a solitary independence. In
the spirituality of ministry there has been a subtle shift: whereas Paul
speaks of the power-source of ministry to be the Spirit of Jesus, Clement
and Ignatius speak of the authority of ministry flowing from the awe-
some authority of God.

3. Primal Ministry: Four Characteristics

Our cursory exploration of both charism and ministry in the New
Testament gives us, if not job descriptions, normative insights, phenomenological parameters for each and every ministry. We should not use
the records of the New Testament world to produce either novel theories or marginal and allegorical piety. We are asking if there is a cluster
of insights true to the different ecclesial structures which are partly visible in the writings of the first century. This "primal theology" offers a
guide for a historical-fundamental theology of Christian ministry which
is serviceable for different cultures and eras. Such characteristics, rather
than defining one or two offices, express guidelines for ministry itself.

(a) *Christian ministry is not sacral office.* Christian ministry is
something new while cultic priesthood is as old as the human race. The
Christian minister in the early church was not principally a ritual litur-

gist, a custodian of God, or a mediator for humanity. Each and every minister was concerned with some activity which served the reality of grace. Ministry took place among people and pointed to moments of God's presence in and after Jesus. Rather than being distant and impotent ritual, ministry was preaching about God's event in Jesus and Jesus' words of justice, love and compassion.

The New Testament avoided sacral words for several reasons. They directly reduce the efficacy of God, they divide people from God, they distract from incarnation and morality by leading people to things and states. Before God sacralization can be idolatrous; after Jesus it is unnecessary. The sacralizing process insinuates an atmosphere of unreality into life; people are manipulated, not evangelized. Paul knew that the minister cannot escape being a public figure, but this public "liturgy" is verified in the conversion of hearers to the Spirit and in the dedication of the minister. Christian ministry knows its identity as service, hearing but rejecting the temptation to become again busy but empty.

(b) *Christian ministry is action.* The early Christians described their service to the kingdom of God as actions and not as honorific offices. The minister is the one who really does this action. Verbs such as announce, oversee, stand forth, teach, serve, describe these ministries. The birth of Christian ministry was a language-event: the *ekklesia* fashioned a language which disclosed its way of life. Prophets speak forth publicly; deacons serve; healers heal. There is no gulf between title and work, no substitution of personage for activity because the name of the ministry is the title of the minister and the service performed.

(c) *Ministry is service to the kingdom of God.* Ministry is doing something among men and women in the public world on behalf of the reign of God. Paul has a variety of terms—"gospel," "grace," "life"—for the loving presence of God towards us which has become clear and tangible in the event of Christ. Ministry, like the church, serves something beyond itself. The church's growth is the goal of ministry, and becoming the collective body of Christ is the norm and power and destiny of ministry (1 Cor 12:1ff; Eph 4:6). The church itself is minister, deacon to the kingdom, and as community and visible sign for the kingdom, the church is never self-centered. The dynamic of the church is one of pointing to, realizing and announcing that which it serves.

There are no examples in Paul where life itself is ministry. Christian life is called metaphorically a liturgy because though silent it preaches for the gospel or points to the presence of new life. Being baptized is not itself a ministry but the origin and goal of ministry; prayer is the background of ministry. Nor are secular jobs ministries for the first communities: being a cheerful slave is not a ministry (although the slave's evangelizing explanation of her joy to another person is); loading ships, weaving tents, dying wool and banking are not ministries. The examples of ministering charisms given by Paul are unambiguous in their connection to furthering the Gospel, to nourishing and expanding the church. Paul frequently resolves ministry by linking it to his metaphor of building up the body of Christ. This metaphor is not only a sociology of harmony in the church but an eschatology drawing ministry into action.

> What is distinctive about the Christian conception is not only that there is in the Christian application of the analogy (of the body) no spiritual elite, but also that the living Christ, and not just his example or his memory, is the antecedent presupposition of whatever organic unity a Christian congregation or, ultimately, the Church throughout the world, may have. . . . In some, parts at least of the Pauline epistles reflect an experience of Christ as a "corporate Person," to be joined to whom is to become part of an organic whole.[11]

Ministry is not concerned with the food supply in the Roman Empire or with improved transportation, although justice and the relief of the impoverished are ministries. The emphasis is upon communication of the realities of the Gospel and for Paul the ministry has a terrible urgency: these services of these insignificant people are the channels of new life and salvation. The ministry does not create the community as something outside or beyond it. Ministry is placed in the community by its Lord to nourish and to build it up.[12] In the records of Jesus' ministry, however, we learn that he placed within the kingdom of God the relief of men and women who suffered with particular intensity the effects of the sinful condition of the human race: the crippled, the diseased, the enslaved, the poor. Relief of oppression and injustice, of hunger and illness, when done as hope-filled services and signs of the presence of God's Spirit, is ministry, for the kingdom is the enemy of the effects of sin—disease, poverty, malice and death. Paul includes charity and healing as ministry. These ministries of service to personal anguish are a sign of the arrival of the Spirit and a promise of its future triumph. A ministry of healing or of social care does not, however, argue that every vocation or social task done well is a ministry. There may well be implicit ministry to the de facto presence of the reign of God overcoming the radical sin of human history. Our interest, however, is in a formal analysis of public, Christian ministry, and that service normally is a visible and verbal expression of the existence, goal and values of the kingdom of God as preached by Jesus and preserved in the church.

(d) *Christian ministry is universal and diverse.* Ministry is for each baptized person, it is charismatically given in a universality and particularity, and it should not disturb a ministerial harmony in the community. These three characteristics have the greatest practical import. Paul says often that the Spirit has given ministry to all and that services are of many kinds. It is not the titles and honors of charisms and ministries which are of value but that Jesus Christ is preached and the churches honestly become his body. Each time Paul reflects upon the diversity of functions in the church he recalls the origin and end of this diversity, a diversity willed by God and is the special work of the Holy Spirit (1 Cor 12:4ff; Rom 12:6). Each ministry is a gift of God who is establishing them within the church (1 Cor 12:28); second, this diversity lives within the church (1 Cor 12:28) and has its goal in the construction of this particular church.[13]

The letters of the churches in the first century were addressed not to individuals but to communities. When individual ministers are mentioned it was within the context of the greater life of the entire church. Since ministry was urgent and universal, charism was not a rare endowment and ministry was not merely an interesting option for the baptized. Belief and baptism were initiation into a religious movement which was accepted as essentially evangelistic. Faith was not gnosis about the occult but an acceptance of the changing reality in the world of sin and grace after Christ. The leaders of the community—who were not the head of the community (that was Christ) but its leading ministers, too—directed their oversight with a real authority; yet all ministry was situated within the community for the world.

Today it is customary to speak of "structure" and to use the word much as the nineteenth century used "system." The structure of the church, if by that we mean the dynamic essence which underlies its various activities and forms realized in culture (models of the church), is found in lines not of authority but of growth as service. Ministry to the kingdom is ultimate; all other structures serve that primal one. Whatever law and constitution there is in the church must aim at holding together a voluntary association of men and women who are both community and service.

4. Communities of Ministries: Expansion and Consolidation

What was ministry in the early church like? Was its typical minister a replacement for one of the Twelve Apostles or was the minister a charismatic miracle worker?

We must be careful not to read our variants of ministry into Greek words which described flexible ecclesial roles in the first century. Exegetical studies on *1 Corinthians* as well as Roman Catholic studies on office in the early church seem to have been advocates of one or another extreme position. The Catholic position argued, or more often presumed, that ministry had always been a medieval priesthood flanked by deacon and bishop, the former a liturgical remnant, the latter a nobleman. Charismatic groups from the twelfth, sixteenth and nineteenth centuries asserted that there was no structure in primal Christianity. Every member of the congregation could explain the Gospel and preside at the Lord's Supper; the life of the congregation consisted not in a sustenance of institutions and traditions but in a display of supernatural powers.

What was the early church like? It was neither the Vatican of the Renaissance nor the California audience of Aimee Semple McPherson. As we have just seen, from the churches of the first century we have only pieces of a mosaic. Our picture of ministry remains a projection made from those fragments, a hypothetical arrangement.

How did the community discover and unleash ministries? How did an individual Christian enter ministry? The community knew well that baptism was an entrance into ministry, that faith and baptism and charism changed the sacral into action, offering a new kind of priesthood, universal and missionary. After baptism came charisms and with them service to and for the churches. The community grew: it wanted to grow, and with its growth came more responsibilities. Elements which seem natural to us in terms of church life and ministry were surely present in the communities of Syria, Italy and Greece: education and training built upon experience, charism and zeal. Christianity was a remarkable network of communities with travel between them. There was a natural bent toward learning from each other, sharing experiences. "Paul himself in his choice of co-workers had to judge their aptitude for service to the Gospel. His companions seemed to have been proved on the job."[14] We can imagine that, as ministers moved into full-time activity, confirmed by the community and by some visible success in the ministry to which they believed themselves called, they took the time and expense to learn from other ministers and churches (1 Cor 9:14; Mt 10:10).

How did the full-time, central minister emerge in the community? Charisms and individual ministry needed to be tested in the Spirit. It was true that ministers were set up by God (1 Cor 12:28) but this had its social forms. In the house of Stephanos at Corinth, Paul judged certain members to be capable of being good ministers; the community recommended them warmly (1 Cor 16:15). There is a kind of mutual control of ministries existing between the community and the ministers, for every ministry is "in the church" (1 Thess 5:20f). H. F. von Campenhausen does not find the early communities so charismatically free that they do not need permanence and education. "That there was a rapid turnover of those who exercised these various ministries is nowhere stated, nor is it intrinsically probable."[15] The interplay of gift from the Spirit with a specific activity pursued gave a role in the community.

The prominence of some fulltime ministries (their names and descriptions differed from church to church but a ministry of leader was present) was necessitated by the expansion of the community. As the first century came to a close, central professional ministry, especially that of leadership, was moving (perhaps unconsciously) many charismata/services to the edge of the ministerial circle. In the expansion of churches the need for leadership naturally drew upon Christians who were fulltime in a central service of the Gospel and who were capable of coordinating all ministerial activity.

Diakonos, presbyter, episkopos—these three Greek terms were in place after 100 A.D. Still subject to different sociological hermeneutics, depending upon whether one was at Antioch, Alexandria or Rome, they survived as the permanent, basic ministries. But this revered triad is itself a puzzle. Each of the three may come from a different socio-theological source, and possibly each may have a global meaning, that is, each may stand for a group of ministers—in "service" or "supervision"—rather than for a specific task like preaching. *Deacon* is the name for the ministry itself and is sometimes so used; *elder* is a generic, Semitic office of leadership and was at first equal to and then later only auxiliary to the imprecise term of overseer, *bishop*.

The fragmentary descriptions coming from the first churches have not told us all we want to know about primal ministry. They have not sorted out ministries into the human and the divine nor have they offered precise offices with canonized names. We have, however, gained insight into the originality of an active community with a life and mission both universal and diverse. Different lists of ministries and layers of ministers compose an early church.

E. Schillebeeckx, after surveying the fragmentary information in the New Testament's gospels and letters, offers his own picture of the late first century.

> Consequently, even after the New Testament, church order remains very varied in the different communities. The fact that the *Didache* emphatically points out that overseers and helpers must be held in as

much respect in the community as the prophets and teachers perhaps points towards a certain restraint on the part of these communities towards these new ministries. In the communities of a Matthaean type the old order (prophets and teachers) was clearly of longer standing than presbyters, and there was even a degree of animosity towards the (later) introduction of *episcopoi* and *diakonoi*. . . . However, on the other hand, it is striking that all the communities of this more charismatic type disappeared completely in the course of the second century, or fell victim to Christian Gnostic sects.[16]

In the place of a precise number of offices we have some characteristics of ministry which build upon our principles of community, charism and service. In the long run, these characteristics of primal ministry may prove of great help to a church which finds itself called to growth and stability, to evangelical fidelity and honesty. We will take these characteristics up again in a later chapter when we reflect upon the nature of the ministry today.

NOTES

1. R. Brown, *The Community of the Beloved Disciple* (New York, 1979), pp. 23ff.

2. L. Goppelt, *Apostolic and Post-Apostolic Times* (London, 1970), p. 56. Cf. H.F. von Campenhausen, *Ecclesiastical Authority and Spiritual Power* (Stanford, 1969); P. Kearney, "New Testament Incentives for a Different Ecclesial Order," *C* #80 (1972) 50ff.; B. Holmberg, *Paul and Power* (Philadelphia, 1980), pp. 96ff.

3. *ME,* p. 10.

4. *MM,* p. 59.

5. The early triad of prophet, apostle and teacher is still witnessed to by the *Didache* with perhaps some unclarity and overlapping. For attempts to identify the form of these ministries which faded away, e.g. prophet, cf. E. Cothenot, "Prophétisme et ministère d'après le NT," *LMD* #107 (1971), 61ff.; "Le prophétisme et le Nouveau Testament: La Communauté Primitive," *Dictionnaire de la Bible, Supplément,* 8 (1971), pp. 1264ff.; J. Panagopoulos, ed., *Prophetic Vocation in the New Testament and Today* (Leiden, 1977); on teacher ("theologian") W. Pesch, "Kirchlicher Dienst und das Neue Testament," *Priesteramt* (Stuttgart, 1970), p. 22.; H. Greeven, "Propheten, Lehrer, Vorsteher bei Paulus," *Zeitschrift für die neutestamentliche Wissenschaft* 44 (1952/53) 1ff.

6. E. Ellis, "Paul and His Co-Workers," in *Prophecy and Hermeneutic in Early Christianity* (Grand Rapids, 1978), pp. 5, 9, 12.

7. Catholic Biblical Association, "Women and Priestly Ministry: The New Testament Evidence," *CSR Bulletin* 11:2 (1980) 45; cf. E. Schüssler-Fior-

enza, "Women in Pre-Pauline and Pauline Churches," *Union Theological Quarterly Review* 33 (1978) 15.

8. R. Brown, "Episkopē and Episkopos," *TS* 41 (1980) 333.

9. *Ibid.*, 338.

10. J. Gnilka, *Der Philipperbrief* (Freiburg, 1968), p. 33. See *MM,* p. 405; E. Haupe, *Die Gefangenschaftsbriefe* (Göttingen, 1902); H. F. von Campenhausen, *Ecclesiastical Authority* . . . p. 68; F. Loofs, "Die urchristliche Gemeindeverfassung. . . ," *Theologische Studien und Kritiken* 63 (1890) 68; A. Vögtle, "Die Urgemeinde," *Okumensiche Kirchengeschichte* (Mainz, 1970), pp. 25ff.

11. C.F.D. Moule, *The Origin of Christology* (Cambridge, 1972), p. 86.

12. *MM,* pp. 23ff.

13. *MM,* pp. 57ff.

14. *MM,* p. 27.

15. H. F. von Campenhausen, *Ecclesiastical Authority* . . . p. 69.

16. *My,* pp. 23ff. "In the history of the church's structure it is clearly not a question of the history of a decline but of a first line of development, of a pursual of certain principles and points of departure which made possible the 'incarnation' of the church in that time. The problem for the student of the New Testament today lies not in the fact of this development (which is affirmed) but in any emphasis upon exclusiveness. The New Testament is open for other forms of 'incarnation' for other possibilities of development even for those which were never tried. . . . That church 'office' sucked up so many, various functions (prophet, teacher, evangelist, leader of the Eucharist) is not unbiblical but only post-biblical. All these functions can of course be drawn anew out of this office." Pesch, "Kirchlicher Dienst". . . , p. 23.

CHAPTER FIVE
The Metamorphoses of Ministry

Two thousand years lie between the pneumatic, missionary churches of the first century and the ministries we need at this moment as history nears the end of the second millennium. This span between the first and twentieth centuries is not a void, nor a linear distribution of museums. History is a living drama where old and new characters act out their play, the one drama of grace. The different epochs of history have touched and transformed Christian ministry. The Gospel in theology and the church in ministry have not hesitated to become incarnate in various cultures.

From what we have already seen of the spontaneity of church forms and of the variety of charismatic ministries in the first century, we know that the first decades of the church do not make up an epoch finished and complete. Rather, the church witnessing its own birth gives an impetus which finds rebirth in later centuries and in our own times. The Spirit behind *ekklesia, charisma* and *diakonia* is not an ideal paradigm but a dynamic fullness.

History is a picture painted by culture and time. As the church makes its progress through Hellenic, Coptic, Celtic and Saxon cultures, the ministry is modified by the worlds it reaches. Ignatius the martyr, Ambrose the judge, Columba the voyager, Catherine the mystic and reformer, Innocent the statesman, Xavier the explorer, Bonhoeffer or Teilhard the thinker—all, often unconsciously, were struggling to be Christian ministers, searching out and even demanding new forms for the Spirit whom they followed.

Ministry is a living organism. When it finds itself blocked from activity it seeks new channels. The external forms of ministry may be reduced or wounded, but the organic nature of ministry as a living *pleroma* in the church is never fully anesthetized. Obeying their inner law, diversity of forms and styles of servanthood struggle for external realization. Charisms for service are not merely one facet of the church but can claim to be inspirations from the Spirit of the Lord, veins for his body which is the church.

For some mysterious reason Christians did not write theologies of the church, much less analyses of the churches' structures until well over a thousand years after Peter and Paul. Numerous theologies of the church appear only at the end of the Middle Ages. It is true that the writings of Hippolytus and Eusebius are sources for seeing how Christians understood their churches, and we can find in the writings and sermons of the Greek and Latin fathers as well as in liturgical documents and early ordination ceremonies information on the church's offices. But a formal study of the church and its ministry is missing. Even that architectonic summation of Christendom, the *Summa theologiae* of Aquinas, not only lacks a composite of questions on the church but it treats the church very briefly in segments on faith and ethical sociology. The past century of theology, on the other hand, has spent enormous energy on questions about the church: about its nature, its teaching office, its authority, its divisions.

In the Preface of this book we described its pages as "an historical metaphysics of ministry," "an exploration of the foundations and horizons of individual Christian life of service which comes from baptism," "a cultural sociology of the church's activity." The first chapter emphasized the importance of seeing groups of cultural forms drawn from diverse historical epochs as the way ministry incarnates itself. Beneath the Visigothic, Romanesque or Baroque there is not one lasting Christian priesthood merely changing its vestments. Cultures bring their own material to the ministry; rather than diluting it, cultural forms free ministry to live. In the colors and symbols, vestments and rituals of the liturgy, polychrome speech expresses the simple beliefs of the Christian faith. In the church's different eras not only liturgy but politics tune the language of the ministry. With the distinction between essence and cultural form we can stand apart from history, avoiding both relativism and schizophrenia, and see that history simultaneously limits and reveals the ministry.

To understand the history of ministry is to understand how and why ministry lives through history. The major periods of the church's life display what was once ministry. What is now taken to be an eternal facet of Christianity may be an aspect of the Baroque, or what is considered to be patristic is upon analysis medieval. What the Reformation vigorously rejected again returns, and what the Reformers advocated Rome now claims as its own. C. S. Lewis wrote, "The unhistorical are, usually without knowing it, enslaved to a fairly recent past."[1]

We will not attempt below a history of ecclesiology nor give another analysis of certain moments in the history of ministry, for instance, when ordination and episcopal office appeared in the second century or when the bishop of Rome became pope and much later becomes the Vicar of Christ. Rather we will sketch six important periods—periods which are both crisis and movement. The ministry underwent a metamorphosis during each.

These six periods give us not only the picture but the process as forces molded the ministry into this or that form. Cultural forces (some from within and some from without the church) make up what we call a *Zeitgeist.* All sectors of cultural life share in the processes of change but share in them asymmetrically. We do not find precise parallels in every era between economics, arts, philosophy and religion; nor do parallels occur precisely on time in synchronicity. Yet, often a great *kairos* of cultural history displays the same thought-forms in areas of science, art and faith. We will see that charism and ministry assumed certain forms not simply out of obedience to the biblical letter but also because society called or even forced the church towards patterns which seemed attractive and useful.

Each of these periods in ministry is a time when ministry worked and each period still exercises some influence upon theory and praxis today. No period contains the ministry perfectly, for the horizon of ministry (which is the Spirit) is capable of bringing ministry out of many cultures. Without advocating either an antiquarianism or a progressivism we want to let the history of ministry stand forth in its broad contours. Edward Schillebeeckx has summed it up well:

> The actual form of the priestly office during the previous period of history is so closely interwoven with the understanding of faith in the same period that without a historical and hermeneutical approach all kinds of premature theological and pastoral conclusions might be deduced from it, conclusions which could completely inhibit any attempt to bring the pastoral office up to date.[2]

Our six periods represent six metamorphoses in ministry: (1) a move from communal diversity and universality to a small number of ministries with prominence given to the service of leadership (*episcopaliza-*

tion), and a further alteration of fulltime ministry to a sacral statement (*sacerdotalization*); (2) the reforming and ministerial expansion of the monastery (*monasticization*); (3) a dominance of one structure in the order of offices (*hierarchization*); (4) the interlude of the Reformation (*pastoralization* of ministry)—a movement which is anti-monastic and anti-priestly but still reductionist; (5) the Counter-Reformation's organization of ministry along the lines of Baroque papacy and spirituality; (6) the *romanticization* of the ministry in the nineteenth century.

Each of these processes has positive and negative facets. Although we can and must evaluate them in terms of their suitability for our times, we must also leave each in its own *kairos*. Each of these periods succeeded as an evangelistic incorporation of the Gospel. The rightness in structure of each was at its birth stronger than the limitations we now perceive.

The process of the history of Christian ministry, however, because it is human and historical, has limits. For the past thousand years or more it seems to have been a process of reduction, not of expansion. Up until 1962, cultural and ecclesial epochs seem to present less and less of the ministry.

1. From House Church to Basilica, from Minister to Bishop

The first example of structure in Christian ministry belongs to the churches of the first half century after Pentecost. Of their communal life we have fragments of information contained in Paul's letters and the *Acts of the Apostles*. Just as Jewish and Gentile, Romano-Gallic and Syrian communities viewed Jesus differently in their Christologies, so we can glimpse that their community life and structure assumed different concrete forms. Exegetes and social historians are now beginning to look not at the churches of Paul and Peter or of *Acts* and *Romans* but at churches of different ethnic and theological groupings, and at churches in different cities, e.g. Antioch, Jerusalem, Rome, about which we have some information.

By the end of the first century ministry underwent a movement toward less rich ministerial life, and this was joined to a growing emphasis upon the ministry of leadership as leadership is more and more drawn into the office and the term of *episkopos*, "bishop." Such a reduction to and centralization of ministry in leadership—what we might call its episcopalization—extends through two centuries. Different decades and different places take part in this process in diverse ways.

In the Syrian church of Ignatius of Antioch the bishop had acquired a dominant role by 110 A.D. There a monarchical ecclesiology with the three ministries we have today (bishop, presbyter, deacon) existed not far away in time from a more fluid church order described in *Ephesians* and then in the *Didache*. There was also the world of Rome whose writings (*Romans, Hebrews, 1 Clement*) show a confrontation with Jewish ideas of authority and priesthood.

After 100 A.D. not only did ministry of leadership become dominant but the elders, who had been collegial leaders of churches, became assistants to the bishop and then later individual leaders of lesser churches. Lesser ministers saw some variety reduced as they assisted the bishop and the community in liturgical and extra-liturgical service.

Persecution and gnosticism led the church to close ranks around their community leaders. The delay of the parousia meant a growth from a movement to a large body and this brought a reduced enthusiasm within the community. In the interim before the eschaton, the church faced the challenge of remaining faithful and evangelistic. The bishop came to prominence as the local church comprehended through its expansion that it was not a cell or a sect, but fully the church—salvation in a dying world, pointer to the eschaton.

In the century after 150 A.D. the church wanted organization; those who followed Jesus as ministers of Christ's people were called shepherds or presiders, then "overseers," and then "priests" of the *Pneuma*.[3] There is no doubt that the three ministries of bishop, elder and deacon find universally a central role, although local churches frequently add a further ministry of deaconess, widow or teacher. The elders had to assume broader roles as the vicars of the leader of an expanding urban church. While the prophets disappeared because of crises like Montanism, the deacon's proximity to the bishop as his social minister enhanced and preserved his position.

By the end of the second century there were Christians in all the social levels of the Empire. The first theological theoreticians had appeared by the turn of the third century—Tertullian in Africa, Hippolytus in Rome, Clement and Origen in Alexandria. The fulltime members of the ministry were occupied with considerable administrative burdens. Around 250 A.D. in Rome there were about fifty thousand Christians out of a population of a million. Carthage, Alexandria, Antioch, Ephesus must have had large Christian populations. Cornelius, the leader of the Roman church, complained about the ministerial complexity of that church with its forty-six presbyters, seven deacons, hundreds of lesser ministers and fifteen hundred people needing daily care.[4] Communities of diverse ethnic origins and theological interpretations employed a Roman centralization around the bishop of the city.[5]

In the middle of the second century, the church in Africa retained

a populist memory of charismatic life and universal priesthood in ministry. By the time of Cyprian's episcopacy in the next century, the bishop
in Carthage and elsewhere, still elected by the church and still consulting the community, is an important figure in both Christian and public
life. As bishop he is viewed, and views himself as priest and high-priest.
We will return below to this parallel sacerdotalization of the central
ministry of bishop. The bishop and his fulltime clergy are rather set off
from the masses. Origen in Alexandria, whatever the pneumatic or
gnostic sources might be, sees a dual movement in the church, one coming from the traditional triad of clergy and the other coming from ascetics, theologians and gnostics. Origen still speaks of a universal
priesthood of Christians (which he counterposes to the distinctly pagan
priestly elites), who live a priestly life created by the priestly function of
baptism.[6] For Origen, there are two factors which contribute to his re-
tention of a wider view of priesthood and ministry. The first is his scandal at the ambition and meanness of some of the Christian clergy; the
second is his natural preference for theology and doctrine realized in
teaching and preaching and nourished by asceticism. As the Roman African Cyprian represents the bishop as leader of the Eucharist and authority figure threatened by martyrdom, so Origen, the Hellenist
Egyptian, describes and encourages an ecclesial community which is re-
taining, retrieving but altering some of the diversity of the past.

The increasingly episcopal church is also a synodal church. The
bishop does not exist ministerially alone but as one joined in faith and
activity to several groups. He is joined to his own co-ministers and to
the church which selected him; he is joined also to the bishops of the
area, and then to those of his region and of the entire world.

If the ministries of leadership were absorbing earlier charismatic
services, by the second century it seems that the office of deacon was
diversifying itself. Readers and caretakers were needed for concrete
works. For a while the centralization and numerical expansion of the
church as well as the introduction of a more impressive liturgy enhanced the numbers and diversity of clergy and ministers. Singers and
ascetics, assisting ministers, readers and widows, swelled the ranks. But
by the fifth century this liturgical expansion of ministry was diminishing.[7]

The growth of the church led, in fact, to the diminution of the ministry. We cannot blame the ministers who were becoming in name and
reality a clergy. They were spending themselves in leading thousands
into the Body of Christ, into the chosen people of God open to all religions and sects and races of the empire. The clergy did not, however,

recognize or solve the problem of how to sustain charism and ministry in so many after they had been baptized.

Numbers brought passivity. The bishop and his presbyterial vicars not only led ministry, they absorbed it. This new style of leadership in an organized church finds a poignant example in the selection of Calixtus from the upper class of bankers to be bishop of Rome.[8]

Parallel to the episcopal centralization of the church with its reduction of ministerial diversity was the sacerdotalization of ministry. Two ministries, bishop (*episkopos*) and elder (*presbyteros*), became "priest" (*iereus, sacerdos*). Thus the radical rejection of sacral buildings and persons by the Christians awed at Jesus' own priesthood at Calvary did not long remain. Toward the end of the second century, Tertullian speaks of the bishop as *sacerdos,* but then adds:

> We should be wary of thinking that what in discipline is not permitted to priests is permitted to the laity. Even we laity—are we not priests? For it is written: "He has made of us a kingdom of priests for God the Father" (Apoc 1:6). The difference between *ordo* and *plebs* is set up by the authority of the church . . . but where the ecclesiastical *ordo* is not established, you offer and wash, you are your own priest; for where three are assembled there is the church even if the three are laity.[9]

A Christian priesthood does not suddenly replace ministries of leadership but cultural movements and theological emphases bring not a sacerdotal apostasy but a new, more sacral and sacerdotal perspective upon the ministry of leadership. Hervé Legrand observes:

> The perception of the president of the Eucharist as an explicitly sacerdotal figure is not attested before the beginning of the third century (Hippolytus, Tertullian, Cyprian). On the other hand, with all the witnesses we note that it is a fact, and most often it is axiomatic (Clement, Ignatius, Justin, Tertullian, Hippolytus, Cyprian and the canonical tradition deriving from Hippolytus) that those who preside over the life of the church preside at the Eucharist.[10]

The ministry of leading the community is not a dignity or an abstract power; ordination is for a community and so in its essence it must bear the facets of communal life—active service, diversity, charism. Two movements led to the metamorphosis of the permanent ministries of leadership into a priesthood. First, there was the natural desire in the midst of *sacerdotes* functioning in the cult of the emperor or in the cults

imported from Egypt to have a priesthood. More important were the
images and words of the Old Testament. In a largely Gentile church,
two centuries removed from the writings of *Hebrews* and *1 Corinthians*
the Old Testament was read ahistorically. An inspired page no longer
struck Christians as a forecast of fulfillment in Christ but as a divine
prescription; the Jewish hierarchy of high priest, priest, and levite was
admired by Clement of Rome, and then assumed as a theology of ministry a century later by Cyprian of Carthage. Of course, a purely sacerdotal hierarchy was what the first Christians had seen terminated in Jesus
Christ.

The role of the Eucharist in the centralization of bishop and priest
is important. The community leader is inevitably the leader of the
prominent, public Eucharist at the occasion when a large church gath-
ers. This priestly appearance has been strengthened not only by the
levitical sacerdotalism but by the image of the priesthood of Melchise-
dech. The emergence of a largely Eucharistic church exercised considerable influence upon the ministry. The Roman gift for distinction and
order ended not in a diversity of ministries within the community but in
a separation into two classes, clerical and lay. At Carthage, Cyprian
spoke of the purity required of the priests whose Eucharist was the continuation of the rites of the Old Testament. The Christian assembly
could be reinterpreted along Jewish lines: altar, temple, priests and cult
provided for the new sacrifice of the Christians. The figure of the bishop
as example and potential martyr and the Eucharist commemorating
Christ's sacrifice strengthened a priestly emphasis. More and more the
Sunday Eucharist was the substance of the community's meeting, the
work of its service. As the churches, large and episcopal, neared their
final persecutions and their liberation in the early fourth century, most
of the baptized met not in a home for word, sacrament, and evangelism
but they assembled passively to take part in the liturgical word and sacrament.

Significant in and illustrative of the shift in ministry to Eucharist
and priesthood is the move from house to basilica. The New Testament
speaks of houses or households which Paul greeted as centers of Christian community. There is the church in the house of Aquila and Priscil-
la (Rom 16:5; 1 Cor 16:19) and that of Nymphas (Col 4:15). In *Acts*
(1:13; 20:9) we gather that Christian assemblies for hearing the word
and for the Eucharist took place in upstairs rooms, a feature of Mediterranean households. Pierre du Bourguet observes:

> Thus, the point of departure in the evolution of early Christian art
> was not a sanctuary modeled on pre-Christian places of worship, nor

even directly on the rites established by Christ or the Apostles. On the contrary, it was naturally determined by the realities of the Christian life, lived within the broader context of life in general. In this respect, the only guidance to be derived from the words and even the example of Christ consists in the two complementary activities of teaching the doctrine and celebrating the Eucharist. The doctrine could be taught anywhere, but more easily in a place reserved for the interested public.[11]

The tendency must have been to prolong such gatherings to discuss the needs of the community; the celebration of the Eucharist which might involve the serving of a meal required the use of fairly spacious quarters available in the home of one of the Christians. The usage was simply an extension of Christ's acceptance of hospitality from a disciple and of his institution of the Eucharist in the upper room.

With the community's consciousness of being the Spirit's temple, there had been no need for sacral buildings. The early Christian apologists boasted that they had "no temple, no altar, no image of God."[12] The Eucharist is not held at any one mythical place. The church is the members with their charisms. Christians met in ordinary rooms in private houses, their own or their masters'.[13] As the number of Christians increased in Rome, tenement apartments of three stories were purchased, and the upper floor cleared for a large meeting room. Only in the third century do we have any evidence that houses were fully set aside for worship and meeting, buildings reserved and decorated. While some of the first Roman communal meeting places were from the world of apartments and guild halls of the lower classes, even these depended upon Christian patrons for purchase, rent and upkeep. Other communities, like those at the Flavian palace (San Clemente), were permitted to use rooms in the palaces of their masters. The micromorphology of the early churches—a morphology of diversity—is only beginning to be explored. We know that the dynamic of the community was one of diversity, and not separation. The assembly of sociologically separate classes as well as the universal gift of the Spirit and call to ministry must have been challenging. The internal and institutional needs of the community were limited precisely because the ministerial expectations were external: a place for instruction, for meditative reading and preaching, for washings and anointings and commissionings, for meals and Eucharist.

In the third century, the expanded house church was still the meeting place of the community, but by the year 300 A.D. Christians apparently had buildings publicly set apart for their use. When the church entered undisturbed into the life of the Empire, it looked for larger buildings. The Christians took over not a model of a temple but the plan of the Roman civil assembly hall, the basilica.

> The Roman civil basilica, especially in view of its extremely flexible plan, . . . could serve either as public building, with or without aisles, or simply as a covered or open space, with or without arcades, while at one end stood a bench for the magistrates or a throne for the emperor or his venerated image. . . . As early as the second century the form was being adapted to the purposes of the religious sects that were free to build. . . . Thus without excluding the possibility of a religious note, the basilica had nothing in common with the official pagan temples.[14]

The basilica offered light, mobility and a focal point for the bishop. The entrance into this large tripartite hall, whose lines drew one forward to the bishop's word, molded the community into laity and ministers. There was still a diversity of ministries but they were distinct from the large numbers assisting at the Eucharist, worship and baptism. Their roles and the growing custom of celibacy enhanced a liturgy ecclesiologically inward-looking and newly sacral.

> The outward life of the church grew ever more specialized. Constantine's conception of his own role—as the thirteenth apostle—and the imperial favor resulted in the grafting of court customs onto religious ceremony. The liturgy became imperial, places were set aside for the most important members of the cult . . . , which led to a sharper distinction between clergy and laity. Christ, savior of the meek, had become the emperor of heaven.[15]

The ministerial climax to this ecclesial process was the constitution in the middle of the fourth century of Christian bishops as officials of the Roman Empire.

From our perspective we can see that success also brought loss: in charismatic and ministerial participation and diversity. For the laity, the expansion of the church and the sacerdotalization of the clergy brought inversely a spiritualization of their Christian faith and life. The symbolic, the sacramental and liturgical, the interior and ethical—these became the touchstones of being a Christian. The Christian evangelized now not professionally through word and deed but through the justice and charity of his or her life. After turbulent centuries the organization of the church brought Roman order, modest diversity, and liturgical membership where earlier there had been community, pneumatic discernment, ministerial diversity, and charismatic individuality.

2. The Monastery as Minister

The conversion of the Franks and the Visigoths to the Catholic faith gave birth to national, regional and ethnic churches for whom Semitic, Hellenist or Roman culture provided little material for ecclesiology. Germanic society offered new forms. These new national churches had to survive centuries of invasions to win their independence from new masters. The papacy became the advocate of the church because the pope was one of the few forces which could sustain the independence of the local church. It is not, however, the power of the papacy which interests us but the source of papal efforts to reform and strengthen the local church in the West: monasticism. Gregory the Great and Gregory VII, popes at either end of a time of turmoil, were both monks. To a church whose diocesan structure was weak and whose local clergy was feebly prepared, the great monasteries and monastic families must have appeared as the church itself.

The ministry of the local church was of course in the hands of priests and bishops. The bishops were in one of two positions: either they struggled against being controlled by princes, or they were themselves part of the feudal principate. The priests, prepared by an almost formless education, were sent to serve in eras of social upheaval and to find a place in a civil as well as ecclesiastical feudalism. Many of the important bishops, popes and theologians—Hincmar, Anselm, Hildebrand—had been monks. Monastic renewal for the local church came not from their ambition but from their desire to revitalize the offices of bishop and priest. In the renewal of these offices the monk became the tutor of the minister. From the fourth century on, certain bishops such as Martin of Tours, Paulinus of Nola, and Augustine of Hippo had favored a monastic life for their priests. By 814 councils were urging the spirit and life of the monk upon the diocesan clergy and this movement reached a further stage in the transformation of the clergy into canons regular. Hildebrand argued at the Roman Council in 1074 for vows of poverty for the clergy, an imitation of the life of the Twelve, and for an embrace of the monastic common life.[16]

In these centuries of instability, local bishops could not have competed with the resources of the monastery. The great cathedral schools were, in format and theology, monastic. Influenced by Origen and Pseudo-Denys there were many proponents of the ecclesiology that monasticism was the first class in the church. In the East and in Celtic Christianity the monastic community was the normal ambiance for church and ministry. As the end of the first millennium was crossed, the monastery set the tone for the church. Monastic sites were frequently remote. Away from centers of a population ravaged by the centuries before 1000 A.D., they were secure islands for prayer, contemplation and spiritual reading. Remoteness discouraged dangerous visitors while austerity both amplified asceticism and nourished life.

In the monastery there occurred both a feudalization of the ministry and a sacerdotalization of monasticism. Ministry was reduced to jobs within the monks' community and to liturgical priesthood. The great liturgies and the private Mass were ministry par excellence. In some ways the monastery itself became the Christian ministry. In the midst of unexplored country or social chaos the monastic group was able to preserve order and learning, aid communication by furnishing hospitality to travelers, and enlarge the borders of Christianity by missionary evangelization. The monastery took on the ministry of deacon by offering aid to the poor, instruction in agriculture and the arts, and by uncovering land and other resources for social growth. The life of faith and grace could be served not only by prayer but by better techniques in the apiary and by new manuscripts arriving for copying in the scriptorium.

The art historian K. J. Conant writes:

> The larger monasteries laid the foundation of economic recovery in Europe after the Dark Ages; they presented intricate administrative problems and were accepted schools for men of business and government. In addition they were the training places for talent in the arts, and the refuge of intellectual activity.

> Thus the monasteries did yeoman service in creating all four of the bases on which medieval civilization was to rest: (1) economic revival, (2) the fusion of the Latin and the Teutonic peoples . . . , (3) the afterlife of Roman law in the monastic rule, the canon law of the Church, and the Holy Roman Empire, (4) the feudal system, which set up new hierarchies of power, and enabled the monastic orders to extend their influence and their benefits generally.

> The great monasteries, thus developing as imposing financial, educational, and territorial corporations, were far larger, more complex, and more influential than they had ever been in antiquity. Since many of their architectural problems were new, their architecture became the living and growing architecture of the time.[17]

The monasteries of the Carolingian and Gregorian eras, of St. Gall and Cluny, were striking in their solid buildings and vertical towers. They were symmetrical arrangements of hotels, libraries, dormitories, gardens, refectories, farm buildings and workshops; the center of all was the abbey church where the monks, and at times the wider community of laybrothers and laypeople, met for the divine office and sacramental liturgy. Some ministries survived only as names in the abbatial liturgy when acolytes, cantors, readers and subdeacons joined priests and deacons around the altar. The liturgy as *opus Dei* was the main ministry to grace—an iconic form in word and sacrament for all levels of Christian society. To serve this world other offices emerged with new names and pragmatic functions: abbot, abbess, prior, hebdomadarian, porter, cellarer and procurator.

The monasteries expanded and developed daughter houses. In good times and bad, the monastery was a fortress or haven not only for faith but for culture. A feudal world existed around the monastery which constituted a city in itself, a sacramental anticipation of the city of God. In short, the direction of ministry was from the monastery rather than to it from the local church. The monastery did send out apostles to evangelize pagan lands, but that meant that the very form of the church brought by Kilian or Boniface was from its inception largely monastic. At home stability and maturity drew Christians to the abbey. As a place of ministry the monastic community was a mentor, an inspiration, a magnet.

With no competitors, monastic theology and monastic spirituality influenced all areas of the church. The cathedral schools of Chartres and Rheims were monastic not only in celibacy and liturgy but in their approach to theology.[18] Even devotional literature written for laity and bishops depicted a Christian life whose model was the Benedictine Order. A new beginning in the life of grace, i.e. a personal conversion in adulthood, usually meant entering not the ministry but religious life. Conversion came not in the style of a Thomas More or a Francis Xavier but in that of entering a cloister. Men and women left behind the worldly struggle of knight and lady, of overseeing keep and lands, and renounced all by entering the separate, monastic island. The monastic monopoly of Christian life could not help but color those in fulltime Christian service and office.

The widespread appropriation of monastic theology could only have an enormous effect upon the ministry. As the life-style of the ministry was monastic, so too was the training for ministry and for ecclesial expression in liturgy. Monastic theology encouraged directions which led away from society and reality also: allegorical and moral hermeneutics of faith, liturgies which were an acceptance of the cycle of life and death or an anticipation of a next, better heaven. Sometimes reality and activity in grace, in sacrament and service, became secondary. Ultimately, monasticism meant separation from the world, and the secular clergy did not always resolve well the dialectic of withdrawal and service.

The results of the monasticization of ministry were several. First, the bishop came to resemble an abbot rather than a coordinator of ministries. He was the father of his people and clergy, the spiritual director of his priests. Coloring this modification of the bishop's role was a second shift from ministry to jurisdictional position. In the West, monasticism more and more defined the leader of the community as a figure of authority and order. In the East, the monastic leader was such because he was recognized as a leader in the life of the spirit and contemplation, but in the West appointment to jurisdiction replaced proven spirituality. A person canonically installed in a church office—whether abbot or bishop—was presumed to have the accompanying charisms. Searching and testing for the right person for a specific position was slowly abandoned. Juridical appointment rendered discernment of nature and grace secondary. We have here the beginning of a great reversal: symbols and legal positions dispensed grace rather than grace begetting life through charisms realized in office and service.

Second, the Christian life was seen not as a life of activity or ministry in the public forum but as an inner spiritual life where all were urged to practice monastic detachment and contemplation. The services of the local community apart from the Eucharist and other sacraments were hours of the monastic liturgy, e.g., Vespers, Matins. Since the sixth century the popularity of urban monasticism gradually replaced the old cathedral liturgies. The prayer of the secular clergy became the monastic office, and by the eleventh the private recitation of the monastic hours was expected.[19] The cleric's clothes and vestments were monastic. Arguments between lack of religious distinction in public image and excessive worldliness were resolved in favor of dress and grooming which appropriated many monastic elements.[20]

Celibacy was urged by Rome, and the monasticization of diocesan life could only be of assistance in this. Cathedral and rectory had the qualities of a monastic enclosure, the cloister. Since celibacy appeared as essential to monastic life, there was an inevitable drive within a secular ministerial group to nourish celibacy, to survive in that style of life through the assistance of community life. The designated model of the canons in the eleventh and twelfth centuries, the reformation of the Oratorians in the sixteenth, the originality of Sulpicians, Paulists and Maryknoll in the modern era—each illustrates this tendency of celibate life to move toward religious life.

Even if official church ministries were drawn into timeless liturgy, the prophetic spirit of a marginal life—a life which had first attracted Benedict and Bernard and other ministers of evangelization—did not die out. Pilgrimage and crusade were a kind of ministry in motion. More important was the large number of Christian men and women who took the road to preach, imitating Christ's poverty and the mission of the Twelve. Around 1144, a German priest complained to Bernard of Clairvaux that these evangelicals would do only what Scripture recorded of Christ and the Apostles. Eighty years later a leader of the "Pauperes Christi" exclaimed to his followers: "If anyone should ask to which religious order you belong, answer, 'the Order of the Gospel of Christ.' "[21] These preaching movements were a temporary liberation for public ministry but they were also a source of error (ignorance more than heresy), disorder and immorality. What could have been a large movement of free ministry was channeled into society and the church through two preachers: Francis and Dominic slowly formed a new, post-monastic style of religious life.[22] Balancing the monastic influence, eventually surpassing it and even rivaling the bishops, for Thomas Aquinas the educated mendicants were ministers. Professors were ministers of the Word par excellence; preachers were to be educated in serious study, and academic teachers were ministers of the official church.[23]

The sturdy romanesque monasteries which preserved and nourished the faith and culture of Europe had an impact on ministry which lasts to this day. Many rubrics, clothes and institutions which appear to us to be eternally ecclesial and deeply Christian are monastic and Romanesque. The monastery, source and standard for ministry, drew people to the inner life of the soul and to eschatological liturgy; it assumed or absorbed the diversity of the ministry. The monastery, which had begun as an exceptional outpost in an expanding church of martyrs and preachers, became the church itself.

3. The Ministry as Hierarchy

During the twelfth century the context of ministry as well as the igneous core of Christian society moved from the monastic to the clerical, from contemplative community to individual priesthood defined by the real presence in the Eucharist. Yves Congar writes of the theological implications:

> The theology of monasticism, for instance of a St. Bernard, remains in the stream of the fathers and the liturgy. The theology of the schools, analytic and dialectical, however, reorientates itself towards the reality of things towards their nature, status, place. . . . In the

theology of grace, for instance, we pass from a point of view which is
dynamic and personal (the act of God) to a point of view more sta-
tionary and reified (our supernatural ontology).[24]

After centuries of chaos, the renaissances of the twelfth and thirteenth centuries brought order. Feudalism had fought simply to hold
together the social fabric, but now the *ordo* of medieval society was
prized for its own vitality and beauty. Parallels were drawn between the
cosmos and the structure of that society. The metaphysicians proclaimed that being, beauty, and truth were one, while political philosophers saw the same harmony in social life. What *ordo* and *scientia* were
to philosophy and theology, *corpus* and *societas* were to church and
state. As in a luminous north rose window where every segment has its
own identity and yet contributes to the blue pattern of the Old Testament culminating in Mary and Child, so the medieval mind delighted in
arrangement; in the "natural places" of peasant, priest, merchant,
knight, prince and pope.[25]

The theology of the church was not of major import for Aquinas
although he treats ecclesiology within the theologies of grace and faith,
Spirit and sacrament. For an explicit treatment of ecclesial forms we
must turn to questions on Lombard's *Sentences,* to the end of the middle part of the *Summa theologiae,* and finally to Aquinas' commentaries
on Pauline letters.

The philosophical source for the ecclesiology of the Middle Ages
was largely the quasi-mythical Denys the Areopagite. The educated citizens of Paris believed the legend of Saint Denys, patron of Paris. This
bishop was the same Dionysius converted by Paul on the Athenian Are-
opagus (Acts 13:33ff); he found his way to Roman Paris and evangelized its citizens; before he died he wrote mystical treatises among
which are *The Divine Names, The Celestial Hierarchy,* and *The Ecclesiastical Hierarchy,* works in fact composed by a Neoplatonist Syrian
monk from the sixth century. As a result of his legend, Denys' synthesis
of Christian and Platonist forms held a singular position not only in
theology but in the entire cultural world of Paris. In mysticism, aesthetics and ecclesiology, in politics and papal theory, the Areopagite's influence was unassailable. His thought-form was hierarchy. "Hierarchy was
the Dionysian world itself . . . hierarchy makes life intelligible and possible."[26]

Hierarchy was the structural model of public and ecclesiastical life
in the thirteenth century.[27] A number of social classes constructed the
corpus of society, and within the church three orders—deacon, priest,
bishop—survivors of time, gave ecclesial aesthetic diversity. There were

other offices too: abbess, abbot, archbishop, archdeacon, pope, canon, friar and provincial. Ecclesial ministry was a public dignity and a state of life inserted into the wider social hierarchy.

From his teacher, Albert, Aquinas learned to prize the Areopagite's works; he commented on them and his first work was a hierarchical metaphysics of the levels of being from rocks to God, the *De ente et essentia*. Hierarchy, Aquinas observed, comes from two words, "sacred" and "principle."[28] In a hierarchy, "a sacred principate," are ordered the apostles and all other prelates of the church. The church's hierarchy does not agree perfectly with the angelic one but there is a similarity in pattern.

The church's contribution to hierarchy is the threefold ecclesial office. Earlier authorities had shown Aquinas the magic in three: three persons in the Trinity, three times three choirs among angels. Aquinas sees three sacred activities in the church: the minister purifies, the priest illumines and purifies, the bishop brings to perfection and illumines in a special way. If monks are on a rung beneath this hierarchy of active office, Aquinas argued that his Dominican friars should approach episcopal rank for they are the pope's preachers.[29]

The highest in the hierarchy is the bishop; at the ordination, Denys observed, the Scriptures are placed over the head of this high priest to show both that he receives the fullness of light and that he illumines all.[30] With the angels as analogue and with a Neoplatonic metaphysics of light as model (and encouraged by his own personal vocation of teaching) Aquinas described the ecclesial hierarchy as a ladder of descending illumination. The lower is perfected, illumined, directed by actions moving downwards but not upwards. The higher illumines the lower because such is the pattern coming from the Trinity and the angels.[31]

When this form and dynamic is applied to the church, office speaks and acts only downward. Diversity is vertical in direction. Service has become authority. A deacon and priest can make no contribution to the bishop. A higher office and order contains the lower *eminenter*. What could a lower order contribute to a higher one which possesses all beneath it? Movement upward in illumination or sacred action is impossible because it is redundant. We see here the pyramid of hierarchy replacing the circle of different charisms. The bishop is a divine or angelic principle within his system of orders, the church. Not only are the other ministries silent before him but he illumines and vivifies (if not creates) them out of his being and grace.[32] Community is not a cooperative diversity, a Body of Christ, but a fixed arrangement, a medieval heavenly Jerusalem.

The second facet in this "sacred principate" is the sacral. One enters the hierarchy to the extent that one has an active relation to sacred things. The center of the sacral world, the *sacrosanctissimum,* is the Eucharist. The three ministries are offices of the hierarchy because each has a real, physical function vis-à-vis the Eucharistic liturgy.[33] There is, however, in Aquinas' thought an unresolved tension. To distinguish bishop from priest, he emphasizes the teaching and preaching of the latter (for both can absolve sins and consecrate bread and wine); and yet, in his drawing of the threefold hierarchy from the sacred, he selects the Eucharist. Scholars agree that Aquinas' depiction of the bishop is complex and even inconsistent, for he instinctively leads the episcopacy to the word while theologically he reduces it to a higher form of priesthood.

Ministerial reduction perdured. Not only was the ministry formally limited to bishop and priest but it has been reduced to serving a single event of priesthood, the Eucharist. Yet, we can see how right this aesthetical ecclesiology was for the Middle Ages. The cathedral was a meeting place for the entire society gathered around a vivifying principle: priest and sacrament. The people rejoiced in the visual transmission of their faith through art, and through art in motion, liturgy. Out of liturgy came theater; out of social order in diversity came a peaceful process of urbanization with a new middle class. All of this anticipated the beauty of a city and a society yet to come; the paradigm of life was not action but being and event, an anticipation of what Dante ascending through hierarchical spheres described as beatitude. Beauty and life flowed from order.

Aquinas' society replaced the biblical *diakonia* (with its overtones of ordinary serving) by Roman legal terms such as *status, officium* and *ordo.* The second part of the great *Summa* treated the human person returning to God, its source and goal in grace. Aquinas offered a psychology of intellectual and emotional life, and on this foundation he built his theology of Christian life. We would expect him to have concluded this graced anthropology with activity drawn from charism and related to ministry. Evidently, in the thirteenth century a different conclusion seemed obvious. "We will now consider," he wrote, "the variety of states and offices of human beings."[34] The Christian life ends not with ministry but with social states of life.[35]

In the thirteenth century a certain ossification of order entered, fixing ministerial activity in the flintier structure of priestly hierarchy. In the patristic age *ordo* had tones of the organic and corporate and collegial, but in medieval life it meant the public transmission of power in ordination. The Roman *ordo* illustrates in metamorphoses of meaning the movement from *diakonia* to *officium*.[36] In the thirteenth century an ecclesiastical office contained two things: the work and the dignity following upon the work. Aquinas placed the action within the public institutional personality of the role; for instance, the dignity which accrues to the bishop is not simply an occasional reward but a position in medieval society. In this difficult section Aquinas strove to show how an individual achieved a stable place to radiate grace. What strikes us is the accomplished shift from charismatic individuality and diversity to single stability, the uncertainty of whether life or role defines an office, and the location of ministerial grace and deed in the bishop. Congar writes:

> Thomas had a vision of a pyramidical structuring of the body of the church from parish to universal church, a dynamic passing through deanery, diocese and province based upon the ideas of the time. But he did not follow the secular academics who pieced out authority to sections of the church. . . . Thomas re-established a hierarchical structure, a structure oriented towards the bishops and the troops.[37]

The facade of a French cathedral contains the thought-forms of its time, and presents a diversity of elements in a vertical unity. The lines of the facade of Notre Dame de Paris express theology and ontology; its beauty comes precisely from diversity within order conveying at the same time an impression of stability and transcendence. A vertical dynamic of lines reaches upwards, diminishing in variety but increasing in a single power, suggesting a society where historicity was not prominent, but where knowledge and belief in the transcendent were. The levels of the facade and the lines present hierarchy, one reaching from the materialistic realism of the new Aristotelianism to the Trinity of the Greek mystics. The finite was shot through with grace; symbol and reality pointed to the next life. The laity are invited to the cathedral not to act but to see. They are separate from the clergy. Yet hierarchical forms, too, were forms for grace.[38] Because he was a genius, Aquinas' theology contains two openings towards other interpretations of ministry. First, he underscored with his thought on ecclesial states, sacramental orders and the gifts of the Spirit a diversity in the Body; second, by casually noting that some treatments of church and ministry belong to the human polity of canon law ("For the study of offices so far as it pertains to other acts is a matter for jurists; and so far as it pertains to the sacred ministry it is a matter of orders"[39]), he suggested a legitimate re-expression of ministry in diverse cultural forms.

For Thomas Aquinas, the church was the effect and the place of

grace. His ecclesiological interests were not foremost people in ministerial action but unity, and harmony, stability, hierarchy and sacramentality. In them the social and the ministerial became the beautiful.

4. The Reformation of Ministry

The Reformation was a religious protest against the localization of
the activity of God in the human and created. It was also a pastoral
program to renew the life of the local church. Not everyone will agree
with the negative picture Piet Fransen draws from the Middle Ages, but
his location of the causes of ministerial decline in early barbarian and
medieval culture is stimulating.

> The priesthood, implanted in a society issuing from the barbarian
> kingdoms, having doubtlessly profited from its involvement in the
> world around it, began to display more and more clearly after the
> dawn of a new epoch, that is, after the end of the 14th century, the
> profound defects of its accommodation to the barbarian world. It
> could even be maintained, though with necessary modifications, that
> from this epoch onwards the history of the priesthood has been re-
> duced—apart from some periods of reform and intense renewal—to a
> slow process of detachment from a shell which was also a burden.[40]

The Reformers were inspired by the description of the early church in
the New Testament and they worked to renew the ministry according to
that model. They challenged celibacy and monasticism so that they
might abolish the class system within the church. Luther preached the
priesthood of all the baptized and the dignity of every human occupation: being a farmer or a prince was ministry. As Luther rediscovered
ministerial freedom and sacerdotal universality in the New Testament
he championed in the early years of the Reformation the admission of
all into the ministry. Baptism into the priesthood of all believers was
sufficient for community preachers and leaders. But when faced with
charismatic and social excesses, Luther, frightened by the *Schwärmer*,
expounded a conservative reformation and insisted upon a distinct pastorate and ordination. He wrote in 1539:

> Let everyone who knows himself to be a Christian be assured of this,
> that we are all equally priests, that is to say, we have the same power
> in respect to the Word and the sacraments. However no one may
> make use of this power except by the consent of the community or by
> the call of a superior.[41]

Calvin struggled to transform a city into a Christian community and to transform Christian life and worship into an assembly of citizens. In the Calvinist reform, there would be no hierarchy, no sacrifice, no mediator. A complete de-sacerdotalization would take place. The ministry focused not on the Eucharist but on the word of the Christian community. The word and its service were priestly, and the minister of the word administered the Eucharist.[42] Calvin drew out of the pages of the New Testament four ministries: pastor (shepherd), deacon, elder and teacher. Yet his churches did not succeed in maintaining a true diversification of the ministry. One ministry, the pastor, absorbed the others. The offices of elder and deacon did involve laity but without successfully eliminating the division between clergy and laity. Deacons, elders, vicars, wardens, even bishops were in the last analysis honorary or parochial pastimes. Entrusted with minimal ministry, the Calvinist laity more and more justified their ministry in the professions of secular life. Paradoxically, the churches of the Reformation were left with fewer ministries than the medieval church. Unconsciously they seemed to have taken in the idea that there was only one ministry—not priest, but pastor.

Reformation ministry cultivated the characteristics of freedom and identity as it replaced the sacral-monastic with the secular. But support by the state could control ministry, and anti-sacerdotalism could end in passive support for the spirituality of the European bourgeoisie. The marriage of the clergy did not automatically liberate the minister from an oppressive monastic world for greater service to the Gospel. The Protestant clergy never lost aspects of monasticism. The manse, the close, the identification of the pastor's life with that of the church buildings and the pressures upon the pastor's family all led to a manner of life which was both married and quasi-monastic.

The Protestant desire to reform the local church along New Testament lines was incomplete, limited by the cultural situation holding sway at the beginning of modern society. Protestant ministry remains a mixture of elements from the New Testament and medieval forms in a context which risks being too secular.

After its praise of the secular vocation, the Protestant church had difficulty halting the identification of ministry with Western profession, difficulty with keeping a transcendence in the sacrament and service of its minister. A certain secularity and bourgeois ethos was a fallout from the Reformation. The minister failed at times to present a clear identity which was different from the family man or emerging social worker. Either the liturgical expression or the apostolic life-style or the depth of diaconal sacrifice might be missing from the minister—a man identified with the middle class. The furnishings of a Calvinist or Methodist church might be little different from those of a law court or theater; the minister's clothes were no different from a banker's suit or an academic's gown. What was the identity of the Protestant ministry, in England in the eighteenth century and in Sweden in the nineteenth? In short, what did the minister do?

The Protestant theology of ministry had embarked in the sixteenth century upon a not yet finished search for a ministry in free, modern society. It succeeded in some periods and countries, mainly within a homogeneous, middle-class pietism in small towns and country. As that breaks up, the ministry is challenged anew from both sides, from the charismatic and fundamentalist movements, from secular and naturalistic presumptions. The minister is challenged by the sacral and by the personal.

Parallel to this secularization of the ministry ran a second current which reacted to a new bondage for the church. It tried and tries today to restore the New Testament vision of ministry. The "radical reformation" and its heirs hoped to form a church which really did resemble the churches in *Acts* and *1 Corinthians.* Pietism, all manner of fundamentalisms, charismatic and healing churches pursued, in a sometimes tattered way, the theology that charisms come to all and lead to ministry for the community, that there are many ministries and that a church had an outer evangelical life as well as an inner one lived on Sunday. In the small congregations praying in simple buildings in towns and cities there survives an appreciation of the universality of ministry; there the baptized give commitment of intellect, money and time. These fellowships of charism and ministry may not understand that bizarre charisms rank below those which persevere in bringing help. In such Christian communities, however, we often find members, at great personal expense, evangelizing in foreign countries, and we find a personal and verbal service in institutions and an eager hospitality. What they lack is the bond to the wider church, past and present. These churches do not often survive cultural change nor do they spread far. Today they become large organizations and undergo the electronic metamorphosis into televised revivals. But beneath the exaggerations and the hucksterism, beneath the narrowness and superficiality there can be found in Protestant fundamentalism echoes of the New Testament's understanding of ministry: a world of ordinary people expecting charisms, and willing to serve their community and change the world.

5. Ministry and Baroque

From fragile beginnings and uncertain hopes, the Catholic Counter-Reformation developed into a major movement in European history. A world-view both religious and aesthetic took shape. The Baroque expressed well the new Roman Catholic spirituality through which a renewed Catholicism proclaimed that grace was indeed present in personality and world. Baroque impetuses produced sanctity and evangelism. Mission into all parts of the discovered Indies sprang up, as did communities and monasteries of renewal in Europe. Baroque sculpture, architecture, painting, theater and literature were employed as the vehicles of the ideas of the Counter-Reformation in spirituality and theology. The architectural formation of space and light resembled the same ethos created by the *Spiritual Exercises* of Ignatius Loyola.

Baroque aesthetics cultivated movement among figures and was fascinated with detail, and yet its works never lost their single focus. Baroque theology paid attention to theological method and arrangement and to the treatise on grace, while Baroque ecclesiology both expanded the Roman church enormously and fastened its organization upon a single bishop. Precise scholastic concepts and Aristotelian logical rigor combined with the Baroque love of detail to organize the theory, administration and law of the popes.

That Roman Catholicism could renew itself was a surprise. This happened less through the procrastinating Council of Trent than through the lives of thousands of people caught up in a new spirituality and missionary spirit. The austerity of Calvinism, the dualism of Luther, in short, the Protestant spiritualities which kept God and humanity apart, were successful as reform but less attractive as on-going Christian life. In the Mediterranean world, where sacramentality was preferred to sober secularity, the new Baroque was a continuation of the Renaissance and it cultivated the interplay of spirit and grace.

The theology and personal spirituality of the Society of Jesus influenced the church greatly for several centuries, setting the tone for much of what was new and vital. Through the creative power of the Baroque and the energy of the Jesuits, the Roman Catholic world gained new fields for its ministries. Because this cultural epoch faded into the theological impoverishment of the eighteenth century it received no critique, was not clearly replaced and never truly ended. So its influence lasted on—often without notice. Much of what Roman Catholics came to perceive as patristic or medieval in the church's liturgy and organization came in fact from seventeenth century Baroque.

The Baroque loved detail and arrangement, striving to express the infinite in the visual; it loved the play of light and water in the context of space and marble. In the Baroque, the hierarchical combined with the organic to give both life and motion as well as the arrangements of many pieces. Whether in a piazza's buildings and fountains or in the interior ensemble of St. Peter's Basilica, we find many diverse elements related to a single point which gives them all meaning.[43] It is not hard to see these Baroque motifs in the theology, ecclesiology and spirituality of the seventeenth century.

Baroque ecclesiology had begun the reform called for by Trent. In a central codification in liturgy and canon law, in catechetics and conciliar teaching we find great diversity arranged around one center. A Baroque theology of the ministry has two principles: first, the organization of the church in detail around the papacy; second, the designation of the interior life of grace as the object of Christian ministry. The structural form of a universal episcopacy and a post-Reformation spirituality meet in their rejection of the Reform itself.

Intent upon church renewal, the Baroque church took organization seriously. The Roman church would be an expression of the Body of Christ, but precisely as a rational, efficient arrangement of all the enterprises of the church around the papacy as its departments, arms, representatives and ambassadors. Just as medieval theology introduced slowly the idea of the pope as vicar not only of Peter but of Christ, and therefore the head of *the* church, so the corpus of the church seems to be in an exemplary way the Vatican. Into new offices of curial administration—for evangelism, for religious orders, for seminaries—the ministries of the universal and local church were drawn.

Trent affirmed in the face of Protestantism that Christ is not only redeemer, he is also law-giver. In this vein, by encouraging a type of bishop who is pastoral, Trent favored the construction of a hierarchical order, not only around the Eucharist, but one around a regimen where Rome was center and summit. In its well-intentioned and successful attempt to salvage Roman Catholicism in Europe and the new worlds, the ecclesiology of the papacy brought an end to its counterpart, the local church. The idea of a fairly independent church (or network of churches) with its own geographical and cultural identity seemed dangerous. Was not diversity the root of Protestantism? Moreover, was not Protestantism grounded in too high an appreciation of charism and upon an experimentation with new forms of ministry? What diversity had survived through the medieval period was mainly ended by Trent. Local meant schismatic; diverse meant Protestant. This era would be that of the church which was "One."

The papacy was the organizing principle and it found diversity in

new religious orders and curial offices, not in ministries. Many new orders for men and women came into being in the century after 1540.
They took as their purpose not monastic contemplation nor the general
goals of the friars, e.g. prayer, study and intellectual life, but they were
founded for a precise work in the church such as the education of or-
phans and the direction of retreats, many embracing the style of the Society of Jesus.

The new emphasis upon personal conversion and method in prayer
led many to the ministry through religious life. Ministry became less the
activity of baptism, charism or local church and more a call to the
vowed life which places the baptized not in a cloister or in a fixed state
of public dignity but in a missionary post. There was a great deal to be
done in and by the church; for the first time in a thousand years, the
church was called upon to be extra-European. Not only was ministry a
gift of the spirit to adults called to religious life, but vocation was a gift
of the papacy and of its representatives. A participative theology of the
ministry passed over the role of the community to find the source of
ministry in the universal bishop of Rome, and in his local vicars, the
bishops. Not only as discerner and coordinator but as a source, a bishop
was seen to share parcels of his ministry, the only real ministry, with
other Christians, i.e. with priests. We can see that ministries to evangelize Indians in Brazil, to the dying in a hospital, to slaves in Jamaica, to
homeless girls, and to the university or rural parish were all in the one
ministry bestowed by the one minister.

Ministry was something possessed by the church like the Eucharistic bread, and it was distributed carefully. The presumption was that
the Holy Spirit remotely guided this distribution, but ultimately the
public aspect of ministry appeared to come not from the charisms of the
Spirit nor from the community. The necessary and healthy introduction
of the Tridentine seminary supported this monoform delegation of ministry. Rather than being called by adult charism to a specific ministry, a
young man was formed in a perennial theology and life-style so that at a
special moment he could be given a share of priestly fire. Charism, diversity and testing by experience and by the community had disappeared—not out of malice or heresy but because Trent empowered
them to act as papal delegates. Rome's task was an impossible one: to be
incarnate in hundreds of cultures. This weight of cultural incarnation
was avoided, however, by clothing the Gospel in a single language, law
and theology—that of Rome. The missions were no longer the world of
the fourth or ninth centuries when Europe was evangelized through
new local churches with their admirable bishops. The faith was propagated in the seventeenth century as the extension of Rome. The minis-

try was tied to a certain form of education, to celibacy, to Western rituals. The leaders of the new churches of Africa, Asia and South America were papal vicars, and local ministry never really surfaced.

There are successes in this approach, and also tragedies. In 1614 in Japan, there were 300,000 Christians, but less than one hundred Japanese priests.[44] The sudden persecution quickly and easily eliminated the ministry, and with it most of the church. The Christians who survived did so in small groups deprived of all sacramental life except baptism. That would not have happened in the third or sixth century, with Cyprian or Boniface, when bishops and ministers could rise out of the communities and adjust liturgy, leadership and theology to local conditions.

What was the Baroque ministry? What did it serve? Like the Reform, the Counter-Reformation was interested in the topic of grace. Ministry was service to grace, and grace was a power which came from God to move the free but fallen human will. Salvation was the believing obedient response to grace. This grace, however, did not find its goal only in faith but, for Catholics, extended through all of life. The individual, whether in the Alps of Bavaria or in the Andes of Peru, walked into a Baroque church and was absorbed into the Baroque theology of grace through the light which poured down into the figures of saints in white and gold. The atmosphere of the church militant on earth reflected the church triumphant in heaven. For the average person, the life of grace was a struggle for a modicum of morality, chastity and charity. For a more serious Christian (and the invitation was open to all) the life of grace was the inner life; the source and goal of ministry was the interior castle; daily meditation led into darkness and then light. The Baroque spontaneously seized upon two groups as exemplary saints: the missionaries who brought grace to nations ignorant of it, and the spiritual directors who guided Europeans into the mystery of the interior life.

This shift in the meaning of grace away from an extra-subjective, public, developmental kingdom of God to the motive force of an interior life assisted in the separation of the public from the spiritual, the secular citizen from the inner believer. Despite the glories of Spanish, Bavarian and the Italian Baroque, much of the world came to be seen as places of dark and stubborn hostility dominated by Calvinism and then by the Enlightenment. The outer world was evaluated in this model of ministry to Catholic spirituality as secular, Protestant, even pagan. The fulfillment of baptism was not ministry to God's reign but an inner call to a persevering life of prayer.

While Catholics struggled to sustain faith and morality in a changing world, for the elect conversion meant entrance into the new religious congregations where external ministry was something added to the inner spiritual life. Ministry was direct but personal: the kingdom advanced from soul to soul (in France or Brazil) much as one candle lit from another glowed in the dark during the Easter Vigil. Priests and sisters, however, had a difficult time reconciling the burdens of Christian ministry with the demands of the spiritual life.

The spirituality of men and women in the ministry rarely escaped a tension between prayer and work. In society ministry faced a hostile world where God's grace seemed present only in the individual. The style of confronting history with God's kingdom was one of infiltration—infiltration into and anger before a world which had unforgivably entertained Protestantism and the Enlightenment. Hence some evangelistic, public and eschatological dimensions of ministry faded.

In the Western church, there are *three* families of men and women who live out their baptism through the vowed life: the *monks,* the *friars,* and the *Jesuits* who formed the model for the *modern congregations.* These are not purely chronological groupings but rather—as all live on through later centuries—three basic styles for the vowed life. With the Society of Jesus the third period entered and it set the tone for dozens of congregations of men and women which appeared for three hundred years after 1540.[45] More or less they accepted the approach (and often the spirituality) to religious life of the Jesuits: a method of prayer, a universal organization with control over and mobility for its members, a replacement of monastic community and spirituality with a modern, professional, ascetic individualism—all at the service of the church.

This style of Christian life was influential not only among men and women in vows but among the laity and the diocesan clergy, among popes and bishops. Just as the monastic schools influenced the education of bishops and priests in the twelfth century, so the Jesuits would assume the training of many future priests throughout the world and of future popes. We can speak of a "Jesuization" of the ministry within the world of the Baroque as religious and diocesan priests were drawn to this new and helpful spirituality. We see this influence in the importance of retreats, in the method of prayer based upon the *Spiritual Exercises,* in the style of dress and in the rise of private devotions and individual discipline.

A secondary influence of the Jesuits upon the ministry was the tendency of the bishop to comport himself toward his fellow Christians in the ministry as a Jesuit superior. The Jesuit rector had more control over the subjects in his community than the earlier abbot or prior. Unlike the abbot he could touch the external life as well as the internal spirituality of his subjects; and, finally, there was the controversial theology of obedience which identified the superior's will with that of God.

In this ecclesiastical atmosphere the Christian of charism and ministry had no rights, no questions, no insight, no appeal. This transformation of the coordinator of ministries, the bishop, into an ascetical religious superior is one further stage in the absorption and metamorphosis of the ministry into the office of authority. Here is the final stage of the episcopalization. On the one hand, the ministry terminated in the person of a single bishop, the bishop of Rome; on the other hand, the bishop ceased to be really a bishop—his charism and work is not realized in preaching, evangelizing and enabling but in administering and controlling. Moreover, he became a religious superior of a post-Tridentine congregation of men who were his clergy.

In the Baroque, light pours down through clear windows into the church and states that God is not distant, utterly different from creatures. God is actively present in the church and in the Christian. In short, light is molded by the Baroque to proclaim that there is sanctifying grace. At first the Baroque church shocks us with its universe of angels, saints, and decorations. The interior of the Baroque church, moving towards the Rococo, with all its figures, is an affirmation that there is a world of grace whence these angels and saints come. Also the church anticipates the next life in the liturgy, in the religious order, in the new spirituality for lay people, in this very church building of pilgrimage or meditation. Grace, in the fresco and sculptured group, becomes concrete; there is grace in humanity.

There was, however, in the mystical statues with fluid robes hewn out of stone, in the openness to light of the windows and dome, in the images of the dove and Fathers of the church, something more: an efficient singleness of purpose, a subjective insistence, and an organizational method typical of the modern world which had arrived.[46]

This ministry became a ministry to grace, to the presence and power of God realized in movements and religious orders. Evangelization and spirituality presented a very real world of church and grace locked in a struggle with Reformation and Enlightenment.

6. The Romanticization of the Ministry

Friedrich Schlegel, early Romantic and convert to Roman Catholicism in 1804, wrote that three events made the modern world: the French Revolution, Fichte's *Doctrine of the Sciences,* and Goethe's novel *Wilhelm Meister.*[47] This triad led the Enlightenment to its climax, and then bore something new: Romanticism. The Romantic saw the world vibrating between nature and mind. Nature was a mysterious power of generation and development, and human consciousness was the creator of the world. Art and history might be tragic, but they were, precisely as the development of individual and collective spirit, the revelation of God. Amid the turbulent world where new powers burst out of nature and new freedom out of consciousness stood the solitary, heroic person: possessed of intuition and freedom, part of the universal, absolute process, yet alone.

Just as there had been a growing monasticization of Christianity and its ministry from the fourth century onward, so after the fourteenth there was a slow process of secularization. The Reformation brought a modern world which found new intensity in Voltaire and Kant. The Catholic Baroque, however, prepared for Romanticism. After the French and American Revolutions new world-views poured forth: Kant, Fichte, Schelling, Baader and Schlegel.[48] A new evolving world was being born, one open to all.

What was ministry in the nineteenth century? In an age calling for universal freedom from ignorance and want, the church appeared to be a relic whose demise was near. What was the purpose of being a Christian, of being ordained a priest, of serving a kingdom in competition with the new kingdoms of humanity? No doubt the German bishops, who were still secular rulers in the year 1800, symbolized this collective vocational crisis as they lost all their secular power a few years later.

The effect of freedom and feeling leading Europe to universal human dignity was to move the church, with its antiquities and lost privileges, away from the center of society. What the Reformation had not accomplished, the ideas of civil democracy and freedom did.

In the decades after 1800, however, a renewal of Roman Catholicism took place before this strong centrifugal force dominated the church. During the period of Romantic idealism in Germany and France, with allied movements in Belgium and Ireland, new views of the church developed among Catholics. The church cultivated the talents of laymen like Montalambert and Görres who confronted authoritarianism in church and state and absorbed the best of the new philosophy and literature. Conversing with the thought-forms of the times as personified in Schelling, theologians laid a base for a rediscovery of church charism and life. Munich and Tübingen, but also circles of thinkers from all walks of life in Bonn, Münster, and Vienna, were centers of a new Catholicism which was very much the product of laity and priests, men and women working together. F. A. Staudenmaier, professor at Tübingen, wrote a book in 1835 on the "pragmatism of charisms" elaborating a theory of the activity of the Spirit in each individual serving church and society. J. A. Möhler's *Unity in the Church* presented an ecclesiology of startling newness: the Christian church was an organism, a living totality whose present and past flowed out of diversity in the community.[49]

After 1848, however, not only the papacy but intellectual life in Europe grew conservative. Gregory XVI and Pius IX, popes from 1831 to 1878, directed again all church life from Rome. Ultramontanism, accompanying the Romantic movement in France and Bavaria, lost its openness toward philosophy and theology and viewed the civil authority with disappointment and the papacy with uncritical idealism. The Romantic spirit continued but in a backward-looking style. The monastic orders were restored along with their art and liturgy. New missionary congregations, for home and abroad, appeared by the dozens. Yet, there was no renewal of ministerial diversity and ecclesial variety. The number of workers increased in the church but an enormous sameness spread over the Catholic Church. Figures like Görres and von Baader were gone; the impoverished position of the laity showed itself in the increasing prominence of catechisms.[50] It was as if the masses of Christians regressed to the state of catechumens, while there were no successors to the rich journalism of Görres and de Lamennais.

Pius IX and Vatican I singled out monarchical power as the aspect of the church worthy of emphasis. Neo-scholasticism replaced the leitmotif of organic community with efficacious episcopacy as the formal cause of the church. Charism was again moved to the side (to the occasional saint), and the independent activity of the baptized relegated to the background.

Nevertheless, the nineteenth century was a time of restoration. In Europe great romanesque and gothic churches were restored, and in England and America there was an assertion of wider ministry in controversies over parish and diocesan direction and in the founding of new American religious communities. In Europe venerable religious orders were restored. Prosper Guéranger brought back Benedictine life while Lacordaire, already a spellbinding preacher at Notre Dame and unofficial spiritual director to the youth of Paris, dramatically left the pulpit and entered a novitiate in Italy to restore the Dominican Order beyond its fragile existence in Italy and Spain. Just as Solesmes' liturgy was a Romantic expression of a patristic and medieval mysticism, so Lacordaire's preaching in his white and black habit was a Romantic confrontation with secularity. Motifs of high emotion, solitary heroism, mystical faith, a transforming vision of society and the renunciation of all that was secular were present in these figures and their communities.

But when hopes of restoration if not renewal and transformation cooled after 1848, other faces of the Roman Catholic Church in the nineteenth century showed themselves. There was, first of all, a distrust of the world, society and state. Since the looked-for renewal and expansion of Catholic life did not occur in the structures of a church again excessively Roman, mysticism rather than ministry was cultivated. The literature of piety in France during the seventeenth and eighteenth centuries prepared for a limitation and individualization of the priesthood. The priest was placed in a mystical niche, exalted, described as metaphysically equal to, even higher than angelic beings. He lost his roots in the community and in the wider, diverse church. His power in the Eucharist and in penance seemed personal gifts without any source in word or community.

Bishops and priests moved or were moved to the edge of society. There they experienced their powerlessness, they nourished a theology of the world as sinful, and they turned inward in their theology of the kingdom of God to a spirituality of the soul in prayer.

The secularity and evolutionism of the nineteenth century brought with it some denial of the supernatural. The structure of church ministry crumbled as the framework of medieval society was dismantled and a new society—the kingdom of God on earth—was planned. The new politics of the secular, democratic state replaced the ministry as teacher of the way to heaven, as servant of charity in this life. An array of thinkers expounded theories which planned that society would render a teaching about a future kingdom of God unnecessary and would so organize the state that there would not be any poor or disenfranchised, the clients of the charity of the church.

In the face of a hostile or competitive society, the church turned inward to the life of grace. Grace became an interior condition of personal life. Christian life was mainly preservative of the state of grace.

A symbol of the marginalization of the ministry is the Curé of Ars, beatified in 1905 as model of the diocesan clergy. The Curé was a saint, but his ministry was not particularly typical. He lived in an insignificant place geographically; his preaching and liturgy were admittedly undistinguished. His ministry was one of personal direction, of counsel and forgiveness, usually in the form of the sacrament of penance. His sanctity was his discipline; his struggle with his own personality and with the demonic was, as all sanctity ultimately is, personal. The church saw in Jean-Marie Vianney a beacon for the supernatural in a time of darkness (a motif his biographers frequently choose). Alone in the confessional he experienced the horizon of the supernatural in life, and he led others to experience, at times dramatically, that power at a time when the supernatural was ridiculed as outmoded, replaceable, illusionary.

The ministry of the Curé of Ars, however, was experiential and individual; it was not a ministry to confront the world with the Kingdom, but rather a ministry to the spark of real or potential grace which lies in an individual. In this ministry of exploration of personal dialogue with grace, the Curé showed himself to be a modern person. Nonetheless, his ministry should not be viewed as ministry itself, but as one particular ministry, one indeed on the margin of history and grace.

In observing how the church recognized this ministry on the margin of society as exemplary for all ministry, we are not looking simply at a French phenomenon. In Italy and Spain, in parts of Germany, in England, Ireland, Australia and the United States, the Catholic Church was embattled. In one place it appeared to be a minority of strong believers while in another place it represented clerical privilege. The church was on the defensive and could not yet understand how it might appropriate the forms of the modern world and still be faithful to Gospel and tradition. So its ministerial stance was that of the sacrament of the supernatural presence of God in grace and revelation.

The ministries of the Curé of Ars or the events of Lourdes nourished the faith of many individuals, but they did not challenge either the hostility or impersonality of the secular state. They did not lead to a Christian politics whose charisms in matters of socialization and war were soon to be desperately needed. The focus of ministry was grace on earth in signs and remarkable individuals. The church of the nineteenth century almost unconsciously prepared various kinds of people for service in the modern world: the mystic, the neo-medieval monk, the political activist, the solitary priest, the conservative churchman, the papal administrator. But it did not distinguish ministry from mysticism.

By 1950 we come to the end of this ecclesial late Romanticism. A new technology and eschatology will dominate the world. The church has discovered or retrieved biblical and patristic ideas for theology, liturgy and mission. Yet, while European theologians prepared for the event of Vatican II, parallel movements preserving the Romantic, antiworldly mysticism of the nineteenth century remained influential. We see them in the novels of G. Bernanos (*The Diary of a Country Priest* draws on the experience of France and Ars) and F. Mauriac; we see them in the lives and writing of mystics, in the philosophy of Maritain, and in the early motifs of Thomas Merton.

We must note one area where the ministry did expand in a particularly forceful way, an expansion which even today has not been fully evaluated: the new forms of religious life for women, and, consequent upon this, the new role of women religious in modern church and society. In the twelfth, sixteenth and seventeenth centuries, women and men had slowly prepared the church and society for communities of dedicated women who, eschewing cloister, would minister through education and varied forms of health care to so many. The nineteenth century saw not only the formation of many congregations of religious women but also of—as we appreciate them from a later perspective—congregations which were new forms of religious life. The congregations founded after the French Revolution, and in the United States in great numbers after 1830, appear first as provinces or foundations of European communities or as sisters of the third orders of Dominic or Francis. In fact, they are something new in the history of religious life. The American sister became something more than a member of a third order; nor is she by any phenomenological standard a lay person but a paragon of ministry. The large and numerous achievements in institutions of education and health-care, and the high level of office in education and in other areas of public life attained by these women indicate that something radically new appeared. From the point of view of quality in education, commitment, and ministry, religious women are the outstanding group in the Roman Catholic Church in America. They raise by their existence as much as by their desire for equality many questions for a theology of contemporary ministry. First, as we have just mentioned, they are the latest revolution in the form of religious life. Second, they do well over half of the public ministry of the Roman Catholic Church and have done so for over a century. Out of these facts and paradoxes come two questions for religious life. The first questions the sense of the previous distinction between laity and clergy when ministering religious women (and men who are not presbyters) are called "laity." Second, this new realization of religious life in women—which in all appearances was ministerial—naturally raises the issue of a public recognition of women in the ministry. Theologians argued for the restored diaconate at Vatican II by pointing out that the ministry and the ministers of the diaconate existed; what was lacking was the church's liturgical confirmation in public. The same is true with the vast and varied ministry of religious women. Their ministry is particularly striking; what is lacking is the public, sacramental affirmation of it by the church which claims to prize sacrament.

The events of the nineteenth century were twofold and paradoxical. There was a new theology of the organic totality of the church and there was the restoration of an excessively episcopal ecclesiology in Neo-scholastic phraseology. There was the emphasis upon the mystical hero and the multiplicity of new religious communities; there were new institutions and services, and there was a new resurgence of papalist centrism. All, including the search for a happier, theonomous time in a restored medievalism, had contributions to make. It was as if, in the decades leading up to Vatican II, the motifs of the great periods of ecclesiology were paraded forth: the church of the apostle, the bishop, the medieval hierarchies, the Baroque and Romantic saints.

Conclusion

The six metamorphoses which ministry has undergone over two millennia are six acts of a pageant. Their variety describes not the entire story but the peaks along the cultural, ontological and pneumatic history of Christian ministry. The triumphs and the limitations of ministry—evangelist, bishop, priest, monk, *Herr Pastor, curé*—all these are the products of culture.

There are always some who claim for their time and style a perennial value. Ministers in every century have argued that their form of *diakonia* fulfilled the Spirit's reality of service to the kingdom. Frequently a period forgot part of the past and failed to imagine the future. The lesson of the history of ministry is that one should not claim an eternal superiority. The life of the Spirit in the church never ceases; the corporate service of Jesus Christ in his Body continues.

We have avoided negative judgments on these past realizations of Christian ministry. In matters of culture it is instructive to contemplate the form but best to avoid comparisons. We have been taught to view history as an evolution toward the better. In fact, history is a chain of different periods where one epoch illustrates one side of ministry and then another period draws out a different style. The six major periods we have surveyed succeeded in the goal of ministry. At the same time, even in their success time and culture imposed limits upon the ministry of the third or thirteenth century.

Second, we have not been looking merely at history. Because of the importance of the primal event of the early church and of tradition, and because of the tendencies in Christian churches to freeze a golden age or to fear change, all of these forms of ministry have survived. They live on; they are our past; they influence our future. We have then been looking not at history but at the roots of our thinking about ministry. We have seen the sources of the church forms we now have.

NOTES

1. C. S. Lewis, "De Destructione Temporum," *They Asked for a Paper* (London, 1962), p. 23.

2. E. Schillebeeckx, "The Catholic Understanding of Office," *TS* 30 (1969) 568. For a cultural hermeneutic of types of ministry and church, cf. A.

Dempf, *Religions-Soziologie der Christenheit* (Munich, 1972); A. Mayer-Pfann-holz, "Der Wandel des Kirchenbildes in der abendländischen Kulturges-chichte," P. Bogler, ed., *Die Kirche und der heutige Mensch* (Maria Laach, 1955), pp. 50f; T. O'Meara, "Philosophical Models in Ecclesiology," *TS* 39 (1978) 3ff.

3. *ME,* pp. 53ff; cf. G. Tavard, "A Theological Approach to Ministry and Authority," *J* 32 (1972) 311f.; R. Schnackenburg, "Episkopos und Hirten-amt," *Episkopos* (Regensburg, 1949), pp. 87ff.

4. Eusebius, *Hist. Eccl.,* VI, 45, 11; cf. R. Grant, *Early Christianity and Society* (New York, 1977).

5. G. La Piana, "The Church of Rome at the End of the Second Centu-ry," *Harvard Theological Review* 18 (1925) 201ff.

6. *Contra Celsum,* 8, 73; 8, 17; *Homilies on Leviticus,* 3, 5; 10, 3; 24, 2; 9, 9; cf. A. Vilela, *La condition collégiale des prêtres au IIIe siècle* (Paris: Beau-chesne, 1971), pp. 43–156; J. Lecuyer, "Sacerdoce des fidèles et sacerdoce min-isteriel chez Origène," *Vetera Christianorum* 7 (1970) 253ff.

7. E. Braniste, "L'Assemblé liturgique. . . ," *As,* p. 101. Opinions vary as to the point of departure, extent and rationale of the variation of the ministries in the second and third centuries. Cf. P. Nautin, "L'évolution des ministères au IIe et au IIIe siècle," *Revue de Droit Canonique* 23 (1973), 47ff.

8. On the changing role of the bishop, cf. C. Vogel, "Unité de l'église et pluralité des formes historiques d'organisation ecclésiastique du IIIe au Ve siè-cle," *Episcopat et l'Eglise* (Paris, 1962), pp. 591ff; J. Lynch, "The Changing Role of the Bishop: A Historical Survey," *J* 39 (1979) 289ff.

9. *De Exhortatione castitatis* 7, 3; G. Otranto observes that Tertullian's text indicates a common priesthood which does not exclude or attack the role of the presbyters and bishops; "Nonne et laici sacerdotes sumus?" *Vetera Chris-tianorum* 8 (1971), 46. On the priesthood of the Christians in the first centuries cf. D. Donovan, *The Levitical Priesthood and the Ministry of the New Testament* (Münster, 1970).

10. H. Legrand, "The Presidence of the Eucharist according to the An-cient Tradition," *Worship* 53 (1979), 407. Schillebeeckx argues that the centrali-ty of the Eucharist alone does not explain the development of the community leader into priest; *My,* pp. 48ff; cf. J. P. Audet, *Structures of the Christian Priest-hood* (New York, 1969); P. M. Gy, "Ancient Ordination Prayers," *Studia Li-turgica* 13 (1979), 85ff.

11. P. Du Bourguet, *Early Christian Art* (New York, 1971), p. 32; R. Krautheimer, *Early Christian and Byzantine Architecture* (New York, 1975); C. Norberg-Schulz, *Meaning in Western Architecture* (New York, 1975). On Cyp-rian, cf. Epistula 62, 1; 65, 2; 67, 1; 72, 2; cf. M. Fahey, *Cyprian on the Bible* (Tübingen, 1972); M. Poirier, "Vescovo, clero e laici in una communità cris-tiana del III secolo negli scritti di S. Cipriano," *Rivista di storia e letteratura religiosa* 9 (1973) 17ff; J. Jacobs, *Saint Cyprian of Carthage as Minister* (Boston University Diss., 1976).

12. Minutius Felix, *Octavian* 32, 1. Justin Martyr in the second century explained that Christians were priestly people because God had set them free

from pagan and Jewish rituals; their prayers replaced sacrifices. *Dialogue with Trypho* . . . , PG 6, 74ff.

13. J. Petersen, "House-Churches in Rome," *Vigiliae Christianae* 23 (1969) 265ff.; Cf. A. Malherbe, "House Churches and Their Problems," *Social Aspects of Early Christianity* (Baton Rouge, 1977); P. Stuhlmacher, "Urchristliche Hausgemeinde," *Der Brief an Philemon* (Zurich, 1975); H. J. Klauck, "Die Hausgemeinde als Lebensform im Urchristentum," *Münchener Theologische Zeitschrift* 32 (1981) 1ff; E. Schüssler-Fiorenza, "You Are Not to Be Called Father. Early Christian History in a Feminist Perspective," *Cross Currents* (1979) 301ff; K. Gamber, *Domus Ecclesiae* (Regensburg, 1968).

14. Du Bourguet, p. 140.

15. *Ibid.*

16. *PL* 148, 771ff. Cf. A. Fliche, *La Reforme grégorienne* (Louvain, 1924), 3 vols.; G. B. Ladner, *The Idea of Reform* (Cambridge, 1959); C. Dereine, "Vie commune, règle de S. Augustin et chanoines réguliers au XIe siècle," *Revue d'historie ecclésiastique* 41 (1946) 365ff; *ESA,* p. 112.

17. K. J. Conant, *Carolingian and Romanesque Architecture, 800–1200* (New York, 1974), p. 34; cf. J. Evans, *Romanesque Architecture of the Order of Cluny* (Cambridge, 1938); R. de Lasteyrie, *L'architecture religieuse en France à l'époque romane* (Paris, 1929).

18. J. Leclerq, *The Love of Learning and the Desire for God: A Study of Monastic Culture* (New York, 1961).

19. G. Dix, "The Coming of Monasticism and the Divine Office," *The Shape of the Liturgy* (London, 1945); R. Zinnbohler, "Die mönchischen Strukturen des Priesterbildes," *Priesterbild im Wandeln* (Linz, 1972), pp. 73ff. On the clericalization of the liturgy and the distancing of the people, L. Bouyer, *Liturgy and Architecture* (Notre Dame, 1967), pp. 70ff. On the privatization of the minister in the Middle Ages, *My,* pp. 52ff; O. Nussbaum, *Kloster, Priestermonch und Privatmesse* (Bonn, 1961); A. Häussling, *Mönchskonvent* und Eucharistiefeier . . . (Münster, 1973).

20. A. Borras-L. Thier, *Ursprung und Entwicklung der Priesterkleidung* (Linz, 1970), pp. 353ff.

21. *PL* 182, 677. Cf. M. D. Chenu, "The Evangelical Awakening," *Nature, Man and Society in the Twelfth Century* (Chicago, 1968), p. 237.

22. Cf. H. Grundmann, *Religiöse Bewegungen im Mittelalter* (Berlin, 1935) and a bibliography in Congar, *ESA,* pp. 198ff; cf. Chenu, "Monks, Canons and Laymen in Search of the Apostolic Life," *Nature.* . . . , pp. 202ff.

23. *Quaestiones Quodlibetales,* I, 14; 4 *Sent.* d. 6, q. 2, a. 2., 2; d. 19, a. 2, q. 3, ad. 4.

24. *ESA,* p. 174; on an ecclesiology of order culminating in the twelfth century, cf. Y. Congar, "Les laics et l'ecclésiologie des 'Ordines' chez les théologiens des XIe et XIIe siècles," in *I Laici* . . . (Milan, 1968), 83ff; cf. A. Darguennes, *De Juridische Structuur van de Kerk folgen S. Thomas* (Louvain, 1949).

25. M. D. Chenu, "Nature and Man—the Renaissance of the 12th Century," *Nature.* . . . , pp. 1ff.

26. R. Roques, *L'univers dionysien* (Paris, 1955), p. 131; cf. J. Stiflmayr, "Uber die termini Hierarch und Hierarchie," *Zeitschrift für katholische Theologie* 22 (1898) 180ff; Interestingly, J. Meyendorff criticizes Ps. Denys for removing church role from the community and locating it in mysticism, *Christ in Eastern Christian Thought* (Crestwood, 1976), pp. 91ff, while Y. Congar argues that the Western churches resisted such a dominance of gnostic hierarchy until the twelfth century; *ESA*, pp. 224ff. Thomas of Ireland, Aquinas' first teacher at Naples, wrote: "The Blessed Dionysius came to Paris so that he might make of this city the mother of studies after the pattern of Athens." M. D. Chenu, *Towards Understanding St. Thomas* (Chicago, 1964), p. 24.

27. Cf. Y. Congar, "Aspects ecclésiologiques de la querelle . . . ," *Archives d'histoire doctrinale et litteraire du moyen age* 36 (1961) 72.

28. *2 Sent.,* 9. 1, 1; *De Divinis Nominibus* 1, 2.

29. *4 Sent.,* 24, 3, 2; cf. J. Lecuyer, "Les étapes de l'enseignement thomiste sur l'épiscopat," *Revue Thomiste* (57) 29ff.

30. *ST* II—II, q. 184, a. 5. "He who preaches should have what he preaches permanently and integrally." *ST* III, q. 41, a. 3, ad 1. On Denys as a source of hierarchy through illumination, cf. Congar, *ESA,* pp. 226ff.

31. *2 Sent.,* 9, 1, 1; *4 Sent.,* 5, 2, 1; 1 *De Veritate,* 9, 1.

32. Aquinas, following Gratian and Lombard, admitted an influence from pagan sources upon the monarchical aspect of the church, *4 Sent.,* 24, 3, 2, qa. 2, ad. 2; cf. *ESA,* p. 154.

33. *ST* II—II, q. 184, a. 4.

34. *ST* II—II, q. 183, a. 1, ad. 3.

35. *ST* II—II, q. 184, aa. 3–6; cf. P. Michaud-Quentain, "Aspects de la vie sociale chez les moralistes," *Miscellanea Medievalia* 3 (Berlin, 1964) pp. 37ff.

36. Cf. Y. Congar, "The Idea of the Church in Thomas Aquinas," *The Thomist* 1 (1939) 331ff; H. Krings, *Ordo* (Hamburg, 1981).

37. *ESA,* p. 239. Aquinas never wrote a treatise on ministry for the *Summa theologiae.* From his commentaries on Paul, though, we can glean some further views on ministry. Paradoxically, Aquinas thought that the ministry actually had expanded since the first century when the lesser ministries like reader were all contained in the diaconate (*4 Sent.,* 24, 2, 1, ad 2). Explaining *Romans,* Aquinas saw that there existed ministerial diversity—"He who receives the grace of prophecy needs the one who has the grace of healing." *Commentary on Romans* (12:5), *In Epistulas* 1 (Turin, 1953), p. 181. These ministries, however, were something other than ordained, ecclesiastical offices. They were in fact charisms, and for Aquinas charisms were temporary, personal graces, lacking stability and so not ending in public office. Charisms ("gratuitous graces") inspired an individual transitorily to a specific work in the church. Aquinas interprets the Pauline metaphor of Body of Christ as a communion of varied graces for lives in the church rather than as ministerial offices (*ST* II—II, qq. 171–178).

To be a bishop or a priest, called in Scripture "ministers of God," was different; they had "a grace and an office." (*Commentary on Romans* 12:7, p. 182). Office is distinct from charism, possibly separate from grace. What distinguishes these ministers? What brings them the dignity of office, the stability of status? It was their relationship to the sacraments, especially the Eucharist. Aquinas interprets the list of ministers in *Ephesians* in this way: The "apostles" were the Twelve; the "evangelists" were the four authors of the New Testament gospels; the "teachers" were the bishops whose main task was to teach and nourish with the Eucharist. *Commentary on Ephesians, In Epistulas* 2 (Turin, 1953), pp. 52f. What gave stability to the religious side of medieval society was the bishop, around whom, as with a magnetic pole, the diversity of charismatics, monks, nuns, friars, lawyers and cardinals found their orientation.

38. *ESA,* p. 232ff. On the structure of the curia today as a pyramid, cf. G. Zizola, "Le pouvoir romain," *Lumière et Vie* 26 (1977) 25; also, W. Bassett, "Subsidiarity, Order and Freedom in the Church," *Cross Currents* 20 (1970) 141ff. Cf. E. Panofsky, *Gothic Architecture and Scholasticism* (Latrobe, 1959); T. O'Meara, "Paris as a Cultural Milieu of Thomas Aquinas' Thought," *The Thomist* 39 (1974) 689ff; O. von Simson, "Die Kunst des hohen Mittelalters— 'Lichtvolle Geistigkeit'," *Propyläen Kunstgeshichte* 6 (Berlin, 1972); cf. W. Dettloff, "Der Ordogedanke im Kirchenverständnis Bonaventuras," *Ecclesia et Jus* (Munich, 1980), pp. 25ff.

39. *ST* II—II, q. 184.

40. P. Fransen, "Orders and Ordination," *Sacramentum Mundi* 4 (New York, 1969), p. 313. "The Christian ministry is in the process of losing its originality and becoming excessively similar to a pagan or Old Testament priesthood. The ministers are so well integrated into the machinery of feudal society that they no longer have the strength to react against the pressure of dealing commercially in the sacral and ministerial." *ME,* p. 67.

41. *On the Bablylonian Captivity, Luther's Works* 36 (Philadelphia, 1966), p. 116; cf. H. Schutte, *Amt. Ordination und Sukzession* (Dusseldorf, 1974); G. Haendler, *Luther on Ministerial Office and Congregational Function* (Philadelphia: Fortress, 1981).

42. A. Ganoczy, *Calvin. Théologien de l'église et du ministère* (Paris, 1964), p. 245. For the United States, cf. D. Hall, *The Faithful Shepherd: A History of the New England Ministry in the Seventeenth Century* (New York, 1974); D. Scott, *From Office to Profession: The New England Ministry, 1750–1850* (New York, 1971).

43. P. Portoghesi, *Roma Barocca* (Cambridge, 1970), pp. 4ff.

44. R. Drummond, *A History of Christianity in Japan* (Grand Rapids, 1971), pp. 58, 112, 115.

45. Cf. R. Hostie, *Vie et mort des ordres religieux* (Paris, 1972), ch. 6.

46. The organic life of Baroque ecclesiology depended, like Baroque art, on a tension between a central focus and independent pieces. "The Counter-Reformation ecclesiology can be seen, in retrospect, to have begun a time of juridicism which dampened its vitality. Theoretical study was replaced by law, and the concepts and words of scholasticism were canonized. There was an insistence on obedience in theology and not just in faith." *ESA,* p. 368. Baroque ecclesiology was not the only theology of church and ministry existing between 1600 and 1900. An ecclesiology of national conciliarism, one of whose forms

was Gallicanism, competed with the papal organization for dominance and was at times of great importance.

47. F. Schlegel, *Literary Aphorisms* (University Park, 1968), p. 143.

48. Cf. D. Julta, "Le Prêtre au XVIIIème siècle," *Recherches des sciences religieuses* 58 (1970), 521ff.

49. Cf. T. O'Meara, *Romantic Idealism and Roman Catholicism. Schelling and the Theologians* (Notre Dame, 1982).

50. Congar, "Laic et Laicat," *Dictionnaire de Spiritualité,* 9 (Paris, 1976), 98ff.

CHAPTER SIX
Ministry and Ministers

The Holy Spirit and a living, faithful community give ministry.

The New Testament has offered us a record of some structures from a few communities fired by Pentecost. Next, history has disclosed the forms (and the limits) of ministry as the church addressed, entered and survived cultures.

As we looked at ministry in Scripture and in its ancient and modern forms, we proceeded with only a general description. Now we need to search out the deeper nature of ministry; otherwise we can have no assurance that efforts to renew and expand the ministry are faithful to the Spirit. If we follow too empirical an approach to ministry, ministry will be whatever a church group decides. When everything is ministry, after a short-term exuberance nothing is ministry. Soon it loses its attraction and fades away. On the other hand, when a definition is too ready—a definition given by a language or ontology which is imposed as divine and eternal—human words control the activity of God. Then there can be nothing new in ministry, for the realm of the prophetic and diaconal tinted with the blood of missionaries and martyrs has been turned into an ecclesiastical assembly line. Our theological method of correlation has struggled first with the revelatory records of ministry and the emergence of the early church, and then with the needs of our own time. The two seem to have something in common. Through both we approach a definite description of ministry.

There are different ways of defining ministry. One approach is to research a metaphysical definition from which all problems might be logically solved. This approach, however, overlooks the fact that while revelation is God's word and event in human history, theological expressions of revelation can never attain the ultimacy of revelation; they are always reflections in human conceptuality and language upon revelation. The New Testament urges ministry, commands ministry, describes the conditions and characteristics of ministry; but it does not define, not does it proffer lists or job descriptions.

A second approach is to search for the nature of ministry in the tradition of the Church and the churches. The Christian churches, our historical survey showed, have received ministry in the midst of various cultural moments. We should take seriously these diverse ecclesial-cultural styles for they give phenomenologically a definition of ministry. For instance, in the perspective of the Syrian church poetry replaced logic, and liturgy and spirituality were more prominent than organization. The ecclesiology of Ephrem's hymns contrasts with the rigor of Bellarmine's tracts.[1]

A third way, suggested by our age of rapid changes, finds the best or sole guide to ministry in what is actually being done. What works is the real; the new is the best. The thought-forms of society and the needs of the world are indeed the forum of ministry, but they do not determine fully its nature or its forms. Times change. When a church commits itself too boisterously to one ministerial style or rejects too forcefully the Spirit present in other ministries, or when it identifies ministry with this style here and now, that church eventually will fight for its life when the next cultural epoch arrives.

Our Western mind longs for unanimity; we are disappointed in our search for one rigorous definition in ecclesiology, just as a Christian is disappointed in a search for one view of Christ. We do not find a single ministry or a single definition of ministry in the New Testament. We can see, however, that plurality and potentiality help the Gospel appeal to a succession of civilizations. Without pluralism the church would already have exhausted itself long before reaching Persia or Ireland. The variety of the New Testament is not a sign of relativism but an affirmation of its ability to present the definitive religious event of the human race in all its richness. For that reason, not only before the mystery of Christ, but before the style of the Christian life and the forms of charism and ministry in the community, we stand as learners, contemplatives, ready to draw forth old things and new.

When we reject literal biblicism or airy scholasticism, complaints are often heard that Christianity, particularly Roman Catholicism, has lost the ability to give certain answers. Some questions, however, are too complex, too close to life or too removed from the Word of God to support one certain answer. Ecclesiology is not at the center of God's revelation in the way the dialectic of sin and grace or the person of Jesus is. Because history and society intrude into the Christian community's life, one way of answering a complex theological question is to sketch the parameters of an answer. To disclose what ministry might be, let us draw forth again the characteristics we saw in the New Testament perspectives on ministry. They establish parameters (positive and negative) for describing the nature of ministry. We can surmise in advance that two dialectics will surface again: diversity and harmony, baptism in the Spirit and varied ministries in the world.

1. Characteristics of Ministry: Toward a Definition

We return to the world of apostolic churches, not to present another analysis of *charis* and *diakonia* but to draw out a phenomenology of ministry from its essential aspects.

Six characteristics stand out in forming all ministry and each ministry. Theologically they compose a nature of ministry. Let us look at each briefly. Ministry is: (1) doing something; (2) for the advent of the kingdom; (3) in public; (4) on behalf of a Christian community; (5) which is a gift received in faith, baptism and ordination; and which is (6) an activity with its own limits and identity within a diversity of ministerial actions.

(1) *Doing Something.* The Christians in the first churches, avoiding any appropriation of sacral language, depicted church life by using words which were ordinary. With only a few exceptions verbs described the offices which were actions undertaken to sustain and spread the Gospel. Over the centuries these Greek action words became sacred offices. We need to rediscover the original language-event of ministry and its linguistic preference for doing. The Christian is not baptized into a tribe or race, nor into a passive group of neophytes or into a gnostic study club; but into action; into church, but also into service. While faith is the milieu of conversion to Christ, that faith-conversion continues in actual service to grace. Because this element of action is essential and yet so obscured in the structures of laity, religious life and clericalism, we will return to it in a later section as we explore the relationship between the activity of ministry and the life-styles of the ministers.

(2) *For the Kingdom of God.* Not every noble movement or good deed is ministry. When everything is ministry, nothing is ministry. Extra-Christian ministries can be services to grace, an implicit annunciation of what is a full revelation in Christ. We are looking, however, for

characteristics of *Christian ministry,* and that ministry has the clear purpose of serving the kingdom of God as brought and preached by Jesus. Ministry makes the kingdom explicit, turns its ambiguous presence into symbol, word, action. Word and deed are offspring and servants of the kingdom of God. The first Christians were intent upon preaching the newness of this kingdom and the public nature of their faith converted or antagonized their world. While Christian ministry has its own patience in leading not forcing to faith, and while ministry serves ultimately the inner conversation of a person with grace and not church politics, ministry normally is public service of the Kingdom. Call it "grace," "salvation," "faith," "Holy Spirit," "justice"—ministry serves the reign of God after Jesus Christ directly and immediately.

(3) *A Public Action.* The New Testament speaks of Christians announcing their faith in God's presence "openly." Public preaching is ministry and liturgy (Rom 15:16). There is no doubt that the first Christians saw the witness of their lives as a service to the Gospel (Rom 16:19; 12:1). When we say ministry in public, we mean that the ministry normally takes on a visible and public form in words and deeds. Its inner dynamics towards clarity moves away from vague gesture to self-interpretation. The communication of the Gospel has not been done mainly through uncertain signs, such as justice in commerce or casual neighborliness although these may be part of Christian life. When we recall the desperate sociology of grace which Jesus sees confronting the world's sin and death, we understand the uncompromisingly public nature of ministry.

We should not accept an interpretation of baptism which asserts that the main activity of the baptized is a relatively passive participation in liturgy and sacrament. The theologies of the laity in this century failed in their attempt to give the laity a place in the community precisely because they joined a passive, liturgical role to a vague witnessing in the world. Liturgy is the nourishment of life and therein the root of the sacraments, but liturgical life is not the single goal of baptism but the background of charisms and some ministerial involvement. It is difficult to restrict, a priori, all public evangelical and liturgical activity to a small group in one ministry and at the same time be realistic about how baptized Christians are active in their evangelical faith. The public characteristic of ministry challenges any rechanneling of Christian service into liturgy alone or into inner piety.

There is no doubt that some Christians, because of age or illness or some other factor, are limited in the public aspect of their ministry. Their limited service in prayer and life-symbol can be a great grace for the entire Body of Christ—but this is not the norm of ministry. Prayer and suffering may be the life's blood of ministers but they are not the ministry itself. With the entry of large numbers into the urban churches, the leader of the Christian community in the third and fourth centuries faced (and, from our perspective, never solved) the problem of how all the baptized could be in the ministry. Today, at a time of expansion in the ministry and of desire to enter the ministry in different ways, we should not present Christians who are active in prayer as the norm of ministry, nor should we easily cloak Christian communities' passivity with a sacral language of offering and suffering in order to locate everyone in the ministry. So, the public nature of the ministry questions members of the clergy whose work is not clearly ministerial just as it challenges the existence in the churches of a passive laity.

The church through the centuries has struggled to overcome this reduction of the ministry. Religious orders served this purpose as did associations of laity. If the religious orders kept alive the diversity of ministry, movements such as *Action Française*, Jocists, third orders, priest-workers and various forms of the "apostolate of the laity" struggled to bring some ministry to Christians who were not in vows.

After the Reformation and French Revolution, the ministerial side of the church's life looked inward. Often the contemplative life was seen as the ministry par excellence. Canonized saints were by and large contemplatives, foreign missionaries or famous converts. The laity had been rendered largely secular or immobile. Frightened church authority did not trust what it could not control. In Christian countries (which were in fact becoming de-Christianized) the ministry was unimaginative, and feeble in its task of addressing the modern world.

In this century, the hierarchy offered a substitute to ministry. The very phrase "apostolate of the laity" shows the deficiencies in many praiseworthy attempts to extend the ministry.[2] "Apostolate" meant a share in the bishop's or pope's ministry, a ministry called apostolate because it was grounded in the Twelve Apostles. The implication was that all ministry came exclusively from the episcopal order and that it had come to the bishops through a historical line with the Twelve. The roles of Spirit and community were overlooked. Church and ministry were seen as a mono-form hierarchy which could share parcels of what they alone possessed fully and sovereignly. No nuances were made between the nature of the early apostles' ministry and that of a local bishop; no questions were raised about the active role for the community in the emergence of all ministries, even in those receiving a commission from the Twelve or from other churches. The legal usage of "laity" froze all Christians who were not ordained priests in a passive state. One could praise the baptized in devotional language, but neither the code of canon law of 1917, nor a modern form of Christian life such as the secular institute succeeded in calling the baptized to real ministry. The apostolate held out to the laity was not a significant one, e.g. collecting old clothes, coaching sports. Where ordained ministers tried to find ministry for laity, it was often trivial; where the baptized took up public service—as with *Action Française* or Catholic Worker, it was significant but kept at a distance by the hierarchy. Nevertheless, in touch with the inner mind of the church and with the Holy Spirit, the twentieth century has seen a generous, genial surge of activity by Christian men and women, often independent of official leadership. This has been a precursor of the present expansion of the ministry.

If charism and ministry are universal, the church must encourage real universality of ministry and not reduce it to symbol, metaphor or trivial beneficence. If the first Christians had exercised only kindness and cheer, the Gospel would still be in the suburbs of Jerusalem. Sign can be ministry, but normally ministry is more than signs. These *ersatz*-movements in ministry lacked precisely a public word. The explicit and audible proclamation of the Gospel had been transformed into marginal, "secular" activity. At the root of this is a devaluation of baptism away from being an initiation into a new eschatological life which intrinsically includes ministry to being a personal guarantee of salvation in the next life. True ministry connects eleemosynary and caring deeds with the values of the Gospel; it distributes money and develops social programs out of the inner dynamic and word of the Kingdom of God.

Christian life is the backdrop to ministry, but service brings something more specific, namely public action directly for the Kingdom. Justice and mercy are incumbent upon all Christians. The bank teller who witnesses to his faith by being joyful and honest lives as a Christian and may even exercise a sign-ministry. But a sign is slow in its efficacy and unclear in its attraction and message. Upon the bank teller too, during stages of his or her life, is incumbent some public ministry for the church and kingdom.

Even as we insist that ministry be both action and public action, we recognize there is room for the ministry of sign. The Christian gesture, an exemplary life, and involvement for good can be symbols which speak to people. Sign is a secondary, a silent ministry. Signs are always ambiguous, they need interpretation. Lack of interpretation is the reason why ministry as sign is an analogous form of service and why sign is not the place to begin a definition of ministry. The interpretation of the sign—the explanation of a Christian's honesty and joy, witness or limited life-style—is necessary for the sign to be ministry. Interpretation turns sign into public address.

(4) *On Behalf of a Christian Community.* Ministry begins with the Christian community, flows out of the community, and thereby nourishes and expands the community. Many ministries sustain a community because there are many things to be done in a communal life of word, sacrament and sustenance in faith. A community, however, evangelizes new members as well as educates Christians young and old. There are ministries internal to the church and ministries from the church into the world to draw men and women explicitly towards the still-dawning kingdom. This brings us back to the conviction that ministry serves the kingdom just as the church does; both are the results as well as the life-giving catalysts and sacraments of the kingdom; both are creations of the kingdom and have their justification not in themselves but in the kingdom. Whether on a university campus or in an urban hospital, the minister ultimately ministers to grace.

Both Biblical faith and ministerial experience show that the dialectic of sin and grace in today's society is not easily mapped. Membership in the church and obedience towards the church and its creeds are not the unalterable lines corralling grace. The rediscovery of the breadth of the kingdom of God around the church and its word and sacrament brings an awareness that ministry is not only the administration and juridical solidification of churches but the enabling of the church itself to serve and to speak the grace of the Kingdom. The minister does not have the responsibility of judging the presence of grace, nor the tiring burden of insisting that salvation is simply church membership. Ministry is not a mandala in black and white but a spectrum of grace's colors; its design is not the church building but the pattern of the human personality permeated by God's plan. For the ministers, the prayer "Thy Kingdom come," is one of commitment, but also of consolation.

Jesus' ministry in the New Testament is not only a ministry of preaching the kingdom, but one of confronting the antitheses of the kingdom. These are evil, sin, illness, madness, want, injustice, and death; they are the visible effects in our human condition of fallenness or sin. They startle us, for ministry to or against them is prominent in the New Testament and yet is not a direct ministry of church to reveal belief or liturgy. Christians have traditionally seen, following Jesus, all human effort which relieves these signs and effects of sin to be fields of ministry. The act of nursing the sick not only imitates Jesus but serves the triumph of love and life over sin. Apparently for Jesus' own theology of our world, illness, injustice and want are not chance occurrences. He views them as endemic tragedies flowing not only from natural or social causes, but from sin: They are opposed to the Father's plan and so the advent of the kingdom cannot leave them unchallenged. In areas of personal and social service we should not be too strict in delineating what is and what is not ministry for the Christian community; not because we want every good deed to be ministry but because Jesus places as service to the kingdom not only words of faith and hope but deeds of justice and mercy confronting sin and death.

A theology of ministry on behalf of the community begins with baptism. As sacramental initiation bestows new life and confirms faith, baptism also initiates a person into charism and evangelical action, into a community which is essentially ministerial. In baptism the early Christians experienced not only a beginning or a confirmation of their charisms but also a ritual with priestly overtones. N. Dahl writes:

> In the baptismal liturgy and theology of the ancient church sacerdotal ideas are especially connected with post-baptismal anointing. The whole, complex ceremony of Christian initiation including water-baptism, change of clothes, anointing and first communion corresponds to the pattern of the Old Testament initiation of priests."[3]

This "priestliness," as we saw, became not a sacral cult but service to the Gospel. The current renewal of the theology and liturgy of Christian initiation highlights the discrepancy between a mature theology of baptism into ministry and an immature theology of passive laity.[4] A Christian church does not have the option to live liturgically but not evangelistically. "On behalf of" means action born in a local church. Each church should be as intent upon witness in the world as upon its own inner life. The church at every level—from curia to a new rural parish—should live a life of zeal for public action. Like the kingdom, the church lives on the boundary between its own institutional sustenance and the winning of new nations to the Word of God. The church leaves the ninety-nine for the one lost sheep, but in our time this lost creature is entire movements, cultures and nations.

(5) *Gift of the Spirit.* Ministry has not one but many sources. Above all, it is a personal call by Jesus' Spirit to discipleship in and to grace. We have already discussed at length the linear transition of charism into service. J. Hainz sums this up in this way. "The Spirit must be seen as the *pneuma* of God and Christ; as the medium of mediation; as the sphere and force-field in which Christians, and too the churches, exist as the 'Body of Christ'."[5] In a society such as ours, a developmental history of personality brings a welcome nuance to the developmental theology of charisms. Not as an automaton of the supernatural but as a modern adult, the minister steps into the hope and ambiguity of ministry.

(6) *Diverse Services.* No characteristic of ministry is more certain (or more controversial) than that there is a plurality of ministries. Jesus himself is followed by different groups—the twelve, the disciples, the women; and, his ministry has a variety to it—preaching, healing, forgiving, confronting injustice. Jesus is interested in the quality of human beings responding to the call to follow him and not in the precise arrangement of their groupings and authority (Mt 20:25). Paul says repeatedly that there are many ministries within a harmony of community life. The mission of the Gospel and the power of the Spirit are such that ministry must explode into diverse forms. The connection of ministry to personal charism grounds the diversity in charism. Diversity in ministry is normal.

The question of the diversity of ministry cannot remain an issue of informally permitting a part-time reader or modest distributor of the Eucharist. Diversification in the ministry has already drawn some parish and diocesan services to the level of fulltime ministry. Some of these ministries begin with lengthy preparation and entail expertise, responsibility and commitment. Cannot the ministry as it exists in presbyter and bishop disclose itself in other district ministries? This question is at the center of a fundamental theology of ministry today and so we will turn later to the issue of diversity.

2. A Definition of Ministry

These six characteristics constitute the fundamental identity of ministry. They are not narrow laws; indeed, richer than ministry as it now exists, they lead us to consider calmly the new possibilities which our own times suggest. These characteristics cannot be easily set aside, although no single region or era may perfectly realize them.

Christian ministry is the public activity of a baptized follower of Jesus Christ flowing from the Spirit's charism and an individual personality on behalf of a Christian community to witness to, serve and realize the kingdom of God.

Is our definition of ministry too narrow? In its intended narrowness we want to challenge several theses.

(a) Every act an ordained minister does by virtue of ordination and not necessarily by the action itself achieves its ministerial goal.
(b) Acts of a layperson which resemble ministry are either secular actions or actions motivated by Christian virtue in the secular

sphere because the layperson by definition is excluded from formal ministry.

(c) The layperson influences the secular order by personal and public ethical stances while the minister acts in a liturgical and teaching sphere.

(d) The ordinary professions done by honest baptized Christians are their only ministry for the Gospel.

(e) In the layperson, neither zealous intention, baptism nor professional preparation can turn an activity into official church ministry; in a presbyter, bishop or deacon, however, a good intention can easily cause grace even through incompetent teaching, preaching and liturgical leadership.

(f) There can be only three serious ministries which deserve ordination and the designation of church office: deacon, presbyter and bishop.

(g) Baptism is only metaphorically a commission to real, formal, charism-grounded ministry; baptism constitutes a person in the Christian laity which is by definition outside of serious church activity.

All of these propositions are upon reflection incomplete if not false.

We must permit the theological definition of ministry to appear diversely in preaching, teaching, social care and leadership. Paul's metaphor of diversity and harmony in the Body of Christ suggests ministry similar to the way Meister Eckhart pictures creatures coming forth from God. The entities, even the persons, of the created world, as viewed by God, are not in competition with each other. They are not morally or cosmically better or worse—only different. A fly is a fly, a human being is a human being; one sees quality and modality but not competition or moral degrees in creatures. All creatures participate in being. Similarly, various ministries (of diverse intensity and ecclesial importance to the baptized and the world) participate through their personalized charisms in ministry. Other fulltime ministries—traditional or new—are not rivals to deacon and bishop.

3. Of Language and Ministry

Language is drawn from human experience and then language returns to determine reality. One cannot help but notice how in the course of history Christian theology in its dialogue with Greek philosophy exchanged some of its dynamism for the static ways of being. Verbs became nouns, actions became social states: e.g. priesthood, leadership, hierarchy, abbacy. This linguistic shift tended to change the church into a reservoir of being rather than a concert of doing. Ministry, as we saw, began with verbs: preaching, evangelizing, being-sent . . . and above all, serving.

Can ministry be constituted and defined by words apart from any consideration of a real activity? Is one truly a bishop who cannot preach or does not preach? There can be, of course, no re-entry into the jungle of Donatism where only a verifiable presence of grace created true ministry: since grace cannot be verified, one was never sure of a baptism or an ordination. If we need formality to join real ministry with grace, nevertheless, ministry as a public action on behalf of the Gospel should be tentatively and empirically viewed and tested. Ministry is not a document or a state but an action.

The expansion of serious ministries and the quest by willing baptized men and women for parttime and fulltime ministries is not in America a return to Trusteeism nor in Africa or Latin America a presumption of indigenous leadership, but an awareness of a richer Christian life than a Sunday routine, and a reluctance in entire continents to be without sacraments for a long time because a celibate, often foreign priest can only rarely visit the community. Today the number of vocations to the pastorate or priesthood is not high, but the number of men and women desirous of entering professional ministry is climbing. What is holding them back is partially a question of language.

Canonical, rubrical or nominalist theologies (where church office exists without a necessary connection to service) obscure the freedom and energy of the church. Meanwhile a determination to use language to control definitions and people is not always eschewed by church bureaucrats.

Ministry's language has ended up confused, sterile, even duplicitous. The word "ministry" is a prize which everyone wants to own and which the older administration of the church wants to reserve. A theological realism respects and nourishes the ministry even as that same realism asserts the empirical to be the master of the linguistic. Realism defines Christian ministry narrowly and yet insists that the defined reality be applicable to more than one or three ministries. Concepts and words from scholastic or Baroque theology have held mastery over ministry while those from charisms and other biblical forms have been relegated to piety. Now diversification in people and ministries questions old regulations.

How will we speak of readers, members of parish councils, theologians and directors of religious education, deacons and pastors gathered together in the same local church? Several merely verbal solutions have been suggested: sets of words which might distinguish one group of ministers from a second. There is *lay* ministry and *clerical* ministry, or *non-ordained* ministry (baptism is overlooked) and *ordained* ministry. One approach is only typographical, *Ministry* and *ministry*.

The problem is that the distinction between each word in the pair is a priori, without much grounding in reality. A prior law or a decision would constitute within almost an ecclesial vacuum the different classes of ministries. The designation of what is ministry at all and what is important, lasting ministry would come from one historical period or one law and would perdure apart from the empirical needs of the community.

All these pairs seem to be rooted not in an ecclesiology of ministries but in a sociology of clerical and lay states. Behind the new and the old terminologies may stand a sincere will to expand—moderately—the ministry, but they convey a nominalism (words disconnected from the actions they should represent), and a solution through terms present both in church administration and theological journalism.

Logic reveals in all these pairs and in the linguistic process itself a theological incompleteness. We have mentioned the difficulties of nominalism and a priori constitution; a third difficulty is the pervasive presence of the word "laity." Lay persons, according to contemporary English usage, are men and women who are not involved in or are ignorant of what the educated, initiated possesses. The exclusion of the majority of Christians (precisely as "laity") from ecclesial power, the traditional counter-poising of them over against a limited clergy, the present and past meaning of the word—all this makes "lay ministry" a contradictory term. Aristotle suggested that words be used as they are commonly understood. The pejorative meaning of laity appears even in the patronage by which minor realms of "ministry" are given to lay people. Laity always appears to carry an intrinsic obstacle to ministry, its lay-ness. In fact, baptism is the essential opening to ministry.

The terms "jurisdiction" and "sacred orders," to the extent that they escape the critique of history, also block the explanation of ministry. All these words are obstacles, opaque or self-justifying. Their meaning is what must be unlocked. For ultimately, as theology repeats from Aquinas, faith and its graced obedience are movements which terminate not in words, but in personalities.[6]

Language is not simply a tool but an expression of life and reality. Modern hermeneutics makes us aware of language as an event, a liberation, or as a propaganda and control. A fundamental theology of ministry should be critical of language, should criticize unsubstantiated or schizophrenic frameworks, and finally should stand apart from every dictatorship of concepts. The theologian has the task of working toward an honest and true correlation of grace in personality and church. The sovereign reality of grace is the ground of all the forms of language which bring together God and human beings.

4. Diversity in Ministry

The issue of diversity in Christian ministry is at the heart of the church today. To bring together an expanded fulltime ministry with bishop and pastor, and to solve confusions about the make-up of the Christian community we need an accurate and incisive theory of diversity-in-ministry. Martin Luther's priesthood of all believers, Aquinas' understanding of a potentiality within the sacrament of orders, Trent's insistence upon not one but three offices are moments in the church's consciousness of a will toward diversity-in-ministry.

Vatican II did not accept the medieval and Baroque reduction of ministry to priesthood alone but took steps to reestablish diversity within traditional church offices. First, the Council established a true ministry of deacon open to men from various manners of Christian life. Although the restored diaconate has not escaped difficulties (the deacon can easily become clericalized, and an extra-liturgical dimension is frequently missing), this restoration is important. In the diaconate today we have a ministry and an ordination which do not lead to priesthood; we have Christians being ordained who are not pledged to celibacy, men who are not members of a quasi-monastic state. Second, conciliar theology located the priesthood as a ministerial representative of the leader of the local church, the bishop. The original meaning of "presbyter" was reintroduced and this gave an identity to this ministry which was other than sacral priest or the lowly parish assistant. Finally, Vatican II described the bishop as a proper ministry and not as a dignity added to or a version of priesthood. We now have three separate ministries with three ordinations; no ministry leads to another nor does one by essence encompass the others. The bishop is the minister to whom presbyter and deacon relate as co-workers.

The new ministries emerging in the church (which in charism and essence are often old and primal ministries) own different degrees of intensity. They are not simply acolytes or parochial helpers. Social action, education, liturgy and health care are areas which seem to be forceful enough to draw Christians to dedicated and complex service. A realistic theology of ministry in today's churches distinguishes between Christians who are in the ministry in limited and temporary ways—readers, weekly leaders of religious education meetings, occasional bearers of word and sacrament to sick and dying—and Christians in the ministry fulltime.

Certainly, parttime ministries are also part of the global expansion of ministry and there is a wide spectrum of these. Ultimately, every Christian at times would be involved in such services. Each ministry should include some preparation and some public commissioning. Some ministries and ordinations (why should we not employ for this commissioning the traditional term "ordination"?) are less intense, of shorter duration, but these are not non-existent.

After 1972, Pope Paul VI and some Vatican departments addressed the issue of the traditional minor orders and indirectly the issue of emerging ministries.[7] Archaic orders such as porter and exorcist were suppressed; reader and liturgical assistant (acolyte) were retained. They were separated from the major orders and entrusted to Christians as a share in the ministry of Christ endowed by baptism. A Christian now enters these restored ministries (they are liturgical services) through an installation which, the Vatican suddenly declared, is not an ordination like that commencing one of the three Tridentine orders. This beneficial renewal joined two traditional services to some real action in the church and it recognized somewhat the ministerial dimension of baptism. There were, however, two drawbacks to this positive move: first, the traditional word "ordination" was separated from these ministries; second, women were excluded from the restored service of reader and minister. The second problem led to ecclesial confusion: an act of ecclesiological nominalism established that women could function in these ministries in an extraordinary way but without the ceremony (and grace) of installation. Consequently, the ministry has expanded among the baptized—but without clear forms. An observer can see behind this hesitant process two fears: one of admitting women to the realm of sacral orders, one of watering down the difference between clergy and laity—a classification taken as more significant than ministerial diversity sharing in common baptism, charism and service.

David Power points out that the effect of this Roman encounter with expanding ministry is minimal if we remain with the documents themselves, but that the documents do recognize a new world-wide situation in ministry. Their contradictions indicate that here praxis has outstripped official theology.

> Whatever the indecisions and ambiguities, the church is working out
> the implications of the Vatican Council's teaching on the laity and is
> trying to do this in conjunction with the facts of church life rather

than in a purely abstract manner. Thus, the ecclesiological principle which states the call of the laity to share in the mission and ministry of the church on the basis of their share in Christ's own ministry, is everywhere accepted. . . . The extent, however, to which these concerns postulate a new ecclesial structure is not often found in statements. It is more the lived experience that calls this to our attention.[8]

Could there be a further diversification of ministry, a diversification into ordained ministries parallel to bishop, priest and deacon, a diversification recalling the early churches? Paul VI suggested to national churches that they might add their own ministries to the lower level of reader and acolyte. "Besides the rites common to the Latin Church, there is nothing to prevent episcopal conferences from requesting others of the Apostolic See, if they judge the establishment of such offices in their region to be necessary or very useful."[9] This suggested expansion of parttime ministries (a suggestion the Vatican subsequently has not approved) indicates a path which could extend to fulltime ministries.

Our fundamental theology has indicated that baptism will lead all Christians to some ministerial activity during their lives, that some of this activity will be in liturgy and some in the public forum, and that then some Christians enter upon professional ministries, three of which tradition holds as particularly central. With the prosaic term, "professional ministry" we delineate ministers who through education and internship, through the church's sponsorship and through mature dedication enter upon an important, specific ministry. This ministry is their profession (but not a job or a status). They intend a lengthy commitment to this public ministry. The word professional contains pejorative overtones from the world of self-aggrandizing, slick or elitist professions. Originally, a profession was a commitment, an act of faith in a work which was often a service, e.g. medicine, social service. By "professional ministry" we mean (1) those services in the church which exist after a serious call and extensive preparation, (2) services which are fulltime and which include a strong possibility of lengthy, lifetime commitment, (3) ministries which draw on such preparation and commitment because tradition and contemporary pastoral practice consider these ministries to be central, important, foundational for the church in its full life.

These professional ministries imply permanence (whose pictorial theology is the tradition of character), responsibility to the entire church, and qualities of leadership. Normally, these ministries would be permanent, although the mobility of Western society threatens the permanency not only of professional ministers in education and peace and justice but also those in the leadership ministries of presbyter.

The distinction between professionally prepared, permanent, important and publicly established ministries, and other baptismal ministries should be grounded upon the real permanence and significance of ministries central to the local church and not upon an arbitrary distinction between groups of Christians, or upon theology of ordination which neglects the dignity of baptism.

The same issue of diversity between ministries exists in their respective ordinations. There is considerable difference between the public entry into an episcopal ministry of leadership for the entire diocese and the training and presentation of a minister of communion to the sick for a few years. The identity of each is ministerial, however, and their considerable difference must be established by the levels of intensity of what is done and how that is viewed by the church. Diversity (with the meaning of theological phrases such as "essential distinction") is to be grounded in the reality of the ministry and the church's life. The baptismal background to ministry cannot be overlooked nor can the distinction of ministries and the identity of the central, ecclesial, professional ministries be phased out.

Some churches may need other, central ministries, e.g. justice; they must be positively related to the ministries of bishop or presbyter. We cannot equate a Eucharistic acolyte with a fulltime minister in the hospital. The acolyte is not in Christian service as intensely as the presbyter, but the health-care minister may well be. A formal Christian ministry, witnessed to in the early church and needed by this region, should not be ministerially ignored or relegated to the vague designation of laity. Christians who are active seven days a week in the improvement of political policy and community life are not less but more than the former subdeacon. New ministries can fulfill the essence of ministry even if there is a difference in service, quantitatively and qualitatively. A solution to the issue of new professional ministries must begin with a theological realism which discerns ministry where the characteristics of ministry are active.

The legitimacy of ministerial diversity is established by research into Scripture and history; the modality of such diversification, however, comes from experience and theology. How is diversity appearing in church structure? Which ministries stand forth to complement deacon, bishop and presbyter? What are the possibilities and needs for a community or a country?

There are different ways by which churches will find other ministries. (1) Some would do it by reintroducing ministries found in past tradition. Ministries from the New Testament or from the patristic periods in churches, East and West, are brought back into church life, especially into the liturgy. (2) Others look at the need and availability of Christians for a ministry and so conclude it should be established. Behind the Constantinian church's clericalization of widows and ascetics and behind the clericalization of the papal household in the seventh, thirteenth and seventeenth centuries there is a discernment and location of people and offices in the official ministry, the clergy. Today there are groups of teachers, musicians and social workers in the ministry. Their talents and good may indicate charism. The ministry, however, is not aided when the organization and function of ministries are left unclear, when a variety of jobs are gathered together into one office without a specific, extra-liturgical purpose, or ignored as lay service. (3) Finally, there are ministries based not upon Scriptural or liturgical legitimation (although both can be present) nor upon a pool of interested people but upon the needs and priorities of a local church (parish, diocese, region, country). Here ministry is viewed teleologically: charism and service are directed without exception toward a specific service of the kingdom, or of the church and the human race. Ministry as a function of building up the church begins not with an extrinsic charism nor with a liturgical restoration but with the community's consciousness of its needs; communal goals lead into an ecclesiology, i.e. into a plan of ministry.

Let us look at some recent examples of diversification in full-time ministries. Bernard Cooke argued for different, more open classes of ministry.[10] He saw five areas as fundamental for church life: groups of designation as important ministries: (1) Christians who form community, (2) ministers of the word, (3) ministers to human needs, (4) ministers of God's judgment, (5) ministers of the sacrament. This classification works at being a phenomenology of church life in growth. There is, however, a problem with an overlapping of these ministers. Are not ministers of God's judgment ministers of the word? Would not those who form community administer some sacrament and preach the word?

The German bishops set up three new ministries. They were selected not by important areas of service to church and kingdom but by secondary aspects of parish life. The pastoral assistant works in areas such as teaching and personal counseling; the community assistant helps the pastor in his work, both in the parish and liturgy, except where the pastorate requires priestly ordination; there is thirdly an administrative assistant who relieves both pastor and ministers of the burdens of administration. There is in all this only a vague teleology, for the emphasis is upon people trained to assist. These assistants may only intensify the lack of ministerial focus in the pastorate as there are now three groups educated to do everything and nothing. There need not be anything formally ministerial about parish administration (an atheist can be a good bookkeeper and secretary). Rather than establish clear ministries in the parish, the single minister has been given assistants. The overall impact of the German plan must be one of a pool of random ministerial services.

Another step by the German bishops is more interesting. They approved for preaching Christians not ordained to the presbyterate.[11] This has introduced a range of men and women into the liturgical preaching of the community's worship and has established baptism as a ground for important ministry. Moreover, while permitting occasional preaching by valued Christians, it has set up theological education and training as the criteria for becoming an ordinary preacher in a German parish. If we could change "lay-preacher" into "preaching minister," we would have an example of the diversification of significant ministry.

David Power, treating ministries other than bishop, presbyter and deacon, suggested a number of levels of ministry arranged not according to their present or potential importance but according to present Roman Catholic recognition.[12] First come the ministries of acolyte and lector preserved formally in the church's law and liturgy; next are the extra-ordinary ministers of the Eucharist, whose identity is unclear; then there are ministries of liturgical presidence, that is, ministries which perform an important work for the community, but are recognized only obliquely: e.g. preaching or assisting the pastor (similar to what was established by the German Church); occasional services, for instance, to the sick and elderly, which occur so often in a parish; finally, daily Christian involvement through sign and word in the course of secular society. Power's sketch is valuable for it illustrates the present lack of recognition of the ministries of the baptized. There is also the interesting downplaying of ministries involved in liturgy alone and a telling location of the traditional lay witness to and transformation of the world at the end of the ministry's spectrum.

In the process of diversification occurring in the diocese and parish the churches can draw from all three sources of diversity—tradition, the ministerial interests shown by educational commitment and service, and broader goals and priorities of the church. In the United States, teaching ministry is particularly important followed by two more recent services: (1) peace and justice; and (2) the broad ministry of healing found in counseling, parochial care of the sick and aged, social advocacy on behalf of the elderly, and ministry in health care institutions. Liturgy and preaching of a wide variety also call forth ministers.

It is not surprising that astonishment, even skepticism or fear, strikes us when we imagine a church with ordained ministers, some of whom are not priests. Would there be order as well as diversity? Would leadership be sustained amid a universality of charisms? An implementation of diversity in ministry is not inconceivable. It would be, for some churches, only a coherent theological arrangement and ecclesial recognition of what is the de facto structure of the parish or diocese. At Vatican II, theologians argued for the restoration of the diaconate by pointing out that the church in fact already had the diaconate active in certain areas; what it did not have was the grace and form given to both community and individual which come from public recognition and commissioning of this ministry. Today this is even more true, and of more ministries.

The preparation of ministers calls for a few alterations in the pattern of ministry.

(a) The leaders of the local churches, bishop and presbyter, find their identity in leadership: this leadership is manifest through preaching, through various forms of leading liturgy, through a leadership of the life (apostolic as well as liturgical) of the community, and through the facilitation and coordination of ministries. Discovering the true identity of this particular ministry leads some previous roles of secular administrator and sacral father into decline.

(b) Certain ministries, considered important by local or regional churches, may be recognized as professional ministry, i.e., they begin after lengthy training. Their permanence and preparation call forth a serious ordination in the church.

(c) If this expansion of the ministry appears too abrupt, diverse ministries could be established as forms of the diaconate. Such a step has the advantage of giving the permanent diaconate an extra-liturgical identity it now lacks. But this would also mean that a deacon (and deaconess) is a global ministry and needs a subsequent interpretation: for instance, deacon for education, deacon for peace and justice. This revives what may be one view of the early churches that *diakonia* was not at first a specific liturgical or eleemosynary ministry but represents (as it does linguistically) ministry itself.

(d) Finally, the ministerial image and service of the baptized should be enhanced. The levels of involvement in the life of the community should be recognized. All Christians deserve a biblically urged participation in the pneumatic reality of ministry which assists, inspires and suggests the professional ministry.

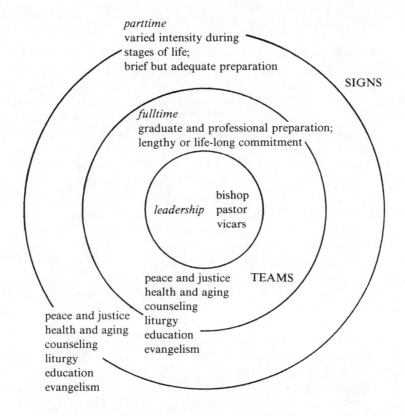

parttime
varied intensity during
stages of life;
brief but adequate preparation

SIGNS

fulltime
graduate and professional preparation;
lengthy or life-long commitment

bishop
leadership pastor
vicars

peace and justice   TEAMS
health and aging
counseling
peace and justice liturgy
health and aging   education
counseling   evangelism
liturgy
education
evangelism

National and regional needs offer the fundamental ecclesiology for adding and diminishing ministries. Into that process goes not only evangelistic need but also the spirituality, liturgy, and cultural sociology of this Christian-people. Just as ministry can assume culturally this or that pattern, so ecumenically the ethos, spirituality and tradition of a particular Christian church influences the spirit and form of its ministry. As both Scripture and tradition show, certain ministries are always present but the pattern of ministry and the addition of ministries, whose preparation and stability implies a public commissioning, can vary from place to place, time to time. Unity in the nunber and description of ministries is not a special way for the churches to manifest their unity. While ministries should not be too easily moved in and out of church order, the nature and number of the ministries expand and diminish as culture and church need them.

5. Doing and Being: History and Critique

Our emphasis upon the activity of ministry may have fed fears that ministry is Christian activism, unprepared and unreflective; a rigid doing-good or a frantic but casual involvement in social change. Should the dignity of Bossuet or Newman, the austerity of a Charles de Foucauld be replaced by minions of HHS? "Doing" is a necessary stage in the liberation of ministry but we must now balance that aspect with some discussion—both positive and negative—about "being." Being and doing belong together. The activity of ministry and its charism are rooted not only in the Spirit, but in the personal life of the minister.

Three areas unfold the relationship of being to doing. The first asks how seriously should our definition of ministry prefer doing over being; the second looks at the life, the being, of Christians in the ministry, particularly in the fulltime ordained ministry and asks about suitable lifestyles to form the milieu of ministry; the third recalls the theme of secular and sacral, for in the classic distinction between clergy and laity, priesthood and ministry, one term seems to emphasize being, the other doing.

Philosophers will tell us that the dialectical problem of being and doing pervades our entire life. Certainly it raises old and deep issues for a theology of ministry. Being can aid ministry or it can challenge, even replace or compromise and then destroy ministry.

Modes of being enter into the fiber of ministry in many ways. Affirming the active dimension as essential to ministry is much like holding a sailing ship's wheel steady in a storm, for people naturally gravitate towards stability. The church has yet to free itself from the step of Christian bishops entering the Roman imperial bureaucracy in the early fourth century—a moment when the waters of salary, insignia and power (all warned against by Jesus) flowed into the wine of preaching the Gospel and coordinating the ministry. Rome, Constantinople, Aachen, Paris, Würzburg, New York—centuries and civilizations have not been able to imagine the ministers of the church without their status in society and politics.

Elements of a clerical state of life have helped at times to make ministry effective, and one can still argue for some of them as helpful to ministry. Clothes, celibacy, a style of housing, certain prayers can be public signs of a mode of being. As elements in a style of life they can serve ministry, but they are not ministry itself.

The Tridentine *seminarium,* etymologically a "hot-house" for seedlings, aimed at producing a lifestyle more than a ministry. Rome of the Counter-Reformation took seriously some of the Reformers' renewal but it ignored others by concentrating upon the discipline of the clerical life. It was hoped that what a dry and foreign liturgy could not accomplish the holiness of its priest could. The atmosphere of the seminary—rules and a meticulous evaluation of their infraction—showed an emphasis placed upon being rather than doing. The amount of time spent upon education for preaching was small compared to that spent in practice of clerical discipline.

There are also less glorious roads by which being infiltrates service. For many historical reasons, ministry itself became a state of life, a mode of being. Over and beyond ordinations to ministry, there developed a first, liturgical ceremony of entrance on the ladder of ecclesiastical orders: tonsure placed a man in the clerical state where he had new obligations and rights without having any ministry. A cleric did not *ipso facto* act significantly for the Spirit or church but nevertheless he existed in a novel form of being. Being had been separated from doing, manner of life from ministry.

Life-style at times absorbed the ministry. A particular style of being had to be maintained while the ministry of doing seemed to be highly desirable but not essentially necessary. We see this exemplified in the evaluation of a priest, whether by bishop or people, as someone who is bound by clerical style. The church tolerates ministers who are ineffective in ministry, men who cannot preach, counsel or celebrate the liturgy except with ineptitude; the official church does not, however, tolerate the minister whose clerical mode of being is compromised. If one must choose, right clothes seem preferable to zeal and ministerial ability; *figura* over *diakonia*. Offenses against the essence of ministry were tolerable—communities suffered for years under ministers who were incapable of any ministerial work and whose guidance in private and from the pulpit was both heterodox and scandalous. Offenses against the life-style, however, were not tolerated. The alcoholic survived, the incontinent did not; the inept preacher was promoted, the dedicated slum worker who had set aside clerical clothes was forgotten. Ordination was transformed into a ceremony of entrance into being a sacred person. The quasimonasticism of the seminary aimed at being.

Life-style is so mixed with ministry now that both have lost some of their meaning. Each has assumed the characteristics of the other. What is approved as priestly life may be essentially optional facets of being a Christian; what is in reality essential to ministry, e.g. publicly preaching the Gospel, may have faded into the background, pushed aside by the demands of an office whose burdens are political and economic. Both being and doing, however, are aspects of the healthy personality. Christian being is the atmosphere of ministry but not its substitute.

6. Doing and Being: Sign and Countersign

Being, Christian being, has a place in a theology of ministry. Being is the ground of all that is done. The Christian life is broader than its services. Although ministry is not the day-to-day life of a Christian, the daily life of every Christian can be ministerial. It is clear from history that the lives of Christian men and women have been voices of revelation, places of hope and care. Lives of radical commitment attracted others to the faith. The Christian life as sign can serve the kingdom powerfully. Being and doing, sign and activity are clarified through the following typology.

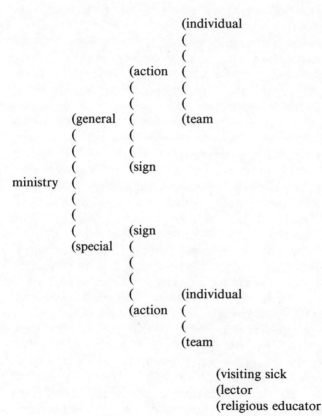

```
                              (action   (
                                 (          (
                                 (          (team (administration
            (from baptism    (                    (volunteer service
                 (          (
                 (          (
                 (          (sign—a Christian life
                 (
ministry    (
                 (
                 (
                 (
            (special   (sign    (contemplative, monastic life
                          (
                          (
                          (
                          (          (individual (bishop, pastor, deacon,
                       (action                DRE, teacher, social action.
                          (
                       (team (school
                             (health service
```

Let us turn to three areas where venerable theology and church practice have mixed being and doing in the ministry and where we are challenged to distinguish the Christian life from the church's public ministry: (a) the monastic, contemplative life seen as ministry; (b) secular, professional life as Christian vocation or ministerial sign; (c) ecclesiastical life without real ministry.

(a) The modalities of being a Christian which we call contemplative, monastic and eremitical are, as such, not ministry. They may be ministerial as a sign. This does not mean they are not important; for those called to it, the monastic contemplative life is a particularly rich way of being a Christian. Contemplatives are ministers when they minister to each other in community, or to occasional visitors, or when they write or teach (ministries not central to their chosen life). But as a life, the monastic and contemplative life is precisely that—a life. Life is not a direct, public action, for life is not clear and explicit. The world can ignore or misunderstand the unspoken words of the contemplative life, of a silent Christian life; society may never even perceive that in silence and symbol something saving is being expressed. Ministerially, precisely in this ambiguous utterance of a witness in being and life, the contemplative life is a sign. In some times and places the signified Gospel of contemplative men and women may be the best preaching of an apostle. Normally, however, the Gospel is communicated through more direct actions, and it is in direct, full-time professional ministries that we must search for the essential character of ministry. If silence is ministry, if prayer is preaching, if solitude is apostolate and social service, ecclesiology becomes a self-defining atmosphere touching only obliquely church or world. We must let the good things of Christian life stand on their own, and also let the analogous complexity of ministry challenge our analysis. Only then can ministry struggle for a wider life.

As we consider the monastic life and its application to church service in areas like education and health care, we must note that Christians participate in the ministry not only directly or by sign, but also indirectly: as members of a group, team or community whose goal is clearly ministerial. "Team" invests daily professions with a ministerial goal and yet safeguards a narrow identity for ministry. The universal church is made up not only of dioceses and parishes but a variety of institutions, particularly educational and health-care ministries. What is not explicitly ministry—maintenance, bookkeeping, etc. (there are no Christian numbers or pipes)—can become an integral part of the team ministry of a group or institution. For the primary ministry of a hospital is not radiation therapy but health in the widest sense just as the ministry of a Catholic university is an education which preaches the values and message of the kingdom. To this primary goal the entire team contributes.

(b) Our insistence that ministry is something the Christian does explicitly for the kingdom and church (and not the justice and love which results from Christian life) leads us to question the theology and ecclesial identity of the lay apostle. We have already alluded to this. An indirect ministry, taking the form of life as symbol, certainly may influence secular life without explicit religious proclamation, but is this the ministry introduced by baptism?

Secular institutes once suggested that in the modern world explicit ministry must diminish while covert and symbolic action would be normal ministry. This may have been true of earlier decades. Roman Catholicism, after the Reformation and Enlightenment, felt that the modern world was hostile toward it. The church could not abandon its view of the kingdom as more than the life of the soul; Christianity was public and social. So without direct control over society, church leaders encouraged the laity formed by doctrine, sacraments and spiritual discipline to transform the secular order, slowly and from within. The theological rationale for this low-keyed ministry was not all that congenial to the Catholic mind. First, it implied that faith was a matter of individuals and of souls; second, it doubted this mission to grace was present in the world; third, it entrusted to the laity what was in fact an infiltration of the worlds of science and politics; finally, it divided grace from nature, giving soul and sacrament to priests, world and history to laity.

Ministry makes explicit the advent of the kingdom of God. Christianity does not monopolize justice or joyfulness but what is unique to Christianity is precisely an explicitness, an exposition of God's plan for our race. Normally, the church expresses the Gospel publicly and explicitly, not by infiltration. It is confusing when Christian ministry becomes no more than a hint of a change in the world's era and future, only an implicit gesture or a slow, patient but oblique reference to what is in fact the Incarnation of God. There are times and societies where only the ministry of sign is permissible, e.g. in Muslim countries or in a refugee camp, in a factory or an Asian village—there a patient ministry of being speaks more loudly than sermons. The ministry of silence and symbol, however, is never the norm of ministry. That would deny the incarnation of God's word and would reduce Christianity to a static sect.

Activities such as teaching French, being a bookkeeper and farming are not Christian ministry. They are the vocations and professions of Christians and as such are good and holy. We cannot continue a universalist theology of ministry in which every legitimate and moral human enterprise is ministry. How does teaching chemistry well announce Christ directly in a manner suited to the age of the Spirit? A lawyer's work should be judged not as ministry, but as the work of a Christian; not every legal transaction is ministry even if legal aid to the oppressed intentionally done as a confrontation of sin by the power of the Kingdom of God can be a ministry. Preaching and teaching are direct ways of spreading the Gospel; farming and mining are not. Producing food, directing the flow of money, and making and selling furniture may be important, but neither ledgers nor fields evangelize directly or publicly. Only those already converted by word and sacrament can perceive what message there might be in a bucolic spirituality.

We do not mean to imply that the way men and women work is inferior or unblessed. Life pervades our work and so do baptism and grace. We are, however, complex beings; we are called to be, to work, to live and to minister. These are not all the same enterprise. Considering all of life to be ministry will ultimately hand over ministry again to a professional class. Defining ministry narrowly does not produce an elite group of ministers but lets ministry challenge the potential ministry of every baptized person. When all is ministry, ministry fades away.

What Luther intended by the priesthood of all believers was the ministry of all Christians. Again, language can be a social and theological obstacle. A sacral priesthood of all baptized is not found in the New Testament; it could not be because priesthood itself (not simply Old Testament priesthood) ended with Jesus. Nor does the New Testament indicate that farming, banking and shipbuilding are ministries; the actions of a ministry listed in the New Testament always have a proximate reference to the Gospel of the kingdom and not simply a remote and preparatory connection. What Luther intended was a liberation of baptized adults from oppression theologically justified in feudalism, an elimination of a sacral caste, and a rediscovery of the universality and diversity of the ministry as found in the New Testament.[13]

The Reformers did not succeed, however, in developing a praxis of universal ministry. Some Protestant traditions show a bizarre switch in universalizing not ministry but the secularized laity, speaking of all Christians being lay people in an attempt to get free of the sacramental. This secularization process can now be seen as the suicide of a church. Christians are not all destined to be laity but to be new creation, a new people whose psychology includes charism and ministry. Luther's conservative reform, frightened by Calvin and the enthusiasts, hesitated and then returned to the single pastoral office bolstering it up. Today some Protestant churches may be frozen in a monoform ministry rooted in medieval office.

(c) Our narrow definition of ministry as more than a monastic or clerical state questions also the way in which the church is administered. Ecclesial administration developed after Constantine into something approaching a sacral court, some of whose actions may be ministry but many of which are not. Churches at the international and local level often employ as administrators those whom the church has liturgically commissioned to be preaching leaders of local churches (bishops) or Eucharistic communities (pastors, presbyters). These men now perform secretarial and administrative functions. Behind this staffing of the church by the celibate and/or the ordained is a laudable desire for honesty and discretion and a questionable desire for secrecy and control. The means to these ends (which are to keep the church from ambition, avarice and power) can lead to a confusion of what we will call a mode of life—celibate, male, quasi-monastic, clerical—and a ministry—bishop or presbyter.

The curias of the church, Roman and diocesan, have been from the beginning administrative circles of men whose dedication and self-effacement recall a religious order. Episcopal and papal households were patterned after religious orders. Tradition tied many administrative offices to priestly ordination as an entrance to the curia, and to episcopacy as a fulfillment. This led to priests who had no real ministry in a local community and to titular bishops who more often than not did not fulfill the ministerial definition of a bishop but existed as such only by virtue of their ordination. There existed archbishops who rarely preached, presbyters and deacons who were secretaries and archivists. Goals of ecclesial administration and not ministerial identity altered the meaning of priest and bishop, while the mix of monastic clericalism and bureaucracy gave another example of a minister who was in fact defined in ways extrinsic to the ministry. This furthered an a priori legal and liturgical definition of the ministry of leadership—the bishop as a juridical leader of a non-existent community and as a solitary Christian with the power to confirm and ordain. Nominalist views of the ministry joining with the clerical mode of living to give arbitrarily a public title to an ecclesial administrator.

What the church needs for its administration is perhaps a religious order (although non-monastic Christians, too, can be trustworthy and efficient). They would serve, without ambition and without any hope of honor and wealth through the misappropriation of ministry, as the curia of the church's leaders. In a healthy religious order, service to the community and its leadership as well as to the world is done not only with dedication and humility but with anonymity. The drives for insignia and power are resisted. We can see how the employment of the semi-monastic clerical state was a quest for this kind of administrator who would retain a dignity and quiet while restraining the noises of modernity which threaten to turn every church into another business. But today, because of the mix of the monastic and ministerial, some evangelical ministries have become titles for administrative posts.

7. Clergy and Laity

For fifteen hundred years the primal structure of the Christian churches, the ultimate form of diversity within that social group, has been not Christ and his Body, not the Spirit with its gifts but clergy and laity. This line of socialized diversification represented differences in people which came from levels of being and which created not services but classes.

Both historical theology and the expansion of the ministry have challenged the claim that the distinction between clergy and laity is basic, perennial and of Jesus' institution. In its historico-social forms it exists as a product of culture; it is a pointer to the importance of ministry.

a. Clergy

The etymology of clergy lies in the Greek *kleros,* "lot," "portion." In *Acts* (1:15f) Matthias is elected by casting lots (*klerous*) to receive the share (*kleron*) of the apostolic ministry which Judas had abandoned. By the time of the *Apostolic Tradition* of Hippolytus (c. 220 A.D.) the word is used for a common state to which bishop, presbyters and deacons belong. A special laying on of hands was reserved for these clergy because of their liturgical ministry. By the third century the higher clergy not only existed as a social group constituted by ordination but their ministry was increasingly sacerdotal and the source of their social status was largely derived from the liturgical side of communal life, a side which was touched by the sacral.

There is another New Testament meaning for *kleros.* In *Acts, Colossians* and *Ephesians,* the word is used for the share which all Christians, all members of a local church have in the word and reality of Christ, "the inheritance of the saints in light" (Col 1:12). Hans Küng notes the strange transposition by which this Greek word for share or lot came to mean not the universal participation of the baptized in Christ but the special allotted task of leading ministers.

> From a theological point of view, then, *clerus* means the share in eschatological salvation which God gives to each individual believer in the communion of all believers. This share is to be understood not simply as "lot" but as a "good thing" prepared for the believer by God. The particular share of the Lord is precisely not just the clergy but the whole people of God; and Christ is the "share" not just of the clergy but of the whole people of God. The word *"clerus"*, too, belongs to the whole church and not just to those who hold office in it; and while the New Testament can support the use of the term as applied to individuals, it is fundamentally the property of the whole church.[14]

In a letter of Clement, a church leader in Rome, written around 95 A.D., we find some appreciation of Christian ministry rooted in the Aaronic priesthood. Clement described how the great Apostles planned that Christians would succeed them in ministry. These bishops and deacons function (as did Moses and Aaron) as leaders of the people. There is an order (*taxis*) among the charism and activities. Nevertheless, Clement did not describe the Christian ministers as priests nor does he use sacerdotal language in referring to Christians. Jesus is the significant high priest. Still we can see that by the turn of the century, work and leadership are giving particular importance to a few ministries.[15]

During the third century the focus of the community began to shift from evangelization to liturgy and orthodox teaching. The external mission of the church was still considerable but the increase of Christians gave liturgy a more central role. The separation of a clergy from the people may have been nourished by the tendency of the churches to want to resemble pagan cultic life. Particularly important was an a-historical reappropriation of the Old Testament. A largely Gentile church looked upon Jewish Scripture not so much as a prophecy of Christ but as a collection of inspired beliefs and ethics. There is Hippolytus' liturgy of ordination and Cyprian's argument for the purity of the *sacerdotes* by citing Old Testament texts. Origen uses *klerikoi* as a term for those in special orders and he contrasts them with the people; he presents the clergy as the maintainers of the church's organization, but with his bias in favor of preaching and theology, he occasionally implies that the most important ministry is accomplished by those who teach and preach at an advanced level.[16]

Class distinctions come in pairs. While the clergy became an elevated, sacral state, the laity became a passive group. What were originally titles of glory, "heirs" and "people" become prisons of status.

b. Laity

At the heart of Israel's faith and revelation was its theological sociology of being the people of God. People (*laos* in Greek) is contrasted with the *goyim*, the nations. Israel is people because of God's involvement in history: his love and care touch them. Aware of both the intensity and universality of the advent of God in Christ, the first Christians saw themselves as the people of God. This title is not withdrawn from Israel, but the reality of being-the-people-of-God in a more intense fashion is open to all, male and female, slave and free, Jew and Greek (Gal 3:28f). God is bringing out of the nations a people (Acts 18:10); those who were once alien from Israel and at war with God, no people, are his people (Eph 2:19). The idea of the new, pilgrimaging people of God, broader and stronger, is often found in the New Testament writings which challenged sacral religion. *Hebrews, Ephesians,* and *1 Peter* display the new covenant giving to all the followers of Christ a priestliness or consecration. In the midst of cults and sects, Judaism, Germanic or Syrian religions, the Christians saw themselves as an elect people blessed by God: unique, powerful, in a sense untouchable.

A derivative form of people in Greek, *laikos,* from which comes the Latin and English "laity," has generally been thought to be simply a form of *laos*—a lay person who participated in the greatness of the new people of God. Critical studies have found that this is not the case.[17] In secular literature and in translations of the Old Testament after the Septuagint, the meaning of the word is much like our contemporary meaning: ordinary, not consecrated, even profane. The word is rarely used in Christian literature before 200 A.D., but by the third century Clement of Alexandria used the term *laikos* of Christians who are not presbyters or deacons.[18] Slightly earlier, Tertullian, recalling previous theology, exclaimed: "*Nonne et laici sacerdotes sumus?*" "Are not we laity priests?"[19] "Laity" soon found a fixed place among Christians as a term for the mass of believers who are not among the sacral elite. The etymology and theology of *laos,* "people," are positive; that of "laity" seems from its beginning to mean people who are profane, outside of the center of interest.

The period from Constantine to Justinian established the clergy as a separate social class endowed with religious and civil privileges.[20] The episcopacy, which was earlier an acceptance of a potentially dangerous and self-denying service of the community, became a privileged state. For the medieval church clerical tonsure was a minor ordination which guaranteed membership in an ascetic and legal state. Feudal and pre-industrial societies prized stability because they had to struggle to maintain existence and society itself. Medieval and Baroque theologies of the church looked at ministry, that is "church office," much as they looked at marriage: to defend its legal rights, its public image, its contribution to a stable society. The being of ministry analyzed by law and the sacramental ontology of structured grace were paramount. Later societies prizing freedom, individuality and action could only find the clergy-laity model not false but sociologically inept.

c. The Breakdown of the Clergy-Laity Distinction

To be a layperson is to have a modality of being, or, better, of non-being; not-being ordained a priest or bishop or deacon (married deacons are often contradictorily referred to as "lay deacons"). The phenomenologically pejorative or at least passive meaning of laity excludes a baptized person from acting publicly on behalf of the community. Rather, that life is one of virtue in an alien world; activity is reserved to the ordained. Yves Congar has written: "To look for 'spirituality of laypeople' in the Scriptures makes no sense. There is no mention of laity. Certainly the word exists but it exists outside the Christian vocabulary."[21] Today, as baptized Christians assume in large numbers ministry to the sick, teaching and preaching in communities where no ordained ministers are available, some churchmen struggle to establish a rationale for how they are *not* in the ministry. They do this because they fear that any entry into the ministry means entry into priesthood, and such access is closed to those who are not male, celibate clerics.

How is the ordained secretary of the chancery in the ministry while the educated, full-time Christian employed in the team ministry in the urban hospital remains in the lay state? We could cite dozens of such paradoxes. Their solution can only come from a coherent theology of the ministry which replaces the clergy-laity structure with a group of concentric circles. Yves Congar describes how this shift took place in his own thinking, and because of his preeminence in the ecclesiology of this century, it is worth quoting him as a summary of many ideas.

> I wrote in my "Introduction" to *Towards a Theology of the Laity* (1953) "It is not just a matter of adding a paragraph or a chapter to an ecclesiological exposition which from beginning to end ignores the principles on which a theology of the laity really depends. Without those principles, we should have, confronting a laicized world, only a clerical Church, which would not be the people of God in the fullness of its truth. At bottom there can be only one sound and sufficient theology of laity, and that is total ecclesiology." That theology I did not write. (I have come to see) that the pastoral reality described by the New Testament imposes a view much richer. It is God, it is Christ who in his Spirit does not cease building the church. . . . The church is not built up merely by the acts of the official ministers of the presbytery but by many kinds of services, more or less stable or occasional, more or less spontaneous or recognized, some even consecrated by sacramental ordination. These services exist . . . , they exist even if they are not called by their real name, ministries, nor have their true place and status in ecclesiology. Proceeding along this line of double recognition is extremely important for an accurate view of things, for a satisfying theology of the laity. Eventually one sees that the decisive pair is not "priesthood-laity" as I used in my book on the laity but much more that of ministries or service and community.
>
> We can say, in short, that Jesus instituted a structured community, a community holy, priestly, prophetic, missionary, apostolic with its center, ministers—some freely raised up by the Spirit, others ordained by the imposition of hands.[22]

Recent defense of the distinction between clergy and laity has its source in a legitimate anxiety that the denial of this patristic and medieval theological sociology will lead to a church without diversity and without ecclesial competence. We would argue that just the opposite is true: the clergy-laity distinction suppresses diversity and standards of competency in the ministry. Church administrators fear that a pietist universalism will appear where anyone can perform any service in the church. In fact, distinction through education for every ministry will increase in depth and rigor as the general Christian population grows in education. Taking ministry seriously according to the criteria of the New Testament includes a distinction of ministries. The identity of and difference between bishop, presbyter and deacon, and also of teacher and counselor in a parish is far greater now than it was twenty years ago. Clear ministerial identity brings not monoformity but distinction and demand for competence. There is more distinction in a church through a diversity of responsible activities than through two levels of class.

Members of religious orders (who are not priests) are canonically laity. The canonical status of brothers and sisters versus their real role in ministry presents a particularly poignant example of the collapse of the clergy-laity division. In the United States perhaps seventy percent of the ministry is and has been performed by religious women all of whom are officially not in the ministry and who, because real ministry through jurisdiction is tied to ordination to one or two orders, have no real public life in the church. They are formally laity. The piety of the official church, when it views them, addresses them out of the context of vowed laity. Certainly their vast accomplishments since the nineteenth century show that they are major ministers in the American church. Religious women present the most dramatic phenomenological "non-compute" in the world of clerical and lay states; for in their "non-ministry" lie great services, and in their non-sacral spirituality are perduring charism and ministry.

Many religious orders of men, dating from the medieval or Baroque period, have built into their constitutional structure a clericalism, i.e. they are primarily communities of priests whom a minority of non-ordained members assist. Now these orders are finding this sociological distinction injurious to their very existence. Because the ministry of presbyter has assumed a new role as community leader and liturgical focus, because the weak spirituality of the private, hyphenated priest has not survived, because opportunities suggest new ministries, and because an educated society does not offer many candidates for menial labor, men enter clerical orders intent upon ministry and scholarship, fresh from practical and theoretical education, but without seeing any reason why all should, as a step towards community and ministry, be ordained to the particular ministry of presbyter or deacon. This attitude is not one of disdain for these two ministries. Even members of religious orders who are ordained to the ministry of presbyter may sense out of theological reflection that this ministry is not quite the same as that of the presbyter/pastor of the local church. Jesuit, Dominican priests are not leaders of local communities, although they are preachers and celebrants. This too questions a single ministry of priest.

Religious life challenges the separateness of clergy and laity. In its own renewal mandated by Vatican II it has rediscovered a diversity in ministry within the community life and services of the larger orders and congregations, male and female.

For these various reasons, the social framework given by the clergy-laity distinction cannot survive. Congar is right in suggesting the model of concentric circles—all of which circles are realms of ministry but which are diverse in goals and intensity.

8. Ministry and Modes of Life

Being and Doing. One way of untangling a theology of ministry from the several contradictions which surround it is to distinguish between a *specific ministry* and a *mode of living*.[23] Both are facets of Christian life but each has its own identity. Role, profession, status, office— different sociologies have different terminological schemata to distinguish between doing and being. By ministry we mean not every Christian charism and activity but those done on behalf of the church, and our theology speaks mainly (but not exclusively) of professional, full-time ministry while including a variety of other true but parttime ministries. By a modality of living, on the other hand, we mean a stable way of being a human person. The conditions which give a mode to individual life can come with birth (race, sex) or they can be freely chosen (marriage, vowed celibacy, divorce). There are also ambiguous and anti-Christian ways of living. All optional ways of living are subject to the dialectic of sin and grace. Living out one's life can be ethically and existentially at the service of *charis* and *diakonia* or it can impede them by sin, error, scandal and neglect.

We are biologically determined by birth. Male and female, of different races and cultures, sprung from economic and social classes— these are all modalities of human life. Can we argue convincingly that ministry cannot join with one or more of these natal styles of existence? What inner dynamic in the kingdom of God would exclude through an aspect of birth the baptized from a particular ministry? Could ontic modalities of life given at birth impede the exercise of ministry in the church? If so, then the theology of freedom and universality of the kingdom of God, so richly exemplified in the Gospels and proclaimed in Paul (Col 3:11), is brought into question. God's Spirit has brought about a revolution in human religion, a word of acceptance to all people, a universal end to barriers between people (Eph 2:19), and so the potentialities of this eschatological people run through every sex or race.

Social consciousness in the past did exclude certain groups—feudal peasant, American negroes—from some or all ministry. But the kingdom of God challenges any a priori exclusivity and elitism in the ministry. When the ministry is seen as a prize, a kind of knighthood or sacral elitism, idolatry is not far distant. If the ministry is an integral aspect of following the Gospel and yet diversified from papacy to liturgical reader according to the charism of the individual and the needs of the church, it is hard to grasp how biological aspects could exclude people from ways of serving the Body of Christ animated by the universal Spirit. The accompanying chart displays the different modalities of life which meet baptism and ordination.

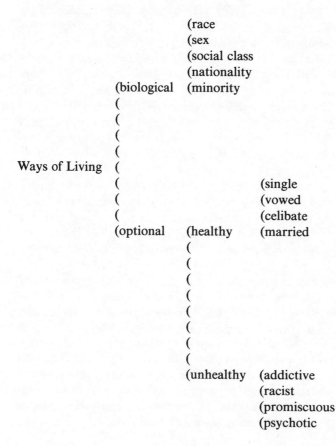

For some reason, the acceptance of basic differences in human be-ings is a difficult task. A rejection of the other is a mark of sin. A real-ization, however, that more than one or two modes of life may unite with being a minister should not begin a rush to embrace any lifestyle. While there may not be biological or ontic states intrinsically opposed to ministry, there are freely chosen life-styles, e.g., addiction, which are not compatable with charismatic activity for the Gospel. Some churches have excluded marriage from being compatible with ministry, but this exclusion has been based upon spirituality and positive law and not upon dogmatically asserted incompatibility. There are profound reasons for the preference of celibacy as a life-style in the West for a millenni-um. Whether that way of living is as suitable to Asia, South America and Africa as it was to the Celts and Germans remains to be seen. Nev-ertheless the admission of ministers to marriage in churches which now exclude it could happen when a particular church desires it. This would not mean that all celibate ministers would marry, for many of them are celibate not by reason of their priesthood but by reason of their vowed entrance into a religious community such as the Franciscans. Protestant Christians know that a reduction of mandated celibacy for Roman Ca-tholicism would bring new dangers; for marriage brings not only its benefits but its modern obstacles to *diakonia.*

It belongs to the spirituality and ecclesiology of an age to select op-timum modes of Christian life which will enhance Christian ministry. This choice has its own hope and its own risk, and is based not only upon what seems normal but upon the charisms and eschaton of the kingdom which ministry serves.

Do culture and history suggest that regions rather than the univer-sal church should make decisions about manners of life compatible with ministry as long as these ways of living display clear fidelity to the Gos-pel? Yet, this seemingly easy argument for regionalization would bring new difficulties in a world whose size media and travel have reduced. As they did in ministry, unity and diversity enter at the level of being. The Christian ways of life which the public ministers of the church as-sume are of the greatest importance, because diaconal action cannot flourish where the broader Christian life is absent or obscured.

Through most of history the church focused upon the ontic as it studied combinations of life and ministry—upon sex, legitimate birth, sexuality and sexual continence, social class. Today we look more deep-ly at human life, not at biological conditions but at proximate, psycho-logical conditions. Chosen styles of life influence not the external make-up of the person in ministry but the entirety of life at every mo-ment. The spirituality of ministry is not less important in today's expanding world but more crucial; psychological health in ministers is not a luxury.

Some optional ways of living—deeply neurotic, addictive—are not suitable. Ultimately, they will impede ministry. We have to take seriously that the desire to minister to grace may in some personalities be the result of religion mixed with sin. False ministry reveals itself as an immature or neurotic will to replace the divine or to engage in a self-serving charade. There are ways of living which demean or impede the power and dignity of the ministry. Of all human endeavors religion is particularly susceptible to neurosis; ministry can be today a refuge for the sociopath, just as in the past priesthood became a refuge of the ambitious.

The addictive personality is not simply a normal person with a problem which will-power can erase. The syndrome of addiction repeats itself in the personality which cannot function freely and actively without a freedom-negating stimulant. Zeal, insight, self-dedication are difficult for the addict because the ordinary trials of life are difficult to sustain.

There is also an elitist personality who rejects compulsively and hostilely segments of the human race: members of a particular race, the opposite sex, the poor. Then there is the promiscuous person who in either a genital or repressed way cannot live chastely whether as celibate or as married. Sociopaths must either dominate (anger) or flee (passivity) personal contact—stances which make ministry impossible for them. For these people, ministry seems to bring status, but it can also bring depression and self-hate. These are only a few examples of styles of being a human person which render sustained service to visible people and invisible grace very difficult. It is hard to combine them with realistic ministry (but, sadly, they can be combined with an inactive, ecclesiastical life-style). Ultimately the unhealthy personality wars against the rigors of full-time dedication. The Spirit cannot unite charisms of prominent ministry with the fugue of deception. Charisms come to all persons but they do not demand what we cannot give.

When we come to divorce, remarriage after divorce, and homosexuality, new problems emerge. Bishops and theologians question their compatability with full-time ministry. The Roman Catholic Church is now preserved from some decisions by its strict requirement of celibacy. Some Protestant churches, with surprisingly little discussion, accepted some debatable life-styles. Does this imply that they view any manner of living as compatible with ministry? Ministry, however, is not a hobby for everyone but a permanent decision to be both servant and sacrament.

The optional but significant choices a person makes in life have a persistent, omnipresent influence upon ministry for better or for worse. Psychology is taken for granted as an assistance in admitting to study for ministry, but it is still a novice in discerning the parameters of the healthy personality for ministry. From the point of view of a spirituality where charism draws forth nature, there should be no conflict between psychological profile and readiness for ministry just as there need not be any conflict between the created person and grace. Nevertheless, between nature and grace stand the masques of sin. The development of an adequate psychological profile of the personality entering into and enduring a life of ministry is not easy but it is very important.

The minister's manner of life in its ethical structure and symbolism is not only an individual decision but an ecclesial decision. Life is the ground of service, and Christian life is, as we said, ministry as sign. The church's approach to life joined to ministry should lie between the remote decision of a seminary to admit this person to ministry and the similarly gnostic insistence by an individual of an infallible call by the Holy Spirit. The community is not simply an object of ministry for ordained church leaders whose private lives are monastic or libertine, as the individual minister determines. The community is not a sick person before a medical team; it is a source of ministry. The charisms of the Spirit, since they are not magic or extrinsic to personality will speak through individual lives, and they will be muffled by sin and illness. As ministers and communities rediscover their external and evangelical essence, they will note that both belong together as body and act, as mind and utterance. When a Christian's life is contrary to the word and sacrament of revelation or contrary to the community as sign (for even the unbelieving and contemning world has expectations of the church and Gospel), there occurs an appropriation of the values of the "world" in the Johannine sense, the ambition, avarice or sensuality of the eon which Jesus opposed even as he evangelized and saved our fallen race. In the Catholic tradition, the minister is not only a word of grace or a remote, mechanical priest, but a sacrament. Ministry does not exist in a vacuum. Desacralizing the ministry cannot mean secularizing it: nor can it mean reducing it to vulgarity or immorality, neglecting the cost of discipleship and the contemplative asceticism expected by the kingdom. As ministry expands, formation and spiritual life must become deeper, more intense.

Both the diversification of ministry and the entertainment of one or two other modes of Christian life as compatible with ministry are part of a single cultural process whose course the church cannot quickly chart. Theoreticians, prophets and church leaders may not, however, ride roughshod over the churches and the universal church in the name of every liberal development, causes which only a segment of Christians now perceive as important. Each church has its consciousness and tradition, and its rights. While consciousness is developmental, and while the process of growth in the spirit cannot be a priori extinguished, a particular stage in development does not immediately reduce the views of other groups to sin or stupidity. Changing social consciousness forms the background for including and excluding people from ministry. The limits of a society are inescapable, and they are not always heretical or evil. Social conflict, though sad and even tragic, is part of our human nature. Church consciousness evolves slowly, at the global level, toward new perspectives. Life in the church is not a rapid set of decisions, for tradition as the collective consciousness of the church takes seriously its past. The tradition of the church is employed not as a barrier to new forms of ministry but as a guide for looking at behavior which the New Testament describes as ambiguous or immoral. The individual minister and church discern not only the legitimacy but the appropriateness in the present moment of this or that modality of life.

It would be a new, relocated dictatorship for individuals to step outside the life and discernment-process of the entire church and to make a serious ecclesial decision to acquire ministry. We must stay with the New Israel even in its vagaries and delays on the paths of cultural history. The community is the milieu and source of ministry, and the entire church must come to new decisions. While the word for an expanded ministry can be urging and prophetic, a solipsistic act is schismatic. The forcing of ordination, the marginal ordination apart from the wide church, can only be a display of an immature theology: such a constitution in orders calls upon a rigid theology *ex opere operato* of external acts, a media-event vibrating apart from the living church.

Entry into ministry cannot bypass the wider church whose servant the minister is. Nor may ministry claim to lie outside the cross or outside a mature, dedicated spirituality of discipleship.

NOTES

1. On the unusual poetic ecclesiology of the Syriac tradition see R. Murray, *Symbols of Church and Kingdom* (London, 1975); on the preference by the New Testament for describing the church in metaphors, see P. Minear, *Images of the Church in the New Testament* (Philadelphia, 1960); Y. Congar, *The Temple* (Westminster, 1962), p. 160.

2. Cf. C. Moletter, "Brève histoire de l'action catholique," *Lumière et Vie*

12 (1963), 45ff.; P. Guilmont, *Fin d'une église cléricale* (Paris, 1969); on the history and nature of lay movements as "papal solutions to secularism" (p. 5) cf. T. Hesburgh, *The Theology of Catholic Action* (Notre Dame, 1946). It is instructive to compare Rahner's classic defense of the laity briefly participating in the work of the bishops in 1963 ("Notes on the Lay Apostolate" *TI,* 2) with his later "A Declericalized Church," in *The Shape of the Church to Come* (New York, 1947), pp. 56ff.

3. Nils Dahl, "The Origin of Baptism," *Interpretationes ad Vetus Testamentum . . .* (Oslo, 1955), p. 46.

4. The theology and liturgical practice in the new rite of initiation raises questions about the relation of baptism and confirmation towards adult ministry; cf. A. Kavanagh, *The Shape of Baptism: The Rite of Christian Initiation* (New York, 1978); R. Coffy, "La confirmation aujourd'hui," *MD* #142 (1980), 7ff.

5. *Ek,* p. 362.

6. *ST* II-II, q. 1, a. 2, ad 2.

7. *Ministeria quaedam; Ad Pascendum* both in *The Rites of the Catholic Church* (New York, 1976), pp. 732ff., 726ff.

8. *G,* pp. 31f.

9. *Ad Pascendum, The Rites . . .* , p. 728.

10. *MWS,* p. xi.

11. *G,* pp. 16ff.

12. *Ibid.,* pp. 51ff.

13. The Roman Catholic tendency is to minimalize all ecclesial activity apart from priesthood. Protestantism made the opposite claim but its theology of universal priesthood eventually had the same minimalizing effect.

Martin Luther developed theologies of wider priesthood and of the sanctity of every vocation. He identified vocation with charism and ministry in order to break the haughty class structure of late medieval society where monk and priest often dominated the social pyramid rather than served it. Luther wanted to end the inferiority complex of secular professions and show that being a farmer or a prince was God's benediction in the world. The vocation of people did not make second class worldlings who lacked zeal or discipline requisite for cloister and pulpit. Luther's theology of the priesthood of the laity was allied to this, rightly rejecting as unworthy of a Christian church the sustenance of a group who did nothing. The passive attendance of most Christians at Word and Sacrament was, he preached, a pale reflection of what discipleship meant to Jesus and baptism to Paul and Peter and John. Luther's priesthood of all believers liberates the baptized from total passivity and unintelligibility caused by the Latin liturgy, and from economic and political passivity before secular powers endowed with sacral functions. It did not fashion a ministerial community (except among Pietist sects) but often challenged the ministerial aspect of *diakonia* to the Gospel into the business of society. From this flows the unsatisfying dialectic of the two kingdoms and the alignment of vocation with ministry. W. Pesch observes of the New Testament in this regard: "In the Old Testament, priesthood is an expressly instituted office but in the New Testament only Jesus has this 'official office' and this in paradoxical, personal and eschatological service. The entire community has a share in Jesus' priesthood according to the New Testament, not in the sense of a general priesthood, but in the sense of a radical binding to Christ." "Zu Texten des NT über das Priestertum der Getauften," *Verborum Veritas* (Wuppertal, 1970), pp. 303ff. Cf. H. Preuss, "Luther on the Universal Priesthood and the Office of Ministry," *Concordia Journal* 5 (1979), 55–62; G. Wingren, *Lutheran Vocation* (Philadelphia, 1977); C. Eastwood, *The Priesthood of All Believers* (London, 1960); P. Dabin, *Le Sacerdoce Royal des fidèles dans la tradition ancienne et moderne* (Paris, 1950).

14. *Ch,* p. 387.

15. Clement's letter is directed at problems of discipline in Corinth, and there is great evidence that its source is Jewish. Clement draws a parallel between the order of the Levitical temple and the Christian community. He intends that Jesus be considered the sole priest, and he employs the word *laikos,* appearing here in early Christian literature, for the Jewish people but not directly for the Christian group to which he attributes in a brotherly spirit a variety of charisms, a universal dignity and function. Yet this harmonious community should obey its bishops and deacons. It is perhaps also that his discussion of church order seems to be public liturgy where order and limited offices would be more prominent. On the analogy intended by Clement between Levitical hierarchy and the Christian community at the end of the first century, see A. Jaubert, *Clément de Rome, Epître aux Corinthiens* (Paris, 1971); cf. B. Weiss, "Amt und Eschatologie im 1. Clemensbrief," *Théologie und Philosophie* 50 (1975), 70ff.; E. Dassmann, "Die Bedeutung des AT für das Verständnis des kirchlichen Amtes. . . . ," *Bibel und Leben* 11 (1970) 198; A. Harnack, *Einführung in die alte Kirchengeschichte* (Leipzig, 1929), p. 95; J. Fuellenbach, *Ecclesial Office and the Primacy of Rome* (Washington, 1980), p. 251.

16. Origen, *On Jeremiah,* 11:3, PL 13, 370, 369. Bishops of large cities are harsh to the poor, insolent like tyrants, *Commentary on Matthew* 16:8, in Origen's *Werke, Die griechischen christlichen Schriftsteller* (Leipzig, 1899), 40, p. 493. On Origen's ecclesiology, cf. H. Vogt, *Das Kirchenverständnis des Origenes* (Cologne, 1974); J. Chenevert, *L'Eglise dans le commentaire d'Origène sur le Cantique des Cantiques* (Brussels, 1969); C. Caspary, *Politics and Exegesis* (Berkeley, 1979).

17. I. de la Potterie, "The Origin and Basic Meaning of the Word 'Lay'," in *The Christian Lives by the Spirit* (Staten Island, 1971), pp. 267ff. On the similar linguistic meaning in the late Roman and medieval periods see Y. Congar, "Clercs et laics au point de vue de la culture au moyen âge: 'Laicus = sans lettres'," *Studia medievelia et mariologica* (Rome, 1971), pp. 309ff; E. Schillebeeckx, "La définition typologique du laic chrétien selon Vatican II," *"L'église de Vatican II* (Paris, 1966), 3, pp. 1013ff.

18. *PG* 8, 1191.

19. *De Exhortatione castitatis* 7, 3f; cf. *De Monogamia,* 7, 8f.

20. Cf. S.M. Onory, *Vescovi e Città* (Bologna, 1933); J. Gaudemet, *L'Eg-*

lise dans l'empire romain (Paris, 1938); G. Tellenbach, *Church, State and Christian Society* (Oxford, 1940). On the rise of the clergy in the second and following centuries, cf. A. Faivre, *Naissance d'une hiérarchie* (Paris, 1977). The separation of clergy from laity is marked in the liturgy from the sixth century while a synodal mingling still is encouraged; *EHM,* pp. 96ff.

21. Y. Congar, "Laic et Laicat," *Dictionnaire de Spiritualité* 9 (Paris, 1976), p. 79.

22. *MC,* pp. 9, 17, 19. Congar is citing his own *Lay People in the Church* (Westminster, 1967), p. xvi.

23. Agreeing that ordination has become an entrance to clerical status, *My,* p. 39. Hans Urs von Balthasar alludes to the separation of personal status from ministry in "Nachfolge und Amt," *Sponsa Verbi* (Einsiedeln, 1961); cf. D. Miller, "Lifestyle and Religious Commitment," *Religious Education* 76 (1981), 49ff. Clothes are closely connected to modes of life; cf. M. Bringemeier, *Priester und Gelehrtenkleidung* (Münster, 1974).

CHAPTER SEVEN
Sources of Ministry

1. Sources of Ministry

The fashion of Greek and medieval intellectual inquiry was to survey the history of the topic of interest and next to discover its causes. Beneath our search for a ministry which is both wider and more active than present church office, within our listening for the primal and present-day inspiration of the Spirit of charisms we have in fact glimpsed the causal structure of charism-ministry.

The nature or essence of ministry is public action by Christians for their church as service to the kingdom of God. The psychological ground or "matter" of ministry is the baptismal and social life of a Christian in the community where throughout a lifetime being and doing intersect. The goal of ministry is to serve not divine idols but God's grace incarnate in Jesus and present in history, often through the Church. The source of ministry is the agent (or agents) who (with the Spirit) is the bestower in private and confirmer in public of those special ministries which flow out of baptism. We are considering here mainly full-time ministries (with their considerable investment of preparation and time) although lesser ministries, e.g., in occasionally bearing word and sacrament and social service to others, look to the same sources.

Does ministry arise from a private vocation akin to a conversion experience? Or is ministry solely constituted by an episcopal ritual? Searching for the efficient cause of ministry should not detract from the dignity and responsibility of ministers in the church. We want simply to disentangle further the phenomena and structures connected to office and ordination; some of them have been claimed as words of divine rule while others have been ignored by canon law.

When we look at neoscholastic manuals and their picture of the church, we find a neatly drawn Aristotelian ecclesiology and we can find causes there too of some ecclesiological myopia and impoverishment. In this theology, the form, the cause and the goal of the church are all the same: the hierarchy of bishops and church administrators. When we recall how passive the material element is in Aristotelian philosophy, we appreciate how constrained in the ecclesiology of the late nineteenth and early twentieth centuries are baptism, charism and laity. This metaphysics of causes presents a framework for looking at ministry which is helpful only if we complement it with level after level of other voices and persons who play an equally important role in the presentation of ministry in the church. There is no one source of ministry.

Is not Jesus the source of ministry? Certainly, but such an affirmation says too much and too little. Jesus' call and his Spirit's charism are different modalities of invitation to ministry. A move from Jesus' individualized invitation to discipleship and then to the activities of the small communities after Pentecost is a move from universality to diversity; from, we might say, prophecy to ministry.

Jesus came to his cross after he had associated individuals and groups not only with his person but with his ministry.[1] The Twelve and the larger circles of disciples were summoned specifically to share in preaching the reign, the judgment, and the hope he was bringing to people. The post-resurrection appearances do not begin the ministerial call to men and women but confirm it. The women, groups of brothers, Galileans, the Twelve, and seventy-two disciples—these are examples of variety and universality in calling. These people are not left as students with—and then without—a guru or rabbi but are urged to share in Jesus' ministry; in its style, even in its divine word and power. Jesus' calling of his first disciples is a forecast of the explosion of charismatic ministry in the churches. How some of these groups survive and how some die out makes up the history of the church from 30 to 130 A.D.

Is not God the source of ministry? Yes, but the difficulty with such a statement is not its affirmation but its analysis. Without going into the question of what is traditionally Jewish and what is novel in the first commissionings of Christians, we see that a constellation of forces was believed to be present at the origin of a ministry. God is active in all of them, and all of them refer diversely to his Spirit, and to his servant Jesus. God chose as the definitive mode of his presence to us the man Jesus—he who is the summoner to and pattern of discipleship. Sustained by an eschatological presence of the risen Christ, believers have the impression that Jesus is coming towards them out of the absolute future which is God. Jesus' second coming is a fire or a magnet which gives further meaning and power to his members' discipleship.

As we saw in the theology of charism, the historical Jesus after his withdrawal from earth remains present under the modality of *Pneuma*. The Spirit which is the source of a commissioning to ministry is not abstract deity but the Spirit of God and of Jesus. By baptism that Spirit is already present as source of all that is to come. Every Christian is a new creation, a liturgy, a part of a living temple. Baptism does not merely mix the clay for the ceramicist's wheel to form into a vessel. The human and divine forces which confirm a Christian in special ministry through public ordination draw on the ontic and charismatic structure given to a personality by birth as well as by baptism.

The presence of the Spirit in liturgy or in church leadership does not compete with other presences of the Spirit: baptism, charism, call, community. Dynamic forces in life and community point to the rightness and hope in a new minister. The church with its leaders either calls forth ministries out of the community or it dies. But individuals test the pneumatic call which may be an invitation to full-time ministry, and the process of training and evaluating the new ministers is a place of the Spirit no less important than the decision of the community's leader. All of these forces come together in placing a minister in the community, and we will look at each below. Canonical rubrics have long held the first place in constituting ministry. They are, however, only of tertiary interest. Ultimately, it is a theology of grace which can explore the sources of ministry.

2. The Activity of God and the Vocation of the Individual

First of all, it is God (in the Christ and his Spirit) who unites and builds the church. It is God who calls (Rom 1:6); it is God who enables people to believe (1 Cor 3:6); it is God who establishes some as apostles, others as prophets and teachers (1 Cor 12:28).

The tendency to reductionism appears in the theology of the sources of ministry developed through the centuries. Unconsciously the bishop drew to his office the different powers at work in bestowing ministry.[2] He called, trained, ordained, assigned. Inadequate theologies of ministry result from the insistence that there is only one source of ministry. Not only church but God and Trinity are neglected by this episcopalization of the source of ministry.

A monocausal theology of ministry neglects the Spirit. The Holy

Spirit is conceived in a non-incarnational way—the *Pneuma* enters life apart from matter, psyche and history. This mechanical style can be magical, and it can also neglect the incarnational core of the Gospel. In the ordering of church life, we do not need to be afraid of diversity and symbol: we cannot have too much visibility, too much sacramentality, for the Spirit accepts our animal nature and it delights to come among our tones, lights, gestures, colors, embraces and applause. It is not the sacramental which is to be feared (and here every iconoclasm and Puritanism is sidetracked) but the idolatrous. A single ministry, a monoform leadership of a passive community often end up in a church not of great worship but of boring sparseness.

Those who attribute vocation and ordination exclusively to a distant God become passive before a temperamental deity. All this has its roots in a Christological monophysitism where Jesus is absorbed into the ineffable and severe deity. The tough demands made by the historical Jesus upon those who would follow him are forgotten, almost as if there had never been a Jesus ministering to the reign of God on the lakes and roads of Galilee and Judea. The ministry is absorbed into a cosmic priesthood identical with that of the risen Christ. This priesthood renders a Christian different in being more than in doing; preaching, Eucharist and social communion are neglected for legal duties which bestow a participation in a divine existence. The minister is not only a sacral figure in a fallen world, he is ontically superior to other Christians. Only the divinity of Jesus Christ is remembered and it alone is reflected in the ministry.

It is difficult for men and women to evangelize or celebrate pure divinity, and so a monophysite ministry ends up moribund before the world. Every baptized man and woman is called to be a Christopher, a Christ-bearer, and Paul's Christic mysticism, "For me to live is Christ" (Phil 1:21), describes us all. The public minister is both a servant and a sacrament of the kingdom. The full Christ, however, includes fatigue and limitation, sin and grace, cross and resurrection. In a monophysite ministry, the incarnation of God comes to be ignored and the minister is either too divine or (in reaction) too secular. An excessively monophysite ministry also runs the risk of a sacerdotalism where the sacral imitation of God appears as a static mediatorship and where the priest is absorbed not by evangelization but by a perfunctory mediatorship. Theologies, liturgies, structures of the church and the institutions of society reflect an implicit or explicit conviction about who God is. Christianity often assumed a neoplatonic ontology which insisted that every horizon of the world should fit into a smooth edged, hierarchical pyramid. Greek ontologies of God's being subtly determined every structure in the church. If, for example, we conceive of God as the pinnacle of a static, ordered universe, then the church will reflect that image. Diversity within the church will be a question of higher and lower status and ordination will be participation in higher powers.

There are also psychological views of God which determine ministry. When our dominant emotion towards God is fear, because emotions are contagious, our ministry will be a ministry in words and deeds of fear. Under the relentless scrutiny of God we can never stop working, never cease laboring for success, never cease forcing people into our version of salvation. We compete not only with other ministers but with God. Pelagian, our charism survives through our efforts. Our spiritual life is one of guilt and exhaustion before the all-seeing eye of God. What a difference there is when the minister accepts emotionally and theologically the reign of God and views ministry as servant to God's grace rather than as grace's lawyer. *Diakonia* contains a whole theology of God; service is not only the imitation of Jesus but is the risky, healthy stance in a world of sin and grace. Ministry can be either tranquil service to sovereign grace or a form of pelagian manipulation which grows into neurosis.

Ministry and Trinity come together. They mirror each other. Not only my vision of church and charism but my view of God depends upon my view of the goal and source of ministry. As I allow God to be truly divine and fully imminent, I make a beginning towards plumbing a fundamental law of ministry: out of dying comes life for self and others. Ordination is a mission into that law of dying and rising. "My one hope and trust is that I shall . . . have the courage for Christ to be glorified in my body whether by my life or by my death" (Phil 1:20).

The Aristotelian philosophy of causality in medieval thought interpreted the spiritual activity of the official minister through the category of instrumental cause. The minister could not be a proper, even a secondary cause of the grace of baptism, Eucharist and ordination because of the propinquity of those actions to the being of God. "Instrumental causality," applied analogously to a living intellectual agent, however, gave the minister in the performance of his office a real, direct role in the life of the Spirit and church—he was not simply an occasion or symbol of grace. The causality and its effect, grace, were real but the mode was modest, instrumental.

> The instrumental cause acts not by its own form but solely in virtue of the impetus imparted to it by the principal agent . . . the way in which the sacraments of the New Law cause grace. For the plan of God has drawn on them to cause grace.[3]

Originally the sacrament, and then by proximity the minister, were viewed as instrumental causes. *Ordinatio* established a person in a sacral-society as instrumental causality constituted the priest to be an instrument of divine action.

By the nineteenth and twentieth centuries both the meaning of instrument and the interpretation of theology had shifted. Theology, and much more important, piety gloried in the instrumentality of the church's actions. Forgetting the original goal of protecting the divine while using the categories of causality, priest and sacrament became forceful, direct, even infallible causes—instruments not only participating in their principal causes but perfectly realizing them. In a scientific society, an instrument is a tool, empty of life and intelligence but carefully crafted to produce the desired effect. A computer, a scalpel are not supposed to interfere with the work given them; to do so is to malfunction. We can see that for the modern scientific world the description of the minister as an instrument of God is questionable. God alone controls the presence we call grace; nor is the human person a pure potentiality awaiting obediently the imprint of form. In short a human minister—with charisms, office, education and talents—is both more or less than an instrumental cause. The *ex opere operato* direction of the sacrament is in fact modified by the psychic conditions of the minister and recipient. What theologies of instrumental causality and *ex opere operato* wanted to safeguard remains true: in serious ecclesial moments and ministers, grace is imparted through the church and its members, but this grace is God's in intensity and certainty. This grace is more than our graced expectation, more than the ecclesial atmosphere could ever call forth.

Vocation is, first, to take part in God's plan for us as it has been begun in our baptism (Eph 1:4ff.) Vocation is not to struggle at any price for every achievement, or to be rooted in unquestioned work. What is a vocation? Myself and my future in the future which is God. God's call is a way for me to move toward his future and to escape the false paths and the dangerous faces of myself which we call sin. While I rush toward my future (including my death) empowered by God's presence, I am also liberated by God's word and action in Christ from the various deaths which would entice and entrap me.

I bring something personal to God's call. The genes and drives which make me to be me—these are not a burden or a responsibility. I am not called to bow down before a vocation: I am my vocation, for the God who created my individuality out of finite potentialities is the same God who has introduced me into his wider plan of meaning and life. It is out of this interweave of my personality and my promise that my vocation, God's various calls, emerge. Thomas Merton wrote: "For me to be a saint means to be myself. Therefore the problem of sanctity and salvation is in fact the problem of finding out who I am and of discovering my true self. Trees and animals have no problem. God makes them what they are without consulting them, and they are perfectly satisfied. With us it is different. God leaves us free to be whatever we like. We can be ourselves or not, as we please. But the problem is this: *Since God alone possesses the secret of my identity, he alone can make me who I am.*"[4]

At this point we can hardly go further, since we encounter that theological puzzle which will not yield a solution: how my free will modifies and fulfills God's sovereign will. Perhaps I must see my vocation, like my life, as a dialogue between the presence of God (who in his powerful vastness cannot be set aside) and my freedom in the years of life. God's meticulous plan of millions of years for billions of people is flexible, yielding to change, but ultimately working out as love.

In the past the theology of vocation or call appeared a cold system fraught with guilt feelings. Theologians neglected Aquinas' principle that "grace brings nature to perfection." Since my personality is the love of God, his signals to me will not be ugly or strange. It is a dangerous and destructive theology that rejoices in evil and suffering, imagining that holiness comes from contradiction rather than, as it does, from harmony.

Life is not uninterrupted joy, but happiness and growth are signs that we have found ourselves, i.e. found our vocation. Of course, no life escapes the cross, but an internal neurosis of suffering and distraction is a sign that my created personality (also a gift of God) is out of harmony with the unfolding of my life. If our image of God is one of a neutral master planner or a judge, then we will imagine that there is an abstract or oppressive vocation for us—computer-produced, unrelated to our self, commanded by the Almighty. God will not crush us by his vocations/charisms for us, but we through a pagan view of God can enfeeble ourselves by guilt.

Mobility is a keynote of our society; mobility seeps into our personalities. Career development, career change, the setting aside (free of guilt) of a career that really never worked—this is part of an on-going view of vocation. Without sacrificing permanancy in ecclesial ministry, along with every other aspect of social stability fiercely embattled by today's values, we must ponder how the charisms of the Spirit can be developmental. Some lives and some vocations are better than others in the abstract. In my own life, comparisons are useless. Jesus, in his portrayal of a last judgment based upon simple acts like feeding the hungry, and Paul, in his hymnic summation of all charisms in love, direct us to the ordinary. I cannot be called to what is "better" than myself. My concern is to find my call from God, not to choose the most difficult ministry or life, or to try to capture a charism which ends in prestige but also in an addiction to sustain that prestige. The place of vocation, charism and ministry is my particular personality.

"Everyone has a vocation!" With our deeper understanding of baptism as a call to ministry for every Christian, we can expand that old slogan. Every Christian has a vocation to ministry, to serving the kingdom of God. Baptism is not an initiation into a frozen state of life; it implies discipleship and ministry.

Some are called to give more and more of their time and energies to spreading the kingdom. This is a special call (but not the only special call) for those for whom it is existentially suited. To be an educator for the Christian community, to be a deacon or a bishop, to be in social justice, or to announce liberation and hope in Africa—these ministries are serving the future of God. But we must return to our original view of God's call to each of us as something extraordinarily personal.

Today we hear frequently of a decline in the number of diocesan clergy, a decline in the number of priests at work in Europe, in Latin and North America. A diminishing diocesan clergy is not the problem, however, and pessimistic statistics may be a camouflage for much larger theological issues, those of an expanding ministry.

Even if the number of priests in large, urban dioceses were to triple or return to an earlier level of numerousness, before the new demands upon ministry by quantity and quality, this would not give the church enough priests. As we have pointed out, the number of Roman Catholics has grown and the expectation of church life has expanded. The crisis in ministry could not be solved by an earlier number of clergy; it touches upon a change within the life of healthy Christian communities.

Moreover, in the past the priest carried out a limited administration and liturgy while sisters attended to schools and hospitals. Now, it is not clear that a pastor or presbyter either can or should perform all of the central areas of ministry, reaching from liturgy through religious education to peace and justice.

It is unrealistic to imagine a golden age of many vocations, for that age did not have to minister to the vast churches of today, and many of those large numbers of priests and sisters never remained within the active ministry. In Latin America and Africa, there never was a period when an indigenous celibate clergy reached an extensive level. These areas have always been dependent upon Europe and North America for ministers.

The expansion of the ministry is not, then, a random or annoying occurrence but an aspect of a new church which is, for the first time in many centuries, world-wide. Size, expansion and potential point out the limitations of the past and the potential of the future.

3. The Place of Ministry and Ordination

The place of ministry is the local church. Whenever we speak of local church, we have the difficulty that neither the North American parish (all that are not rural) nor the diocese fulfills many of the qualifications for being the local Christian community. The local church should be large enough to contain within its resources the ministries for life and expansion, and it should be sufficiently limited so that its ministers and communities can have real contact with each other; its local nature is not only geographical and sociological; it is theological, liturgical and ministerial. Because the dimensions of the local church have changed little since Christianity's appropriation of Roman and Germanic structures, most dioceses are too large to have any local identity or real cohesion. Enormous parishes are too small to offer in their staff ministries the variety of ministry expected of the full church, the diocese. Western Roman Catholic ecclesiology is less episcopal than it seems, for the bishops can never enter very deeply into the personal and ministerial life of their dioceses. The real ministerial structure is presbyteral—a network of pastors.

While the Roman Catholic local church suffers from being caught between two large assemblies, urban parish and diocese, the Protestant parishes are either real communities or parishes which are too small; and the Protestant synod, district or diocese is a cluster of small parishes and not an ecclesial organism in itself.

Ordination is not just an act of witness by the local community but comes out of the local church. The Spirit turns the diversity of the Body of Christ into a milieu where ministry can emerge and be judged. Even if it seems normal and traditional, the idea that ordination creates passively in the material of a human being a quasi-divine form is theologically immature. The church does structure the ministry, but it should not treat ministry as its creature, magically dispensing it into a void. Theology should not identify *ordo* or *officium* only with institutional ministry, and *charisma* with personal spirituality. The purpose of aligning ministry with charism is to avoid favoring a dichotomy between the personal and the episcopal call (both of which have their extreme, irrational forms), a division leading to an arid separation of priesthood from spiritual service. Such dichotomies encourage a dictatorship over ministry by a structure uncontrolled by humanity or divinity. The schizophrenia which separates institution from charisma, though well meaning in its desire for the location of charism and for the clarity of structure, ends by embracing only structure and by merely tolerating charism.

Through history the ministry of bishop has increased control over ministry. History shows that usually the bishops (and especially the bishop of Rome) drew ministries into their orbit for laudatory reasons, e.g., to save the ministry from control by the state or by transient movements. Ministry evolved away from being an ordered and effective diversity of services from the Spirit for the kingdom to being a sacral, liturgical administration. The theology of the fullness of ministry residing in the bishop (and then in the priest) flourished under Platonic and Aristotelian metaphysics. As one ministry had absorbed the plurality of ministries, it soon returned to redistribute parcels of ministry out of its own fullness. If it rejects the idea that there is only one ministry (the priesthood shared by presbyter and bishop), a theology of ministry looks critically at the idea that ministries are shares in the episcopacy, in a potentiality of ministry residing in the leader of the church. Does episcopal ministry contain in itself *virtualiter* all other ministries? If so, then a description of ordination is rather simple, for it is thoroughly episcopal. All other Christians, including the ones to be commissioned to ministry, own a highly passive role. Today this theology of a single ministry whose participation is dispensed by the bishop is widespread: only the bishop is publicly and effectively a charismatic and a minister; before him, not only the "laity" but the "clergy" are passive, for in their origins all ordained depend totally upon the bishop's causality, much as the medieval theologians, following Pseudo-Denys, would have explained that all creatures depend upon God for being.[5]

Does every ministry come from the ministry of leadership? Does the pope share his ministry with bishops? Does a bishop share facets of the one priestly ministry with other Christians? This is a question of considerable import, for it touches upon whether the ministry is an objective reality, whether it can expand, and whether ministry is charismatic in origin and diverse in form.

A ministry of leadership stimulates, discerns and orders the charisms of the Spirit as they come to a community. This is not the same as one ministry sharing ontically facets of its ministerial pleroma with others. In the first case, it is more and more not the charismatic ministries of the Spirit in the Christians but the occupations of the bishop which are ministry. This encourages an excessive control, only a pretended generosity in the theology of shared ministry.

The Holy Spirit's perspective on ministry is more generous, more creative and more effective. No doubt the bishop's ministry remains at the center of other ministries. It belongs to the Spirit, however, to initiate and direct the full process of call to ordination. If this seems too "charismatic" in the pejorative sense of being at the whim of non-empirical forces of psyche and Spirit, we should add that charism and call are subject to strict judges: to performance (Is this person excited about this ministry, clearly capable of preaching or consoling well?) and to the community (Can this person be an effective minister to others?) and to the ministry of leadership.

What was the source of the theological opinion that episcopacy creates and bestows rather than recognizes and enacts all ministry?

The rise of the Roman papacy coincided in the centuries after Gregory the Great with the decline of ministerial diversity, and one source of this theology of ministerial participation lies with a medieval (canonical and theological) interpretation of Peter and his relationship to the other Apostles. Dominicans such as Thomas Aquinas (with papal sympathies) observed that the Apostles as Apostles are equal to Peter, but as sheep (all Christians before Peter are sheep) they are not his equal. Hence the powers and services of the ministry ultimately rest in Peter, a monarchical focal point. Turrecremata and Bellarmine (but not Aquinas, Cajetan and Suarez) argued that Peter alone was consecrated by Christ, which commission the Twelve received from him.[6] Monarchy, neoplatonism, and the organization of the Baroque encouraged this theology, and in a ministerial void where only priesthood and its episcopal form existed it triumphed. Our world of diversity and independence renders such a theology of episcopal ownership of ministry questionable. Just as it appears less and less real to claim that the reality of a Brazilian or Ugandan church is derived totally from Rome (as the theology of missionary vicars apostolic implied), so a bishop with a position of total possession of ministry risks being threatened by the expansion of the ministry, or risks dividing his church into two groups: "lay" and "ordained" ministers.

In 1896, Leo XIII wrote that bishops were not to be regarded as simple vicars of the pope, thus preparing the termination by Vatican II of a reduction of world-wide churches and bishops to be branches and ambassadors of the papacy.[7] The papacy and episcopacy have as a special ministry the union of the church and the interrelationship of churches. The bishop is also the stimulus, commissioner and center of local ministry. As the bishop is not in fact a derivation of the papacy, so ministers in the diocese and parish have their own identity. Full-time ministers are not pawns or parcels of the bishop (or pastor) but rather different co-workers. While the bishop and pastor have rights with and over them, their birth and being comes from a variety of causes, of which the church leader is one.

We have looked at the place where ministry begins and acts, the human personality and the local church. Now we want to look at the actors in the ceremony of admission to ministry, to spotlight those movements and people who have traditionally formed the event of sending into ministry. Ordination is a constellation of actors and actions. The church's liturgy, which is frequently an unconscious mosaic of rich and sane theology, has preserved sparks of this multiple event. We are not introducing new causes of ordination to ministry but rather coaxing reluctant channels of the Spirit's grace onto stage center, and turning the klieg lights up higher to reveal the diversity which traditionally surrounds admission to ministry. The Spirit always enters and speaks through many and so it is not only the solitary mystic but the social consciousness of the church which prays, "Do not extinguish the Spirit" (1 Thess 5:19).

4. The Constellation of Ordination

People and actions prepare a Christian to enter ministry in the church. For public, full-time ministry especially, but also for other part-time or assisting ministries, symbols, words, people and movement come together in the constellation of public commissioning. That moment is both climax and beginning, both charism and the source of further charism. We call it ordination.

A new theology of ministry cannot (as some Reformation traditions intended) turn ministry into laity nor eliminate ordination and liturgy as excessively cultic. Just the opposite is needed. The social and animal facets of our human nature call for sacramental liturgy. Ordination is a visible affirmation and invocation of charism, a celebration of the church's diverse life and risky mission, a symbol of the Spirit truly present in the church. Ordination is sacrament: celebratory liturgy and communal structure. Ordination should be enhanced, not diminished.

What has always been central in Christian ordination is the action of the leading minister. His prayers and sacramental gestures (laying on of hands, anointing, entrusting with book or cup, robing) hold the attention of the community and join Spirit and creation. But ordination is more than an act by a church leader constituting others in leadership. Does ministry come solely through ordination? Is the church (conceived of as an institution) the sole source of ministry personified in the single office of bishop? Can ministry come into existence by the written rescript of church administration apart from human factors?

The opposite extreme is to argue that only the inner word and grace call forth ministry. Some pentecostals hold that a call heard and followed gives ministry and a personal charism discerned gives the right to ministry. Roman Catholic and main-line Protestant churches can tend to the opposite extreme, offering a legal-liturgical apparatus which ordains to ministry as it wills.

Community and Spirit meet in solemn commissionings. Ordination is an ecclesial act involving the entire community.[8] Whether this liturgy of ordination presents clearly a multiplicity of charisms or not, they are still there seeking voice and recognition.

Liturgy symbolizes polity. The event of ordination is not the apotheosis of a sacred personage but is a sacramental reminder to all Christians of their ministries and a presentation of all leading ministries such as teaching, oversight and evangelism. The liturgical act of ordination is a community event among Christians whose baptized lives are for a moment focused by the bishop. Just as the leaders of the local church, bishop or pastor are not monopolizers of ministry but catalysts and coordinators, so all those in ministry, in service limited or fulltime, take part in the public life of the community. Part of that life is the discernment of charisms of service in others, the education and approval of new ministers and the ordination of ministers. The present laying on of hands by the presbyters present stands for the welcome of the fulltime ministers; the voiced approval of the congregation sounds not as polite social applause for a relative but as the climax of a long discernment process within the local church with the new minister. Now these elements of a richer community life are weakly present in the venerable ordination ceremony—a liturgy which is to be an enactment of grace giving insight through word, symbol and person into the Spirit's vision of the church.

Initially a Jewish (and perhaps Greek) laying on of hands expressed public commissioning in the church. Drawing on *Deuteronomy* and *Numbers* where Moses established Joshua in leadership, the Mishnaic literature expressed the importance of a laying on of hands for rabbis.[9] In later Judaism the scribes of the first century B.C. received into their group and confirmed the wisdom of ready pupils by laying on of hands. If this approach towards communal commissioning entered the wider churches through Judaeo-Christian churches, the New Testament signified the advent of charism with a laying on of hands. In *Acts,* with church led by prophets and teachers, Paul and Barnabas were prepared

for a missionary trip by fasting, prayer and the imposition of hands
(13:1ff). The Twelve constituted the seven full of wisdom and the Spirit
for an office of service by prayer and imposition of hands (6:6). Paul
and Barnabas in Asia Minor designated elders in each church through
prayer and the imposition of hands (24:23). In terms of theology and
chronology, the ecclesiological meaning of these texts is open to discussion. Nevertheless, they show a commissioning to serious church office
based upon prayer and a symbolic-sacramental action related to Judaism. As presented in *1 Timothy,* the leaders of communities through the
imposition of hands accept worthy candidates into ministry; indeed
charism is said to have been given by the imposition of hands of the
church leaders, given through prophecy (meaning perhaps the gift of
leadership) (4:14).

Every language brings cultural insight and cultural limitation. In
its drive toward arrangement the Latin *ordo* bespeaks office, status, being rather than doing. In the Western church, ordination may mean vi-
sually a liturgical ceremony involving signs like the laying on of hands
but the word does not bespeak either diaconal charism or a commissioning to mission but the ecclesiastical structure of power. The act "to
ordain" constitutes someone in a new position in the order of a society
through the power of a higher personage. After Tertullian, and more
solidly after the peace of Milan, a terminology of *ordo* drawn from the
political and social life of the empire was applied to the church. "*Ordo*"
refers to the bishops; next, to the church's hierarchy over against the
faithful (*plebs*); finally, to all levels in the church, priest or not. All of
this remained within the sociological usage of the time.[10] In the patristic
period there was a flexibility in the usage of *ordo* in the Roman Empire.
Augustine views the church as existing in groups of *ordines* which he
presents also as offices and grades. He arranges them in a descending
hierarchy which ends with married people and people active in the
world.[11]

In the word "*ordo*" grounding the theology of ordination and orders lie linguistic, theological alterations: an activity has become a social state; a term of group-relations has replaced a network of activities;
one word has replaced many powers. To the extent that the derivatives
of *ordo* represent legitimate arrangement and variety, they are sound.
At present, behind this word lies a sociology which has largely been
passed over by historico-critical reflection. We cannot ignore the influence which the linguistic metamorphosis from apostolate and commissioning to order and ordination exercised upon the church.

The community's active presence in selecting and educating its
ministries comes to a climax in the liturgy of ordination. An ordination

cannot be only a priestly or a ministerial class welcoming someone into a brotherhood. It is a diverse community placing its hopes upon someone designated for a specific work. The community does not witness a ritual of initiation but creates a sacramental event of mission. Ordination need not assume any appearance of casual secularity but should possess in its liturgical sacramentality a realism of dedication and service.

Ordination is a *sacramental liturgy performed by a Christian community and its leaders during which a baptized, charismatically called and professionally prepared Christian is commissioned into a public ministry within and on behalf of the local church.* The elements of this definition sum up a theology of ministry. The sacramentality of ordination exists in a multi-faceted liturgy; the background of baptism and charism, of education and discernment; the candidate for ministry, a community with its fulltime ministers and leadership; public service in the realms of kingdom and society.

Ordination brings together several forces. First, one must discern theologically the prologue to the sacrament: a symbolic declaration of a ministerial charism and a petition for grace to enact that ministry. Ordination should not be a pure beginning ignoring baptism and charism. Second, this particular ordination and ministry exist within a diversity of ministries and ordinations. In some way, the community ordains and all the baptized ordain but also the focus of ordination, the leader, ordains. As Yves Congar expresses it:

> A vocation to ministry is not only a personal attraction, controlled and verified by superiors, and then consecrated. It is the recognition by the community and by its leader of a person's gifts and it designates someone to receive a mission from the ordination by a bishop.... Since the Middle Ages, with its scholastic analytic and its canon law, things have been separated which were previously moments of an organic whole.[12]

Ordination is a sacrament not as a creation of grace *ex nihilo* but as a prayer for grace, a communal celebration of graces promised and received. Karl Rahner writes:

> The conferring by God of the office ... must therefore also necessarily imply the gift of grace without which the carrying out of the functions of the office would be impossible. Otherwise God would be requiring something to be done, and at the same time making it impossible, by refusing the necessary means. The gift of ministry is therefore necessarily a proffer of grace to exercise the office. As,

however, this conferring of ministry is, in fact, always a fundamental act of the indefectible Church and therefore is and remains a valid and true transmission of office, and can never be emptied of its significance and become outward show of such a transmission of power, the gift of grace on God's side in the rite of handing on of ministry is absolutely promised, it is opus operatum, a sacrament.[13]

The leader, the bishop, proclaims and sacramentalizes grace through the belief that a charism has been discerned.

5. Diversity in Ordinations

Which ordination have we been discussing? Is ordination one or many? Should some liturgical acts be "commissionings" or "installations" and others be "ordinations"? Does the diversity we found in ministry extend to ordination? Can the tradition of different orders reaching back to the third century support ordaining traditional ministers such as reader and acolyte and newly begun ministers of healing, counseling and social justice? Can the expansion of ordination be done without weakening the identity of bishop and pastor?

Ordination is a derivative event. As a liturgy and a public commissioning it refers to some deeper, more stable reality. As a sacrament it is a causal sign of some deeper reality both in the person and in the church. More than legal fiction, ordination is the correlate of ministry because the commissioning event recognizes and begins a significant ministry. Ordination is a recognition not that a Christian will heretofore exist essentially differently, but that this individual manifests a charism for service which the church needs.

Because there is a variety of ministries in a healthy Christian community, there is a variety of ordinations. The three ordinations of deacon, presbyter and overseer in their separateness no longer form one priesthood or dismantle one episcopacy; rather, each points to diverse identity. Ordination is not an abstract constitution of a Christian for a ministry universal; the verb "to ordain" is incomplete—someone is always ordained to something. As correlates, ordination and ministry cannot be defined alone; ordination is the liturgical and communal bridge between personal charism and a particular ministry.

Before we insist further upon a diversity of ordinations we will contrast two theological positions on the diversity open to ministry: (a) nominalism and (b) potentiality.

(a) Nominalism. Several times in this book we have criticized a rather widespread nominalist stance present in the post-Tridentine practice and theology of ministry. Nominalism is an intellectual view-point wherein a priori, legal voluntarism determines reality, human and divine. Nominalism constitutes reality by words or mental forms which are rooted not in created reality but in the increasingly arbitrary will of God. Nominalism, presuming that law is more significant than reality, selects certain church forms from the past as eternal; ordination and ministerial title are bestowed not by charism or service but by juridical decree. Eventually this stance becomes in the church the harbinger of revolt: a kind of schizophrenia, it would play with reality and control much that cannot be controlled. This world view—and every legalism and nominalism is a psychology and an ontology—affects ordination by reducing it to a liturgical exercise of episcopal power. The role of the bishop seems cut off from the realities of Spirit and community as his will or that of superiors in the hierarchy determines every aspect, divine as well as human, which touches ordination and subsequent ministry.

Yves Congar points out the theological implications of the legal or nominalist stance.

> There is ultimately no insistence upon an actual intervention of God's grace, nor on the need for man to pray for this intervention and to prepare for it by discipline. There is no explicit relation of authority to sacred acts such as charity and prayer. In short, legalism is characteristic of an ecclesiology unrelated to spiritual anthropology, and for which the word *ecclesia* indicates not so much the body of the faithful as the system, the apparatus, the impersonal depository of the system of rights whose representatives are the clergy, or, as it is extensively called, the hierarchy—ultimately, the pope and the Roman Curia.[14]

A serious example of nominalism is an arbitrary designation of some ministries and ordinations as given by divine institution and as worthy of sacramental liturgy. We have already rejected immature divisions of ministry which have no foundation in reality but only in terminology. There are distinctions to be made between the intensity of Christian ministry, but such distinctions flow out of the empirical service of each ministry and out of the visible life of the church. Since ministry is not a sacral state but an action, anything touching its definition must take into consideration what this ministry does.

Absolute ordination is ordination without ministerial limits, that is, without a precise community, a precise goal of service. Christianity, because its roots lie in the limited local church, has always rejected in theory absolute ordination. Yet its history is filled with bishops, priests, archbishops and cardinals whose link to any real church or ministry was tenuous. Protestant churches often allow ordination only after a call to serve a particular community has been received, and their national administrators are not considered to be active in the ministry. Roman Catholicism appears to have, in practice, a large number of ministers whose ordination is absolute, without clear reference to a local church.

To repeat, distinctions like "Ministry and ministry," "lay ministers and clerical ministers," "hierarchical and pastoral offices," and (pertinent to our present inquiry) "ordained and non-ordained ministries" find their foundation in legal decision and not in essential distinction in church service. "Lay minister" involves a linguistic contradiction in terms of action; "clerical minister" combines futilely action and class. These issues of kinds of ministry cannot rest with changes in law and terminology but demand a new fundamental theology of ministry.[15]

(b) *Potentiality*. Three ministries have survived the storms of centuries—bishop, presbyter, deacon—but they are really not such impressive travelers. History shows us that one (priest) had changed its identity, another (deacon) had been informally suppressed, and a third (bishop) was partly absorbed by its partner. Nevertheless, under the guise of these three sacred nouns (whose etymologies were forgotten or altered) different offices and services for the community have been exercised. To pursue this motif of the historical disguises of ministry, the reality signified by deacon, for instance, is different in the first, third, thirteenth and twentieth centuries; moreover, a diaconal reality existed among many men and women who were not ordained to this office. So, the three ordained ministries are not survivors of divine institution of forms maintained in a pristine state, but they are, rather, the meagre remnant—polyvalent in identity and imprecise in purpose—of a larger group.

Ministry is not three eternal offices but a fullness given to the church. History draws out of the potentiality of a ministerial pleroma (sustained by incarnational charism) three or six or nine particular ministries.

Documents from the early third century confirm the privileged place which Ignatius, a century earlier, had given to three ministries—overseer, elder and minister—and to their ordinations. Whether through the second century these three still competed with prophet and teacher, or whether it was more the case that the terminology of *episkopos* and *presbyteros* came to include roles which had been also described as prophet, shepherd or teacher, we do not know. Hippolytus' *Apostolic Tradition* (and the Syrian *Didascalia Apostolorum*) gives us two groupings of ministers: there the first triad receive an important laying on of hands; the others, readers, widows, etc. do not. While the bishop is described as priest, elders and deacons are still diverse ministries assisting him.[16]

In 200 A.D., there was still distinction among ministries and their public commissionings: different churches valued presbyter and deacon differently while the non-ordained ministries differed from region to region expanding and diminishing according to regional conditions. The *Didascalia* urged:

> Honor the bishop as God, for the bishop sits for you in the place of God Almighty. But the deacon stands in the place of Christ and do you love him. And the deaconess shall be honored by you in the place of the Holy Spirit; and the presbyters shall be to you in the likeness of the Apostles; and the orphans and widows shall be reckoned by you in the likeness of the altar.[17]

As the *Didache* gave an unclear picture of prophet and apostle, so in other churches there was an echo of the earlier ministry of teacher.[18] As theological schools begin, the important teaching ministry is enhanced and yet separated from ordination. The Christian who had suffered physically for Christ was not ordained (suffering has substituted for the laying on of hands) even if it is not clear to us whether this confessor could act as bishop.[19] Not in Rome, but in some churches the deaconess received a solemn, ordaining laying on of hands.[20]

Hippolytus' ecclesiology of church order does appear to be filled with organization and cult, and yet B. Botte cautions against such a conclusion.

> What is the church in the theology of St. Hippolytus? It is first of all a charismatic church. We must not forget that the *Apostolic Tradition* was preceded by a tract, "On Charisms." We do not know much about this treatise except that it spoke of the gifts by which God returns to the human person resemblance to the creator lost by sin. The *Apostolic Tradition* which begins by the consecration of a bishop evidently presents the institutional aspect of the church. We must not oppose these two forms as irreconcilable. . . .It would be erroneous to see in the institutional church only an arbitrary juridical organization . . . In virtue of the prayer of ordination, the bishop is a charismatic just like the priest and the deacon; each has received a gift adopted for his proper function. The church of Hippolytus is truly a church of the Holy Spirit for both faithful and hierarchy have been inspired by the same Spirit. The Christian receives the gift of the spirit in the rites of initiation . . .The Christian people (receive it) after the Eucharist.[21]

The early third century shows us a transition to selecting some ministries for special status, a selection based no doubt upon personal training, upon the importance given to work and upon permanence in the ministry. The community still introduced baptized men and women into ministry. More and more, the members of the community rather than the bishop evangelize; his ministry is becoming liturgical; he teaches by sermon and catechesis, summing up this ministry of the word by baptizing and by focusing the Eucharist of the entire community.[22]

Our fragmentary knowledge of the second and third centuries leaves us with questions about their ministries and ordinations. Why did some disappear? Or, did only their names disappear while each role was absorbed by other lasting offices? Why were there two classes of laying-on of hands? Why did less important ministries arise, services which are designated by a manner of life (widow, ascetic) rather than by a work? There was clearly a shift of ministerial focus from external public life to community, and above all to liturgy. This prominence of the liturgy was soon joined to a liturgical prominence of the Eucharist as sacrifice. Without pursuing this, we can surmise the considerable repercussions this would have had on the theology of ministry.

To return to the theology of ministerial potentiality. Despite the commandeering role in his society played by order, office and hierarchy, Aquinas presented orders theologically as a potentiality, "a potestative whole." "The distinction of orders is not that of an integral whole into parts nor of a universal into individuals but of a *totum postestativum.* . ."[23] Aquinas, moreover, will not admit that only the major orders are sacraments; rather, all of the levels or orders are realizations of a single *ordo.*

An argument against a wider diversity of ministries (which in their important service, extensive commitment and preparation deserve ordination) is the theology that three orders—bishop, priest and deacon—are of divine institution. This divine establishment could mean either an express constitution by Jesus on earth or a decision by God communicated later to the church. Some theologians after Trent have presumed that Jesus communicated to the Apostles only three important ministries, instituted by *"divina ordinatione."*[24]

We interpret the teachings at an ecumenical council through its historical context and theological language. The hermeneutical key to the Council of Trent is the Reformation as it has progressed up to 1560. Trent did not present a complete doctrine of orders nor a full theology of priesthood or episcopacy. Its statements were replies to the denials of the Reformers. Luther, Calvin, the Anabaptists and the Zwinglians had given the impression that the ministry was purely human, a legal creation of the church; they identified ministry with actual preaching and seemed to neglect the ministry of Eucharistic leader. Furthermore, they accepted only one ministry, that of the preacher-pastor actually functioning in office. Ordination, character, episcopal power and cultic priesthood were minimalized by the Reformers.

There is no doubt that Trent insisted upon a real distinction between important ministries and baptized Christians, and that it searched for the ground of that distinction in sacrificial cult or hierarchical power (which at best can be particular sources).[25] With regard to the question of the diversity of ministries, however, Trent was arguing precisely for a diversity: *"Plures et diversi essent ministrorum ordines."*[26] Its list of three received with veneration is presented as a rejection of the Protestant idea that there is only one church office—a view upheld by the Reformation to attack the magisterial and jurisdictional power of the bishops. Trent affirmed the sacramentality and the permanence in character of ministry, objected to a reduction of office to laity, but insisted that "the hierarchy (of orders) includes by divine institution bishops, presbyters and ministers." Trent argued for the distinct identity of important ministers; the laity were not to move *"promiscue"*[27] in and out of orders. It is unlikely that the conciliar fathers intended the following meaning, but the letter of the text admits of an extension of ministers under the third, vaguely categorized group, *"ministrorum."* The burden of Trent is to affirm real, stable offices; more than one office; and ministries other than preaching. The line of argumentation is away from monoformity in orders.

Ecclesial changes suggested and made at Vatican II prompted theologians to retrieve the theology of fullness in the ministry. Karl Rahner points out that Christianity is "not a castle of truth with innumerable rooms which must be occupied in order to be 'in the truth' but is the opening from which all individual truths (even errors) lead into *the* Truth which is the inconceivability of God."[28] What is true of expressions of revealed truth can be applied to forms of church life. Rahner's method is to look for the historically manifest essence behind the forms which are claimed to be *de jure divino.* Ultimately, history illumines and critiques what the church holds to be divinely important. In terms of ministry, Jesus established a reality of ministry with certain characteristics of service, detachment, authority and universality. The Spirit in history enlarges or focuses this *pleroma.* Theology is interested not in quantitative control but in fullness and quality.[29]

Rahner distinguishes between a single potentiality ("one pastoral ministry") and its "degrees." He views *jus divinum* positively, for it allows the survival of ministry in the ages.[30] But simply because a church form does not now exist, need not mean it is lost or has no right to exist anew. The parameters of the apostolic period and the limits of the time of primal revelation in Christ are unclear. When we compare the historically conditioned forms for a specific office (or ministerial title) we see both an ecclesial essence (*jus divinum*) and a history. Is there an ongoing revelation of the Spirit and a penetration into the unique message of Christ which encourage both discovery and rediscovery of different forms of ministry? Can a later church alter—improve, diminish—the forms of the past given by the Spirit? Theology tutored by history responds affirmatively to both questions.

For Edward Schillebeeckx, too, Jesus and his Spirit did not bestow one or two offices on the church but a fullness of ministry. He argues that the church not only has the right but the duty to determine its structure in each period. A single structural arrangement may be *jure divino* for one age but it should not be used as an obscuring hermeneutic for the past or as a procrustean bed for the true. The *jus divinum* of ministry is not the judge but the gift of history; it looks backward through tradition but also forward to mission. " 'Divine Origin' includes a historical growth of various forms and divisions."[31] The sociological process within the church which brought forth church office is not rooted in plans from Jesus or Peter. Yet important ministries do go back to the apostolic church, and ministry is present in the early church not only in charism but in an inner drive toward order and effectiveness. Consequently, the pneumatic process of naming and describing, of creating and arranging ministries has a sociological and historical dynamic.

Like Rahner, Schillebeeckx points out puzzles in the history of ministry. Why did some apostolic ministries fade away if a primal constitution established them? Why did others remain but, while preserving their name, change their role? The history of ministry is not a progress from good to better: there is gain and loss, and ministries which were once of crucial importance might appear again. Preaching might be separated again from community leader and healing evangelists might emerge. If ministries can be lost, ministries can also be regained. A single present-day order of the church can never set forth in a closed essential definition, "since different orders of the church are dogmatically possible."[32] History shows not only more than three ministries but different arrangements in church order which nevertheless guarantee all that is necessary for service, evangelization, order and tradition.

6. Variety in Ministry and Ordination

Ministry begins normally with public and liturgical recognition. Since there are already distinct ordinations for distinct ministries, as ministry expands, public commissionings—some of which are ordinations—should be increased and enhanced. There are certainly important distinctions between ministries based upon the duration of this service, upon its object and significance for church and kingdom. These characteristics will influence the seriousness of the commissioning (which is part of every ministry) and the expansion of the number of ordinations. We already have three distinct ordinations; it is possible to have a few more.

The distinction between baptismal ministries and ordained ministries is not fully satisfactory, but unlike the other pairs it does avoid the difficulties inherent in the clergy-laity distinction and allows baptism to ground ministries differing in import but having a common nature and theological aetiology. Baptism is the opening for all ministry; but because church is a celebratory and sacramental community, various kinds of admissions to ministry should be encouraged.

Our interest, however, is not only the expansion of the ministries within the community (although that is an important aspect of the general expansion of the ministry and challenges past theologies of the ministry) but the expansion of the fulltime ministry. Churches are asking how the energies of many Christians can be channeled through their baptismal and diaconal charisms, for we have thousands of Christians entering into fulltime ministry not as presbyters and deacons but as teachers, workers in peace and justice and potential preachers. If through theology and preparation, through tested charism and action they are in the ministry, they too should enter ministry through ordination—through an ordination to their specific ministry.

Essentially an ordination is a communal liturgy of public commissioning to a specific ministry. If one who occasionally reads at the liturgy or bears the Eucharist to the sick can be publicly designated for that limited ministry, cannot teachers and ministers whose preparation and personal sacrifice, parochial and diocesan employment bespeak ministry be ordained? When new ministries assume importance and permanence in the eyes of the church of an area or nation, they should begin with an ordination. For ordination does not create the ministry, but a Christian prepared and approved for ministry calls for, at the beginning, an ordination. It may be that different levels of service should be distinguished by levels of ordination. Yet words such as "installation" and "ordination" ultimately reflect not rules and sacral states but degrees of service, all grounded in baptism.

7. Reversal in Ministry and Ordination

The event of ordination is the point for us to recognize that a new theology of ministry will introduce a reversal. This reversal is not a novelty but an understanding of ministry and ordination taken for granted in the first centuries of Christianity. The reversal is a move from symbol to reality, from church building to world, from liturgy to service. The reversal is: affirming the liturgical side of ministry to be only one side of ministry—the symbolic-sacramental side and source of ministry—and recognizing ministry to be more than liturgy, preaching is more than preaching during the Eucharist, love more than the kiss of peace. Service to the kingdom of God must have a real, public, social facet as well as a liturgical enactment.

Sacrament presumes reality. A Christian is not ordained exclusively or principally for liturgy. Ministry is not exhausted by the services of Sunday morning. Liturgy is not the only preoccupation of Christians; rather sacraments and worship were intended to confirm and nourish their ministries in the world. Ministry partakes of this deep but obscured principle—revolutionary and essential to Christianity: first ministries, then liturgy.

With the entrance of hundreds of thousands into the Christian churches, the early leaders failed to develop wider baptismal ministries within or without the community assembly. There was still a social diaconate and still some diversity in the ministry, but the universal call to ministry was replaced by a call to a virtuous life in the empire. The Christian found himself or herself partaking in what was mainly a liturgical religion with weekly Eucharist, liturgical feasts and special moments of human life heightened by the sacraments. It would be interesting to pursue whether the elaboration of the liturgical year with its anticipation of the Heavenly Jerusalem was not a subconscious replacement of the diminished ministry, where liturgy confronted symbolically the eons of this world and their powers for evil.

Not only did the ministry become the activity of a small group of Christians but ministry itself tended to appear as liturgy and ministers sought out their places therein. It is hardly surprising that the diaconate should have suffered as a result of the process of sacralization. The field of social welfare that had been the diaconate's chief *raison d'être* now began to be entrusted to priests or lay-people. In 595, the Synod of Rome complained that the deacons were no longer looking after the poor but were chanting psalms instead: the liturgy had become their main sphere of activity.[33]

Today it is difficult for Christians to see their church outside of the liturgy and word of Sunday morning. It is difficult for fulltime ministers to step outside of a liturgical or administrative role and to place themselves in the midst of the destitute, psychotic and desperate who make up a large percentage of our population. In any meeting between horrendous social abuses born of politics and the bishop, priest or pastor, a tension appears because most Christians, regardless of their church tradition, view the fulltime minister as priest, as liturgist. Liturgy replaces or cloaks the ambiguities of life.

The past fifteen years have witnessed a struggle to let the ministry flow back into more public spheres. When we compare two ecumenical councils, Trent and Vatican II, we see a move from defining church and ministry in terms of Eucharist to a wider perspective including liturgy and pluriform mission.[34] The presbyter and bishop, correctly defined, are not the same as prophet and deacon: not because their role as community leader sets them apart from extra-liturgical ministry (indeed they are the center and enabler of all ministries, not just liturgical ones), but because the role of the leader of the community is not the same as the community's social prophet. Only with an expanded ministry, with new ministries realizing the old services of prophet, teacher, evangelist and deacon in the public sector can the tension between liturgical and communal leader and social evangelist be eased. While it may be desirable for the Christian church and churches to send members into government service, for instance, into the forum of legislatures, the correct ministry for that is that of public speaker and interpreter of faith and society ("prophet"), not that of priest or bishop whose ministerial identity has the limits of church leader. Similarly, the young churches still need the resources of the older churches in education, planning, theology, spirituality; however, these personnel would come to Zaire or Peru not ordained as presbyters—for the young churches should have their own leaders—but as teachers and evangelists. These two examples illustrate the world-wide confusion generated when the churches have only one ministry . . . and that ministry has been for a long time a liturgical and then an administrative one.

The movement by which Christians withdrew from public ministry to liturgical attendance must now be reversed. Christians do not enter the world as ministers because they have been consecrated as liturgists. Just the opposite is true; offices and roles in the liturgy are justified by public service. Liturgy reflects real ministry.[35] A deacon has a liturgical role because of an external social ministry.

The sharpest example of this is the leader of the community. The leader presides among the ministries of a church in their public services. Hence, this coordinator is thereby the normal minister to preside at that special aspect of the community's life, the Paschal liturgy of Sunday. Hervé Legrand observes that most Christians believe their Eucharistic assembly is possible because it is enacted by a priest whose personally possessed and unique power fashions this. In fact, the bishop and then the presbyter preside at the Eucharist because their ministry is one of leadership and spiritual discernment in nourishing and building up the community. "Thus presidency of the eucharistic assembly is seen as including the liturgical, prophetic and ministerial dimensions in the pastoral charge of building up the church, a charge conferred in ordination."[36] Legrand finds in a variety of patristic and liturgical documents from the first five centuries of the church that reversal by which not sacral priesthood but leadership in charism, liturgy and public life is the foundation of bishop and later presbyter, of Eucharistic leader.

To turn briefly to the deacons, although their identity and origin seems pluriform, the dominant work which characterized them in the ages of the martyrs and of the Constantinian establishment was extensive programs for the urban poor or the Christian needy. Whatever liturgical role they had was derived from this. This reversal by which diaconal action in the world grounds liturgical symbol is a central facet of a realistic theology of ministry.

While liturgy is symbolic, ministry is functional. Beautiful and profound theologies have been written about the sacramental representation of grace in the motions of the liturgy but there is also a real, corporeal incarnation of grace in other ministries. Liturgy serves the spirit of the Christian by word and symbol, by silence and sacrament, by sounds and colors. There is a way in which liturgy remains secondary (for even sacrament is not full reality) and the symbolic and verbal nourishment of the Christian has some further goal, beyond the church building and Sunday morning. Thomas Aquinas concluded that the result of the Eucharist was the external unity of the community; in our active society we could paraphrase that theology and say that an ecclesial source and effect of liturgy is ministry.[37]

Again we are aided in the development of a fundamental theology of ministry by pondering the priorities of grace. Charism precedes ordination whose sacrament that liturgy is. And, just as the varied graces of the community fashion the constellation of a public commissioning for a ministry, brief or permanent, baptismal or professional, so the goal of ministry, service to the kingdom in the world, permeates every service and every liturgy.

NOTES

1. K. Schelkle. *Discipleship and Priesthood* (New York, 1965); J. Quinn. "Ministry in the New Testament." *Lutherans and Catholics in Dialogue* 4 (New York, 1970), pp. 69ff.; S. Freyne, *The Twelve: Disciples and Apostles* (London, 1968); R. Schnackenburg, *Nachfolge Christi* (Freiburg, 1980).

2. Y. Congar, *ESA,* pp. 110, 124, 253ff, 271ff. For an arrangement of models in ecclesiology drawn from patterns in Christology, see J.P. Schineller. "Christ and the Church: A Spectrum of Views," *TS* 27 (1976) 545 ff.

3. *ST* III, q. 62, a. 1; cf. E. Schillebeeckx. *Christ, the Sacrament of the Encounter with God* (New York, 1963), pp. 118ff.

4. T. Merton, *Seeds of Contemplation* (New York, 1949), p. 26.

5. "For the priestly power itself flows from the episcopal power.... As the church is one, so must the Christian people be one. Therefore, as for the specific congregation of one church, one bishop is called. He is head of that church." Thomas Aquinas, *Summa contra gentes* 4, c. 76.

6. Thomas Aquinas, *ST* II- II, q. 33, a. 4. ad 2; Cajetan, *De Comparatione auctoritatis papae...* , c. 3; Bellarmine, *De Romano pontifice* 1, 33. For a discussion of the issue, cf. C. Journet, *The Apostolic Hierarchy* (New York, 1955), pp. 389ff.

7. *Satis cognitum* in Leo XIII, *Acta* (Rome, 1897), p. 197. "To the bishop is fully committed the pastoral office in its normal form. He cannot therefore consider himself to be the mere recipient and executor of commands received from higher quarters. He has an independent duty and responsibility . . . (and) must strive to recognize for himself the scope of his task and the right moment for acting . . . , discover solutions which are not the mere application of universal norms. Only in this way can his diocese and the fulfillment of his office contribute to the good of the 'whole body' of the Church, for this Church is not a homogenous mass but an organic structure which possesses a real variety of members." Karl Rahner, "Episcopacy in the Teaching of Vatican II," *TI* 6, pp. 362f.

8. Thomas Aquinas does not omit the role of faith and ecclesial life in the event of the sacrament; *4 Sent.,* d. 1, q. 2, a. 6. On this theology lying between Donatism and nominalism, cf. Schillebeeckx, *Christ, the Sacrament...* , pp. 102ff.

9. Cf. K. Hruby, "Las notion d'ordination dans la tradition juive," *LMD* #102 (1970), 32ff.; E. Lohse, *Die Ordination im Spätjudentum und im Neuen Testament* (Göttingen, 1951); E. Kilmartin, "Ordination in Early Christianity against a Jewish Background," *Studia Liturgica* 13 (1979) 42ff.

10. Cf. P. van Beneden, "Ordo," *Vigilae Christianae* 23 (1969) 175.

11. Cf. J. Folliet, "Les trois categories de chrétiens . . . ," *Augustinus Magister* (Paris, 1954), 631ff.

12. *MC,* p. 21. "The older ecclesiology looked at the church as the united fellowship of all the faithful and saw there the validity of the sacraments conditioned by this unity of fellowship. The active consent of the people was expressed in prayer and was an indispensable element in celebration." S. Tromp, cited in Congar, *Lay People in the Church* (Westminster, 1965), p. 219.

13. Karl Rahner, *Church and Sacrament* (New York, 1964), pp. 105f.

14. *PP,* p. 64.

15. During the first centuries of the church, the notion of local church was so prominently linked to diverse ministry that there could be no idea of ministry existing apart from building up of a particular church. Then by the fourth century we have indications of bishops moving from one church to another and absolute ordinations (office without community as source, milieu or goal) are unequivocally condemned by the Council of Chalcedon. Despite this, under the influence of the imperial organization of an expanding church, and then of monasticism, absolute ordination in practice if not in theory attained a strong foothold.

A fundamental theology of ministry must inevitably examine and question any absolute distinction between orders and jurisdiction. Far from reflecting the word or dogmatic expression of revelation, this distinction emerges in the twelfth century with Gratian. On its history, cf. M. De Roulers, "La notion de juridiction dans la doctrine des décrétalistes," *Etudes Franciscaines* 49 (1937) 420ff; M. van de Kerchkove, *La notion de juridiction dans la doctrine des Décrétistes. . . .*(Assisi, 1937); L. Hödl, *Die Geschichte der scholastischen Literatur . . . der Schlüsselgewalt* (Münster, 1960); U. Horst, "Das Wesen der 'potestas clavium' nach Thomas von Aquinas," *MThZ,* 11 (1960) 192ff. K. Mörsdorff, "Die Entwicklung der Zweigliedrigkeit der kirchlichen Hierarchie," *MThZ* 3 (1959) 1ff; *ESA,* pp. 148ff; J. Cuneo, "The Power of Jurisdiction," *J* 39 (1979), 183ff. It has undergone what G. Alberigo aptly describes as "grand semantical oscillations" ("La Juridiction," *Irenikon* 49 [1976] 167), finding a place in official church documents mainly during the time from Pius IX to Pius XII.

The introduction of absolute ordination presented the opening for such a distinction. The Papacy's extension of its power in the church and world, competing spheres of ministry and community (e.g. between itinerant Dominicans and the local clergy) and the utility of a distinction which would explain heretics with orders and laity with ecclesial powers were occasions for finding the distinction helpful. But these very issues along with a division of ministerial life into orders and authority played havoc with the essential framework of church life: charism and ministry. Ultimately jurisdiction, like the clerical tonsure, reached a fragilely independent state where it gave aspects of ministry to individuals who, without charism or ordination, functioned purely juridically in the world and service of grace.

The documents of Vatican II were influenced by theologians such as Karl Rahner who insisted that orders/jurisdiction could not describe in a fully adequate way church life and ministry and the texts use the terms rarely, locating both powers in the church and not in one office.

Absolute ordination apart from community presented cases where sacramental orders destined solely to confect sacraments formally existed without preaching and teaching. Then, too, a desire to permit some ministerial activities to Christians who were not priests fostered an ecclesial reality called jurisdiction. In a sense issues about jurisdiction in the medieval and Baroque church replaced the theology of ministries other than priest and bishop. But the cases which ground the distinction are now either anomalies or disciplinary problems. Jurisdiction is not a solution to diversity in the ministry. All ministry is sacramental and touches the realms of order and jurisdiction. It is not helpful to continue to tie the multiplicity of ministry in the baptized to jurisdiction, to support a legal creation of occasional preaching or teaching as coming solely from the ad hoc delegation of bishop apart from the wider structures of the church and the real qualifications (education, experience) in the individual. Such a procedure prohibits ministry from qualified Christians and entrusts it temporarily and abstractly to those who may be unqualified.

The distinction between orders and jurisdiction is a legal framework and not a theological one like charism-ministry. In our society, jurisdiction could be viewed as accreditation, accreditation in the sense of continuing education and competency in ministry by the Christian community and leadership. Traditionally examinations were part of the entrance to jurisdiction. Today continuing education holds an important place in the life of the church and rightly nourishes and determines ministers in a changing world and church. This continued competency is the inner core of what was intended by the ministry of leadership extending its authoritative role (jurisdiction) to other Christians.

A second hermeneutic of jurisdiction is "relational power" (Cuneo, p. 206). Jurisdiction is the harmonious communion among ministers within the community and with local and wider leadership. Jurisdiction does not create activity out of random material, but coordinates the increasingly complex ministerial life of a parish, diocese, region and nation.

> The power of jurisdiction is the *power of communion,* a power to function in the Church which is based upon the relationship of indiviudals to the unity of the Church and to the unity of its mission. Co-responsibility for the *missio* of the Church is not exercised by everyone in the same way.

> Developing a correct concept of jurisdiction seems quite important for understanding increased participation in the Church's mission and ministry. Jurisdiction is the principle which unites the person (bishop, priest, minister, persons with a particular share in mission or function) to the community and to the rest of the ecclesial communion. It is a relationship principle in the realm of the visible unity of the Church's communion (flowing) from recognized relationship. . . . Valid ministry is not merely individual; it must flow from a correct relationship to the Church (Cuneo, pp. 217, 209).

Canonists still argue for ministers of the community who are part-time, who function part-time or in non-sacral ways to be well commissioned by jurisdiction (Cuneo, pp. 218f.). But this seems myopic from the point of view of ecclesiology: it defends a structure which in source and practice is not fully ecclesiological and theological but juridical, and it fails to critique the juridic dual sources from theological approaches which seem to be both primal and fruitful for the Christian community.

16. Cf. C. Vogel, "Chirotonie et Chirosthenie," *Irenikon* 45 (1972), 7ff., 201ff.

17. R. H. Connolly, *Didascalia Apostolorum* (Oxford, 1929), pp. 88f.; cf. E. Braniste, "L'assemblée, liturgique décrite dans les 'Constitutions Apostoliques' . . ."; B. Botte, "Peuple chrétien et hiérarchie dans la tradition apostolique de S. Hippolyte," *As,* pp. 79ff, 93ff.

18. C. Renoux, "Les ministères du culte à Jérusalem au IVe et au Ve siècles," *As,* p. 254.

19. C. Vogel, "La chirotonie presbyterale du liturgie comme condition de la célébration liturgique?" *As* pp. 307ff; cf. M. Lods, *Confesseurs et martyrs, successeurs des prophètes* . . . (Paris, 1958).

20. Cf. R. Gryson, *The Ministry of Women in the Early Church* (Collegeville, 1976), pp. 109ff.

21. Botte, *As,* pp. 79f. Elsewhere Botte writes: "The bishop and the priest have nothing in common with the Roman *sacerdos* . . . nor do they have much in common with the priest of the Old Testament. . . . In spite of the typology, the Christian priesthood is of another order: it is charismatic and spiritual. . . . The episcopate, the priesthood and the diaconate appear less as ritual functions in the ancient documents than as charisms aimed at the upbuilding of the Church." "Holy Orders in the Ordination Prayers," *HO,* p. 22.

22. *Ibid.,* p. 81. For a detailed analysis of the development of the clergy and the distinction between ministries in the third century see A. Faivre, *Naissance d'une hiérarchie* (Paris, 1977) who nevertheless interprets the sparse data as indicating a decline of the ministries before 200 A.D. and then an expansion fifty years later—an unlikely theory which overlooks the fragmentary nature of the documentation used to support it; see also *P,* pp. 59–87. P.-M. Gy observes the diversity of ministry shown in early ordination ceremonies as well as the shift from the evangelical to the pastoral after the third century. "Ancient Ordination Prayers," *Studia Liturgica* 13 (1979) 82, 85.

23. "Orders is . . . a potestative whole. The nature of this is to be fully in one, but in others by participation. So it is in this case: for the fullness of the sacrament is one order, the priesthood, but in the others there is a participation of order . . . and so all orders are one sacrament." In *4 Sent.,* d. 24, q. 2, a. 1. quest 3. Cf. W. Croce, "Die niederen Weihen und ihre hierarchische Wertung," *Zeitschrift für katholische Theologie* 70 (1948) 257ff.

24. *DS* 1776.

25. *DS* 1764; cf. H. Jedin, *Krisis und Wendepunkt des Trienter Konzils* (Würzburg, 1941); J. Sustan, *Die römische Kurie und das Konzil von Trient* 4

(Vienna, 1914), pp. 100f; A. Michel, "Trent," *Dictionnaire de théologie catholique* 15:1, 1414ff.

26. *DS* 1765. ". . . esse hierarchiam, divina ordinatione institutam, quae constat ex episcopis presbyteris et ministris." *DS* 1776.

27. *DS* 1767; cf. *Ch,* pp. 418ff.

28. "Intellectual Honesty and Christian Faith." *TI* 7, pp. 67f.

29. K. Rahner, "Meaning of Ecclesiastical Office," *Servants of the Lord* (New York, 1968), pp. 21ff.

30. K. Rahner, "Open Questions in Dogma Considered by the Institutional Church as Definitively Answered." *Journal of Ecumenical Studies* 15 (1978) 215: cf. "Reflections on the Concept of 'Ius Divinum' in Catholic Thought," *TI* 5, pp. 233ff.

"What 'divine law' is and how we should understand it cannot be presented mainly as a means of forcing others to remain in a moribund and anxious status quo. Rather, it must be measured against the historical situation and the text of the New Testament (responsibly and accurately understood) and the Spirit of Christ living on in the church. This Spirit acts today, too, in a diversity of gifts: they do not exclude the hierarchy but they also do not exclude the baptized living in different times and regions. In historical divine vitality, this *jus divinum* is the unifying and liberating element within the movement of human ministry in which the church also shares. . . .The appeal to a 'divine institution' is therefore—at least in these cases (the distinction of laity and clergy, the precision between episcopacy and papacy) to be understood as a juristic formula and description and not a kind of dogma." J. Neumann, "Das 'Jus Divinum' im Kirchenrecht," *Orientierung* 31 (1967), 8.

31. E. Schillebeeckx, "The Catholic Understanding of Office," *TS* 30 (1969), 569. Yves Congar asks: "What does the usage of the expression 'divine right' signify in terms of ministers: their existence/the distinction between clergy and laity? the distinction between pope and bishop? Does not history oblige us to envisage the idea, proposed by some of a 'divine right' submitted to historicity, and so, in a sense, 'reformable.' " "Ministères et structuration de l'église," *LMD* 102 (1970) 8.

32. *Ibid.,* p. 570. "The church does not enjoy just any liberty over its own structure; it cannot deny apostolic ministry nor the global ministry constituting it. But it does enjoy considerable freedom with regard to the form and organization of the fundamental relationship between some and all. The liberty is not a caprice but a task. It is a duty to give for each epoch out of the apostolic ministry the form capable of making its witness heard and of enabling its efficacy. This also involves discerning and creating new ministries which the People of God needs and which the Spirit suggests." *MM,* p. 415; similarly, Piet Fransen, "Orders and Ordination," *Sacramentum Mundi* 4 (New York, 1969), p. 306.

33. R. Nowell, "Why Did the Deacon Disappear?" *Ministry of Service* (New York, 1968), p. 34.

34. H. Denis, "La Théologie du presbyterat de Trente à Vatican II," *Les Prêtres* (Paris, 1968), pp. 193f. "It is by being a local church that a community

enacts a liturgical prayer. . . . This (church) must verify in itself the essential aspects of church (convocation, institution, communion). . . . But if the church is realized to a high degree in liturgical action, it is nonetheless not reduced to it. The church is also mission, kerygma, teaching, service, political critique and action." Y. Congar, "Reflexions sur l'assemblée liturgique," *LMD* 115 (1973) 8ff.

35. "The principal roles in the Christian celebration manifest the very structure of the church. The functions in the assembly have two sides: on the one hand, they are (liturgical) functions; on the other, they reveal that which the '*ecclesia*' is, its structure." P. Gy, "Ordres et fonctions dans l'assemblée liturgique," *Bulletin du comité des études* 52 (1968) 185.

36. H. Legrand, "The Presidence of the Eucharist according to the Ancient Tradition," *Worship* 53 (1979), 430.

37. *ST* III, q. 82, a. 2,3.

CONCLUSION

This book is not the last word in a theology of ministry as the Christian churches approach a new century. It may be a first word in a theology which in imagination and tradition would be equal to today's crises and opportunities. It was fitting to begin this book with a passage from a sermon of Leo the Great: our times too stand at the end of previous forms and at the edge of great forces and large populations within the church.

The local church with its structure and liturgy, diversity in language and symbolism gave the forms of the church for four centuries. The subsequent long move towards universal monoformity, which had its own reasons, reached its climax not in Boniface VIII or Urban VIII but in Pius XII. Now, precisely through Vatican II, the deeper dynamic of the momentum is back to the local church to meet the needs of Christians.

A few principles emerge from these chapters.

1. The context of a theology of ministry for today is not decline but expansion: the expansion of the Christian population, the expansion of their precise needs, the expansion of the number of Christians interested in various levels of ministry.

2. The context of ministry itself is grace, that multifaceted, active presence of God which Jesus calls God's "kingdom." In a time of rapid change, theology must be rooted in realities or it becomes absorbed in conflicts over past and present words. Grace brings a certain reality to

ecclesial issues, for ultimately grace is the source and the goal, and the judge of all that the church is and does. Bursting forth and dying away, ecclesial forms come out of an encounter as the grace of the Spirit meets the patterns of human life.

3. The church is ministerial. Ministry is not a rare vocation or a privileged office but belongs to the nature of the new covenant; God's religious destiny happens in community but is intended for the entire human race. As with its universal source, baptism, ministry exists in the churches as an aspect of every Christian's life.

4. The diversity within the church (and there is considerable diversity) comes not in states of membership or biological modes of human life but in the choice of levels of ministerial activity. Christians are invited to degrees of ministry according to their particular charism. That charism looks both to the Spirit's plan for each Christian and to the needs, structures, leadership and discernment of the community.

5. The ministry of leadership in parish, team, diocese exists to serve ministry as catalyst and coordinator. This leading ministerial role, within similar but diverse ministries, grounds the responsibility of presiding at Eucharist and of focusing and maintaining union with the church's tradition and universality.

There are limitations in expression in the previous pages, and ideas which are incomplete. From my fallible perspective, there is nothing which is contrary to the New Testament nor to the tradition of the church. Whatever its deficiencies, this book does present a theology of the ministry which is coherent, realistic and evangelistic Old and new facets of the ministry find a coherent framework as theology insists that neither the world nor the Spirit is misguided.

This theology has been a critique of nominalism, of excessive sacralism and legalism, in short, a critique of every theology which eliminates culture and development from the forms of the church. On the other hand, the theology in these pages is haunted by a ghost. It is the spectre of puritanism and secularism; the self-destructive spirit of Christian churches who have substituted laity for charism, organization and conversation for liturgy, suburbia for sacrament. By sacramentality we mean not the seven sacraments and their liturgy but what medieval theologians contemplated: the mutual interpenetration of the divine in the human, the fallout of the Incarnation. The expansion and diversification of the ministry cannot mean a diminishment in the rigor or mystery of service to grace and church. Rather it means that new spiritualities must arise, new ascetic forms of education must be developed, and proven traditions of discipleship must remain. The expansion of the ministry should have not only form but depth. While ministry must be rescued from the realm of "being" the New Testament makes it clear that ministry is crippled unless the minister is a healthy branch of the vine, a true place of the Spirit's presence.

This theology of ministry seems to confront the traditional (but in format largely medieval and Baroque) offices of priest and bishop. Vatican II, as we saw, has already drawn them back to an earlier distinction and identity. In fact, priest and bishop are here not reduced but intensified. Each no longer has an exclusively liturgical role or a role too vague because it includes so much, an impossible general ministry which covers every aspect of diocese and parish. These ministries have become, essentially, ministries of demanding leadership. Consequently, they are of vital import as they coordinate a panoply of ministers—fulltime and part-time.

Recalling the Pauline motif of building up the Body of Christ, the churches and their leaders find their office as a service of an active grace, a diaconal charism.

BIBLIOGRAPHY

It is neither possible nor necessary to reproduce the vast and yearly expanding bibliography on ministry. Articles and books in English, French, German, Spanish, as well as writings from Africa, South America, India are producing vast literature. The following publications contribute to a bibliography of bibliographies in this area.

A. Lemaire, *Les ministères aux origines de l'église* (Paris, 1971); "The Ministries in the New Testament. Recent Research," *Biblical Theology Bulletin* 3 (1973), 133ff. (Revised edition in *LMD* #115 [1973] 30ff; *Bibliographie choisie d'études recentes sur la prêtre* (Montreal, 1969); B. Cooke, *Ministry to Word and Sacraments. History and Theology* (Philadephia, 1976) (the bibliographical data is scattered through the critical apparatus); *Lutherans and Catholics in Dialogue: Eucharist and Ministry* (Washington, 1970); R. Goldie, "Laity: A Bibliographical Survey of Three Decades," *The Laity Today* 26 (1979) 107–43; L. Doohan, "Contemporary Theologies of the Laity: An Overview Since Vatican II," *Communio* 7 (1980) 255f; Y. Congar, B. Dupuy, H. Legrand and others, "Bulletin de théologie" in *Revue des sciences philosophiques et théologiques;* Y. Congar's surveys from 1932 to 1962 are collected and reprinted in *Sainte Eglise* (Paris, 1963); V. Pnür, "Kirche und Amt," *Catholica,* Beiheft 1 (1975); *Teologia de Sacerdocio* (Burgos, 1969) 3 vols.); Y. Congar, *L'Ecclésiologie du haut moyen âge* (Paris, 1968); *L'Eglise de S. Augustin à l'époque moderne* (Paris, 1970); "New Forms of Ministry in Christian Communities," *Pro Mundi Vita* 50 (1974).